Why I'm Not a Democrat

ALSO BY MICHAEL J. MONGE

Concealed Within Scripture: The Diary of Jesus

Why I'm Not a Democrat

And Why You Probably Shouldn't Be Either

Michael J. Monge

Irvine, California

ISBN 978-0-9831884-0-7

Αγchιωεδες
Publishing

Archimedes reportedly declared that given a long enough lever and a place to stand, he could move the Earth from its position.

Visit us at www.archimedespublishing.com

Cover Image and Design by Michael J. Monge. The author would like to make it clear that the cover art is in no way intended to indicate any negative view toward donkeys or the beautiful creature, Stella Bella, pictured in the image. The image of a donkey is intended to refer only to the ideology of the Democratic Party.

To all those who love Truth,
Even when they disagree with it

Contents

Preface

Shortly after my wife and I were married, she gave me the book *Why I Am Not a Christian*, which is a collection of essays by Bertrand Russell. She knew I was an atheist who was raised by Catholic parents, and I appreciated the book. I was profoundly disappointed with it, however, since most of the essays were related to various negative criticisms of Christianity and religion in general, and what I had expected was more of an atheistic apologetic. I guess I wanted to see more of why he was an atheist, if he was, rather than why he wasn't a Christian. I guess I should have taken the title seriously.

Although I think Russell's book fails as a complete justification for atheism, I have no interest in providing a more fulfilling apologetic. I am an atheist, and my reasons for being an atheist are defensible, I think, and I am happy to debate the issue with anyone. But I just don't think the issue of God's existence is very pressing or urgent. I suspect I could turn the world more atheistic if I put my mind to it, and I think that such a world would be more factually correct, but I don't know for sure that it would be a better world. I do think it is important for Christians and other religious people to know that an atheist can share many of their deepest values, or at least respect them, and I do hope this book will help accomplish that task.

So, I am not all that interested in convincing people that Theism, or a general belief in God, is mistaken. There is another religion in the world, though, which I do believe is pernicious and does make the world a worse place. I am very interested in diminishing its power and influence. It is not usually considered a religion, but it seems to me that it is. It is the religion which we in America call the Democratic Party.

If you are insisting that the Democratic Party is not a religion, I have to ask you what you think a religion is. If you think that religion necessarily involves belief in God, then you have a very provincial definition. Scholars have realized for a long while now that the term "religion" is very difficult to define, but the consensus is that it does not require belief in a God or gods. This kind of definition might be adequate if we only consider the ancient religions of the Western world, but when we expand our view to the entire world, there are worldviews we generally identify as religions which do not include the theistic presumption. Buddhism and Jainism are generally recognized as religions, yet they have no gods. Jainism is explicitly atheistic.

To see another difficulty, try to describe what kind of thing a religion is, metaphysically speaking. Is it a set of principles or beliefs? Is it a scripture? Is it a list of commands? Perhaps it is a group of people? Or a group of people over time? It could be a set of practices, or maybe a particular way of living? Maybe it is a particular way of worshipping a deity, but then again, that would exclude Buddhism and Jainism, which we generally recognize as religions.

The truth is that a religion is an amorphous thing, and maybe no single definition will completely encompass every religion in the world. One attempt to define religion is to consider the various attributes we associate with religions in a very general sense. We generally think religion includes the following:

1. Belief in God or gods
2. a worldview, or system of beliefs
3. Characteristic rituals or ceremonies
4. A set of values or ethical precepts
5. Scriptures, or writings which are considered sacred
6. A community, including people who are vested with authority

One aspect of this kind of definition is that a thing need not have all of these attributes in order to be a religion, but the more it has, the more confident we are in calling it a religion. The Democratic Party may not have a belief in a God (although the majority of Democrats no doubt do), but one might think that the Democratic view of government borders on an all-powerful divinity. It seems to me, however, that the Democratic Party has all of the other characteristics.

The Democratic Party has a worldview (which tends to be a secular one) although it may not be as well-defined as in other religions. Primaries, caucuses, and elections are kinds of ceremonies, although we might include other things as well. There is certainly a shared ethical viewpoint among Democrats, although they often seem to think that the views they have about the proper behavior of human beings does not fall under ethics. There is not a canon among Democrats, but there are literary works which are reasonably said to be considered sacred among many Democrats. *An Inconvenient Truth* by Al Gore comes to mind, as well as Michael Moore's movies. We might also think of the Democratic Party Platform as a scriptural document, which spells out the values all Democrats are expected to support. And there is clearly a community of Democrats, including a hierarchy involving people who make decisions for the community as a whole.

We might define a religion more simply as a worldview which allows its holders to make sense of the world, which provides a sort of ultimate reality, and which invests its holders with purpose in their lives. I think it is clear that the Democratic Party would serve as a religion under this definition as well.

I don't want to overemphasize the point. Perhaps other considerations would push the Democratic Party more toward being a religion and other considerations would push it further away. Whether the Democratic Party is a religion or only functionally equivalent to a religion, the important thing is to recognize that its continued existence is insidious. More precisely, the worldview and ethical standpoint with which the Democratic Party has associated itself is the insidious thing. Should the Democratic Party divorce itself from this worldview, then perhaps I would not object to it, but I don't see that happening. For this reason, I will not make any real distinction between the Democratic Party and the worldview it currently supports.

I believe that this worldview, and the organization which holds it and is attempting to spread it, is contrary to my own political philosophy. I believe that it subverts justice, that it leads to less happiness, and that it undermines the value of liberty. It is for these reasons that I have decided to write this criticism of the Democratic Party. I will explain why I am not a member, and how it goes against my deepest convictions. To the extent that you share those convictions, I would argue that you also should not be a member.

I do not consider myself to be a conservative. I consider myself a hardcore liberal, but that term has become twisted so that it is unrecognizable to most people. The bottom line is that I suspect that most of my political values are shared by most of the people reading these words. Look down the list of chapters, and you will begin to see what those values are. For many of those values, most people seem to think that the Democratic Party exemplifies them; I hope to show that nothing could be further from the truth.

One issue I will deal with throughout the book is what to call the ideology I associate with the Democratic Party. I refuse to call it liberalism, because I think it is the antithesis of liberty. I also refuse to call it progressivism, since that implies that the changes it wants to impose are signs of "progress", when I actually think it is fundamentally a reversion to a view which was prevalent before the founding of the United States of America. If I have to give it a name, I think I will just call it "leftism". This term is admittedly unclear, but it seems to me to be the best term we have in America to refer to the ideology in question.

I should attempt to clarify what I take "leftism" to be as much as possible in this short preface. One way to do so is to outline where leftism stands on a variety of public policy issues. I have no doubt that leftist ideology is vague, so that not everyone will agree with every aspect of my list, but I believe it is a fair representation. Here is my list, in no particular order:

Issue	The Leftist Position
Gay Marriage	In favor
Prayer in Schools	Against
The right to abortion	In favor
Minimum Wage	In favor
Welfare	Strongly in favor
School Vouchers	Against
Social Security	In favor (& against privatization)
Inheritance Taxes	In favor
Capital Punishment	Against
Affirmative Action	In favor
Animal Rights	In favor
Income tax	In favor of a progressive and high tax
Role of Judges	Activist
Punishment	Primarily for deterrence/rehabilitation
Eminent Domain	In favor, with few restrictions
Racial Profiling	Against
Gun control	In favor

It is of course true that each one of these issues is complicated, and that this list is a simplification, but that doesn't mean that it is inaccurate. It is also true that not every Democrat adopts the leftist position on every issue. In fact, there may be relatively few Democrats who adopt every position on this list. But that only goes to show that not every Democrat is a complete leftist. Yet, the Democratic Party as a whole seems to be leftist on nearly everything.

I would also say that the positions one holds are not as indicative of one's political ideology as the reasons behind why someone holds that position. Addressing the reasons behind one's positions is more than I want to do at this point. For now, a rough division is enough to give a vague sense of the political philosophy against which I will be arguing.

I have nothing to say here about the Republican Party, or any other political party or organization. I am not now, nor have I ever been a member of any political party. Some of those groups may be objectionable, or despicable in light of my values, and some may not, but that fact can in no way excuse or ameliorate abuses of the Democratic Party. I suppose it is possible that of all political parties, the Democratic one is the most in line with my viewpoint, but if so, then I am glad that I have remained independent politically. I find the offenses of the Democratic Party so egregious that even if no other political party is any better, there is still no way I could join it.

So now you know why I am writing this book. I hope to be as dispassionate and objective as the material will allow, but my goal is a polemical one. My aim is to show that although I share many values with people who consider themselves Democrats, in many cases, it is those very values which make me refuse to join the Democratic Party. I understand that many of those same Democrats are Democrats precisely because they believe in those values, and they have been convinced that the Democratic Party upholds those values as well. It is precisely this presumption which I wish to analyze, and ultimately reject.

To that project, we now turn.

Why I'm Not a Democrat

Introduction

Imagine that there is a small group of prisoners who have been chained since birth so that they cannot even turn their heads. They are imprisoned underground in a cave, and behind the prisoners is a large fire, with people passing on a walkway in between. All the prisoners can see are the shadows cast on the wall, and those shadows are the only reality they have ever known. When the people speak, the prisoners think that the sounds are coming from the shadows themselves, and in fact, they believe that the shadows are all of reality, and that there is nothing more in the world.

This scenario was first presented in Plato's Republic over 2,500 years ago. It is called the Allegory of the Cave, and it is an analogy which makes us reconsider the distinction between reality and appearances, knowledge and mere belief.

Plato continues by asking us to imagine that one of the prisoners is released, and is allowed to leave the cave. At first, he turns away from the wall of shadows and is puzzled by what he sees. For the first time in his life, he sees people, although it is difficult for him to make sense of what he sees. He doesn't even recognize them as people at first, and he certainly doesn't realize that the actual people on the walkway are the causes of the images or shadows of people on the wall. But he begins to realize the truth as he observes things.

He then walks toward the outside of the cave, and emerges into the full sun. His eyes take a while to acclimate, and he can hardly believe his eyes. What he thought was true for so long was finally revealed to be only a silhouette of reality. He had taken an appearance to be the real thing, and he finally understands the truth.

Plato thinks that the prisoner would feel compelled to bring his newfound knowledge to his former prisonmates. Of course, it would be very difficult for him. For one thing, when he goes back into the cave, his eyes would take time to adjust. But besides that, the prisoners who are still in chains would strongly cling to the image of reality which they already had. It would be very hard to convince them that their viewpoint was not reality, but only a hazy copy of the real thing.

Plato was discussing reality in general, and not any particular aspect of it. When I read about the prisoner and the cave, however, I can't help but think of one specific aspect: the reality of political values. I think that Plato was right that even political values are objective in some respect, but I don't want to address such a difficult concept here. I only intend to address the connection between having certain political values, and consistently endorsing policies and politicians who adhere to those values, or, as we will see, the failure to do so. I only want to address the conflict between reality and appearance in the political realm. Does the Democratic Party, in particular, support policies which match the political values to which they purport to adhere?

Too often, people who should be teaching our children are instead indoctrinating them with what I now realize are shadows. Appearances do not match reality. I attended private catholic schools, but even there the indoctrination was heavy. Many of the things which I was taught, which I was expected to absorb and regurgitate, are false. Not only false, but in fact are almost the exact opposite of the truth.

Let me provide a few examples. I was taught that the Democratic Party values individual minorities as human beings, while Republicans do not. I was taught that Republicans were conservative in the sense of mistrusting anything new, while the Democrats were liberal in that they wanted to move to a new system which would be fair for all. I was taught that Democrats believed in an enlightened philosophy where no one imposed any of their personal moral views on anyone else. I was taught that Democrats were the protectors of religious freedom, and that they valued freedom of expression of all kinds.

I don't think I ever fully accepted any of these things completely, but when one is young one usually lacks the experience to see the claims of authorities for what they are. I was no exception. Now, however, I think I am beginning to see them for the distorted falsehoods that they are. With older ears and more experience to fall back on, I can hear the echoes reverberating endlessly within the empty rhetoric used to cling to them.

I follow Plato in valuing reality over appearance. I don't care who says they support certain values, I look for who it is that actually supports positions which are congruent with those values. Many of the values I endorse, and which Democratic politicians claim to endorse, are too often ignored by those very same politicians. I have exited the cave, and seen the light of day, and I have returned to try to help others emerge into the light.

It's one thing if someone disagrees with my values. I may still try to persuade them that they should change their values, but at least then I can understand why they support different policies. But when someone says that they support certain values, and then they support policies which directly undermine those values, well, I just get angry.

I really don't like hypocrisy. Of all human vices, none provoke a visceral reaction in me except for a willful inconsistency. I can no longer stand by while Democrats tell voters that they value the same principles and ideals as me, and then routinely support policies which spit in the face of those values.

As an atheistic community college professor who teaches in the humanities, it would be much easier for me to be a Democrat. A large majority of my colleagues are unabashedly supportive of Democrats, and of the policies supported by Democrats.

Things would be so much simpler. I could have comfortable conversations about politics at work. I could feel welcomed and valued by my colleagues. I wouldn't have to couch every position I express in the safest of ways, so as not to offend anyone. I could announce my support for the candidate I support (who is often a Republican or Libertarian, though not always) without having those around me groan, or worse. And yet, in spite of all that, I refuse to become a Democrat.

Even though it would make a lot of things easier, I just can't do it. While Democrats say they value things like fairness, rights, property, and individuality, they support policies which undermine all of them, at least as I understand them. So, I cannot become a Democrat, at least not as things stand. Ever since I can remember, I have been an independent voter, and I will not change unless I see a good reason to do so.

If you are a committed Republican, I hope you enjoy the book. You will no doubt be enthusiastic about the many instances where I point out blatant hypocrisy on the part of Democrats. Perhaps you will also come to understand political values more deeply. But I suspect there is not much here to change your mind.

Instead, the aim of the book is Democrats, especially young Democrats whose minds are still open, or young indecisive Republicans and independents who are still clinging to the false image of Democrats which was foisted upon them in school. I want to make you really think about the things you value, and your political philosophy in general, and ask whether the Democratic Party is truly supporting those values and respecting your philosophy.

I don't want you to just accept the crass rhetoric foisted upon you in most simplistic political debates. I want, and expect, that you will travel with me and dig deeply into the meanings of words themselves. We will constantly be on the lookout for inconsistency, and we will only accept definitions which are consistent. Then, and only then, will we engage the more difficult task of deciding which policies are most congruent with our values and viewpoint.

Anyone is welcome, as long as your aim is uncovering what is real. I won't usually argue for values themselves, but will take them for granted. I support values such as respect for individual autonomy, a government which is restricted by a Constitution and which has in place checks and balances, respect for others, responsibility, and the idea that no one in our government should favor any one individual or group in our society. If you accept and support these same values, then I invite you to read the rest of the book to see how I think Democrats and the Democratic Party violates or is at odds with each of these values in their practices and the policies they support.

Ultimately, it is up to each reader how he or she reacts to these arguments. If you accept the arguments, it doesn't mean that you must leave the Democratic Party. Presumably, however, you will begin to put pressure on your leaders to change their positions on policies. I suspect that should you do so, you will be far too exasperated to continue on that course.

Keep in mind that should you decide that you cannot remain a Democrat, that doesn't mean that you must become a Republican. Being a political independent has a long and honored history. There are numerous other political parties as well. I simply urge you to make an informed and careful decision that any party you join shares your values and actually lives up to them before you do so.

Lastly, should you disagree with any of the arguments contained within these pages, feel free to let me know. My goal is not necessarily to convince you that what I think is right, but to tell you why I believe it. If I am mistaken, I would be nothing but gracious and thankful to anyone who corrected me (at least that would be my aim). You may send me your comments at mikemonge@archimedespublishing.com. Please do not be offended if I cannot respond to each message that everyone sends.

I look forward to hearing from you.

CHAPTER ONE

Democrats Don't Really Value Democracy

The best argument against democracy is a five-minute conversation with the average voter.

—Winston Churchill

In spite of the name of their political party, Democrats do not value democracy, at least not in its pure form. The real problem I have with Democrats, however, is not that they fail to value direct democracy, but the fact that in their rhetoric they seem to pretend that they do. I say pretend because the Democratic Party accepts large numbers of non-"democratic" institutions within our government, and because I believe that nearly every Democrat would reject pure democracy for a broad range of issues. The problem is that Democrats use "democratic" rhetoric to rally voters to their cause, and against their political enemies, even though they absolutely reject the appeal to "democracy" for a great many issues.

The words "democracy" and "republic", while often used interchangeably, do not mean exactly the same thing. More specifically, the word "democracy" has a second, more specific meaning which the word "republic" does not share. We can think of a republic as a type of democracy, but should recognize that there are democracies that are not republics, at least conceptually.

A republic is a form of government where the supreme political power and authority is vested in the people generally, but political decisions and law-making is done not by the people directly, but by representatives who are elected by the people. A republic is a form of democracy, since ultimate power is vested in the populace generally, and not a single person (a monarchy), or a special group of people who are considered natural rulers (oligarchy or aristocracy).

When democracy was first practiced in Greece, there were no elected representatives. Every citizen could vote on every law or issue which was brought before him. The term "democracy" originally referred specifically to this form of government. Later on, it came to include the republican version of democracy. This original or pure form of democracy is often called "direct democracy" to distinguish it from republicanism.

In America today, both Republicans and Democrats support the idea of representative democracy, where political leaders are elected, and the popular will is expressed only indirectly through them. So, ironically, every Republican is a democrat (in the broad sense), while every Democrat is a republican, and not a democrat (in the narrow sense). Or at least that is what I will argue in the remainder of this chapter.

What Does "Democracy" Mean?

In both direct democracy and republican, or representative, democracy the basic principle of majority rule applies. Whatever the deliberative body in question, a resolution is passed when a majority of the people in the body agrees to it. This principle, that the decision of the majority rules, seems to be at the heart of democracy, or perhaps of any governmental or authoritative body which includes more than one person. Sometimes the term democracy is even used synonymously with the principle of majority rule.

There is an associated use of the word "democracy" which is related to true democracy and majority rule. The concept of one man/one vote is often considered a core principle of a democratic state. The phrase may be a little misleading, however, as it has always meant one citizen/one vote. In most modern democracies, however, there are few to no restrictions on who is a citizen. In the past, there were many criteria, including racial and gender requirements, as well as the requirement to own land. Sometimes "democracy" is associated with the idea of the expansion of citizenship to groups who had previously been denied it.

Today, at least in America, we have universal suffrage: one is a citizen and allowed to vote merely by being born in America or to an American citizen abroad, and reaching the age of maturity. Expanding citizenship to new classes of people will be hard to do, unless we start allowing sixteen year olds to vote. In some states, ex-felons are permanently barred from voting. I suppose one might argue that it is more "democratic" to include them in the process.

The term "democracy" is also sometimes used in an even fuller sense, often when paired with values. In this case, "democratic values" or "democratic ideals" can point toward a system with constitutionally guaranteed rights and freedoms. These ideals have also come to include the value of a society without a segregated system, where only some members of society count as citizens. Some people use "democracy" to refer to a state where discrimination has been eliminated. Others use it to refer to a society where justice is reliable, and people can disagree with those in authority without being punished. I have even seen it used to mean more tolerance, or more equality, or for some version of government neutrality. Efforts to merely increase voter participation are sometimes identified as democratic.

Often the term "democratic regimes" is simply contrasted with repressive regimes. The assumption here seems to be that democracies are not repressive, or are incapable of being repressive.

Exactly why all of these things have come to be subsumed under the term "democracy" is unclear, but it seems to me that people like the term "democracy", and like to lump other good political institutions together under one banner. None of the features listed in the previous paragraph are essential to a democratic state, which is why states which are representative democracies are still sometimes called "undemocratic." On the other hand, repressive dictators such as Hitler, Castro, and Hussein were all elected by a majority vote of citizens, at least ostensibly.

The upshot of all this is that when someone calls for "democratic" reforms, it is not at all clear exactly for what he is calling. It could be a call for the expansion of the franchise. It could be a push toward majority rule. It might be an appeal for a more general vote, as opposed to a representative vote, or it might be a call for a representative vote, as opposed to some other system. It could also be a call for more rights, or for less discrimination. Or it could be a call for freer elections, for some other change to the electoral process, for more tolerance, or for more equality in some way. It might even be simply a push to try to get individuals more involved in electoral politics, or to increase the number of people voting.

The really interesting thing, as I will argue shortly, is that several of the ideas contained under the concept "democracy" are actually contrary to each other. The "fuller" definitions mentioned above are not equivalent to the basic definition, and in many cases, though not all, will actually call for the opposite of what is called for under the basic definition, by which I mean the notion of direct democracy and majority rule. I want to establish that many Democrats, especially people I would consider leaders of the Democratic Party, in their rhetoric and in their pleas to voters, make appeals to a more democratic system, in the sense of direct democracy.

They may sometimes call for "democratic" reforms along the lines of some fuller conception of "democracy", but these appeals do not in general lead to any logical or consistency problems. As we will see, the appeal to a direct democracy does.

Democrats Call For "Democratic" Reforms...

The clearest example of where Democrats have pushed for a more direct democracy is in their call for the elimination of the Electoral College. It may be true that it is not only Democrats who call for the elimination of the Electoral College, and not all Democrats do so, but the call for its elimination runs deep in Democratic circles. I note that the repeal or revision of the Electoral College was not part of the Platform of the Democratic Party, but it seems many people who have publicly called for its repeal have been Democrats, and in my personal experience, it seems to be mostly Democrats who call for it to be abolished. Some prominent Democrats go even further, saying that it is not only time to get rid of it, but that it is a reprehensible institution which never should have been created.

There was a great deal of discussion in Democratic circles about doing away with the Electoral College immediately after the election in 2000. In that election, Al Gore received more votes than George W. Bush, but George W. Bush was still elected to be the President. This outcome was the Constitutionally mandated result, as was made clear by the decision of the Supreme Court to let it stand. Some might consider the impulse among Democrats to do away with the Electoral College to be just sour grapes, but I think it goes beyond that. The timing may have been suspicious, but if we take the words of prominent Democrats seriously, it will become clear that the call for getting rid of the Electoral College is more than just a matter of resentment at Republican victory.

One of the most prominent politicians to comment on the elimination of the Electoral College (at least after the election in 2000) was Hillary Clinton. According to Dean E. Murphy, writing for the New York Times[1], after Mrs. Clinton became Senator Clinton, she "called for the abolition of the Electoral College. She pledged to be a co-sponsor of legislation that would provide for the direct election of the president and vice president." Murphy quoted Mrs. Clinton as saying the following:

> "I have thought about this for a long time. I've always thought we had outlived the need for an Electoral College, and now that I am going to the Senate, I am going to try to

do what I can to make clear that the popular vote, the will of the people, should be followed.

We are a very different country than we were 200 years ago. We have mass communications, we have mobility through transportation means to knit our country together that was not conceived of at the time of the founders' proposals about how we elect our presidents. I believe strongly that in a democracy we should respect the will of the people.

There is no escaping that we are now in a situation where I think most Americans of either party would have to admit we should try to create a national consensus to do away with the Electoral College so that everybody knows that his or her vote will count."

At the time, Mrs. Clinton had appeared with Representative Michael R. McNulty, a Democrat, who sponsored a resolution in the House for a constitutional amendment to eliminate the Electoral College. She praised him and his bill. I just note here that she seems to think the Electoral College fails to be democratic (in some sense) because it fails to respect the will of the people and that it means that people's votes do not count. Presumably, she also thinks the Founders who adopted the Electoral College did not respect the will of the people, or that perhaps they didn't care about it because they didn't have mass-communications. Perhaps I am missing the relevance.

That same year, Lani Guinier wrote a column for The Nation, an independent, but left-leaning publication. In 1993, Lani Guinier was nominated by Bill Clinton to be the Assistant Attorney General for Civil Rights. Her nomination was eventually withdrawn in the face of some controversy, but it is undeniable that her ideas were honored by prominent Democrats.

Her column was mostly about the fact that our winner-take-all system is undemocratic, and should be replaced by a proportional voting one. She did, however, include a criticism of the Electoral College. In her column, entitled "Make Every Vote Count," Guinier first argues that the Electoral College had a racist justification, in what I think is a genetic fallacy, and then criticizes it directly. She points out that:

"under the Electoral College, voters in small states have more than just a voice; indeed their say often exceeds that of voters in big states. In Wyoming one vote in the Electoral

College corresponds to 71,000 voters; in Florida, one electoral vote corresponds to 238,000 voters.

Before the lessons of Florida are forgotten, let us use this window of opportunity to forge a strong pro-democracy coalition to rally around 'one vote, one value.' The value of a vote depends on its being fairly counted but also on its counting toward the election of the person the voter chose as her representative."[2]

Although no newspaper would claim allegiance to the Democratic Party, the political ideology of most major newspapers seems to match Democratic political ideology. In 2004, the Chicago Tribune wrote an editorial which seemed very representative of the position of Democrats generally. The editorial condemned the Electoral College, and then called for its end. After saying that the founders only created it because "they had only a hazy idea how their creation would work," the editorial went on to add that "When it comes to the central event of our national polity, it's hard to justify a system whose only function is to periodically deny the American people the choice they have made at the ballot box. Abolishing the Electoral College would be a welcome step toward a more democratic democracy."[3]

If this call for abolishing the Electoral College were just Democratic griping at losing the election, then the fervor for abolishing it would have died down shortly after the 2000 election, but that does not seem to be the case. Although Democrats have recognized how difficult it would be to amend the Constitution so that for practical purposes it is nearly impossible, some of them have devised plans to undermine the Electoral College without amending the Constitution. One of the most prominent approaches was publicized in a book co-authored by Stanford professor John Koza, who ironically served as a Democratic elector in the 1992 and 2000 elections. Koza's efforts were written about in an article in the San Francisco Chronicle by Matthew Yi. The idea is for the States themselves, who constitutionally retain the power to select electors in whatever way they deem fit, to enter into a compact that will give all of their electors to the winner of the nationwide popular vote. The beauty of the plan is supposedly that it will ensure that the winner of the popular vote will be the winner of the Electoral College, and thus the President, without having to amend the Constitution.

Yi also writes that in 2006 a bill was introduced in Sacramento to implement Koza's plan, called the National Popular Vote plan, in the State of California. Assemblyman Tom Umberg, a Democrat from my original home town of Santa Ana, introduced the bill, and it was approved in the Assembly on a largely party line vote. Yi quotes Umberg as saying "I think that the Electoral College no longer serves a useful purpose. I think direct election of the president by the citizens of the U.S. is a better way to go."[4]

Koza's plan was also glowingly endorsed in a Los Angeles Times editorial. Here is how The Times did it:

"A proposed experiment with majority rule has generated plenty of naysayers who apparently think that some nations are simply too immature to let people directly choose their own leaders. But we say the United States is ready for real democracy.

The experiment is the National Popular Vote campaign, which intends to undermine the Constitution's anachronistic Electoral College. If the campaign succeeds, future presidents will take office only if they win the popular vote nationwide.

…It thus renders the Electoral College moot without eliminating it.

This kind of end run is necessary because the only way to get rid of the Electoral College entirely is via a constitutional amendment, which would be nearly impossible to pass.

Any method besides majority vote empowers some citizens at the expense of others and makes the president beholden to minority interests.

At its inception, the United States was, well, a union of states. But it is now one nation, and our president should be elected by the citizens of that nation, not by its constituent states. To argue otherwise is to say that some Americans should have more power to elect a president than others simply because of where they live. Remember, all men are created equal. Including Californians and New Yorkers."[5]

Throughout these examples, I think it is clear that there is a strong impulse among Democrats to argue for direct democracy. It also seems clear that among this small sample, supporters of eliminating the Electoral College do not see any benefit to it at all, and think that anyone who would support it is blatantly non-democratic, and probably irrationally attached to tradition.

We also see some of the major themes involved with the Electoral College and direct democracy, such as the principle of "one citizen/one vote." Another theme is the criticism of the disenfranchisement of voters. Direct Democracy pushes for more enfranchisement, to the point of universal suffrage, so it would make sense that someone pushing for direct democracy would criticize any effort at disenfranchising voters.

We have also seen that this has been some pretty strong rhetoric. These authors have been making an intense appeal to some of our basic intuitions about the foundations of our society and our core political values. In their eyes, they are simply calling for us to fully implement the promise of Democracy: that all people are created equal and will be recognized as equal and as having an equal say in electoral politics. How could anyone argue against that?

I aim to do exactly that, but I think I better do so slowly, and in stages. I believe that all of this rhetoric betrays a simplistic understanding of our political institutions and a lack of understanding of some basic realities of political philosophy. The truth is, I will argue, that we do not want anything approaching direct democracy, and that all the arguments for it, including the call for the elimination of the Electoral College, are fallacious and inconsistent appeals based on emotion.

Before I do that, however, I want to show that Democrats who use an appeal to direct democracy in some areas are perfectly fine without it in other areas. I want to show that I am far from alone in supporting very non-"democratic" political institutions.

…But Not Even Democrats Support Direct Democracy

One of the easiest ways to see that Democrats do not support direct democracy is to point out one simple fact: Democrats support representative democracy. It may sound odd, since we call them both democracies, but the very notion of representative democracy is to avoid the pitfalls of direct democracy. They are in direct conflict, such that to support representative democracy is necessarily to oppose direct democracy, at least in some respect.

After all, when it comes to actual legislation in the United States Senate, my vote counts for nothing, while Barbara Boxer's counts a great deal. It seems like her vote is infinitely more valuable than mine. Yes, in representative democracy we each vote for our representatives, and every person has an equal vote there, but we are voting for a system in which not every vote counts equally! If it sounds paradoxical, I meant it to be.

When it comes to sentencing convicted felons, my vote does not count as much as the judge or jurors in the trial. Does this disparity violate the principle of one man/one vote? In a very real way, it does. But that is the system we have, and I do not ever recall a Democrat, or anyone else for that matter, arguing that we should get rid of representative democracy generally.

One could perhaps argue that we only accept representative democracy for practical reasons. For example, we can't all observe every trial and then take a majority rule vote. We can't all read every proposed law and then vote, on the internet perhaps, on whether to adopt the law. Such a system would be impossible to administer. Yet, many states have state-wide referenda, in which exactly the thing said to be impossible occurs. On election day, the people in these states actually do vote as a direct democracy, and the majority of the people do decide.

Even so, there may be times where practical necessity forbids us from meeting our obligations to justice, but we should at least attempt to get as close to them as we reasonably can. If our fundamental principles of justice required direct democracy wherever possible, but allowed that we might accept some lesser form of democracy for overwhelming practical reasons, one would think our system would be largely based on direct democracy, except for those instances where we couldn't reasonably achieve it. Instead, our system of government, at the Federal level, at least, never even attempts to incorporate any aspect of direct democracy.

One might also argue that we can retain representative democracy even though we employ direct democracy in one specific area. I would agree, and think that the States which allow referenda or initiatives for *some* laws are beneficial. Yet, I would expect an argument of this nature to include a comparison between direct democracy and representative democracy, as well as an analysis of the strengths and weaknesses of both. Perhaps that might be too much to expect from a politician's stump speech, but a book-length treatment would be woefully inadequate if it didn't include such an argument. Let's see how well Professor Koza's book meets this standard.

Professor Koza and his co-authors, as we saw above, wrote *Every Vote Equal: A State-Baesd Plan for Electing the President by National Popular Vote*.[6] It is a 590 page effort to change our electoral system to guarantee that when there is a conflict, our President is always the winner of the popular vote and not the Electoral College. It's complicated, but it asks states to award electors not on the basis of what that State's voters want, but on the basis of the national popular vote. I presume they would prefer to eliminate the Electoral College altogether, but that would require a Constitutional amendment, which would be too difficult to achieve.

Out of the 590 pages, I count 11 pages which address why the current system is problematic. There are also several forwards, by either Democrats, Independents, or very moderate Republicans, which offer some reasons for changing the system. I find it a little odd that people would launch a quest to fundamentally alter our political institutions involving countless hours and enormous effort on the basis of eleven plus pages, but I am a philosopher. Besides, there could be some incredibly cogent reasoning in those pages.

In section 1.2, Koza lists three "Shortcomings of the Current System", which are that "Voters Are Effectively Disenfranchised in Two Thirds of the States in Presidential Elections", "The Current System Does Not Reliably Reflect the Nationwide Popular Vote", and "Not Every Vote Is Equal". Let's consider each line of argument in turn.

I am concerned about voter disenfranchisement, as we will see, but I don't want the term to lose its force. Jim Crow laws, enacted exclusively by Democrats, truly disenfranchised voters. They were disgusting and deserve scorn and I am grateful they were removed. But I don't want the term to refer to anything other than real efforts to deny a person the ability to vote. So, when Koza argues that voters are currently disenfranchised because under the current system "candidates ignore states where they are far behind because they have nothing to gain by losing those states by a smaller margin"[7], I am troubled. Are Jim Crow laws really comparable to a situation where a candidate doesn't campaign in one's state? I would compare that to calling a kissing bandit a rapist. Actually that analogy is not quite right, because a kissing bandit might still be said to have done something wrong, while I can't say the same thing about deciding to only campaign in places one thinks are most advantageous to one's campaign.

According to Koza, "a vote matters... only if it is cast in a closely divided battleground state". Apparently, Koza and his co-authors believe that a voter is "effectively disenfranchised" if his vote doesn't have a chance of altering an election. I am afraid I might be attacking a straw man, but Koza continues: "the question of whether a voter matters in presidential politics depends on whether *other* voters in the voter's own state happen to be closely divided"[8].

I do want to be careful. I don't think Koza is saying that a vote which won't change an election doesn't matter and disenfranchises the person who cast it (or else every person who votes in an election won by more than one vote would be disenfranchised), but that voters are disenfranchised because the presidential candidate will not visit that voter's state. Personally, I don't believe that this argument is really that much better.

It is truly unbelievable, but Koza's position is that unless a Presidential candidate polls, advertises, or visits your state, then you are disenfranchised. He tells us that "the remaining two thirds of the states are, for all practical purposes, *excluded* from the campaign. They are mere spectators in the election process."[9] [emphasis in original]. This is truly warping the concept of voter disenfranchisement.

Koza states that the "effective disenfranchisement" of these voters has additional effects, namely that "the absence of a meaningful presidential campaign in two thirds of the states diminishes voter turnout in those states". It strikes me that this claim is his evidence for his assertion that there is disenfranchisement, and not an effect of it, but perhaps I quibble. The real problem is conflating a person who is not motivated to cast his vote and a person who is truly barred from voting. No person has the right to have the government offer him a sufficient inducement to get him to the polls, yet that is exactly what Koza is presupposing. No one has the right to have presidential candidates visit them personally, or their vicinity, nor do they have the right to a presidential candidate who excites them sufficiently to get them to cast their vote. Yet, without such rights, there is no way to justify a claim of voter disenfranchisement simply because the Presidential candidates don't campaign in every State.

So the first line of argument fails miserably. It depends upon a distorted idea of what counts as voter disenfranchisement, among other flaws. Sadly, the second line of argument is even worse; it simply begs the question.

There is no thought given at all about the issue. Koza details instances where the popular vote lost out to the electoral vote, and instances where it was close, but he assumes throughout that this outcome is a bad thing. No one disputes the facts in this regard, only whether it is good or bad. Koza just assumes that it is a bad thing, and he is apparently incapable of understanding that some people might disagree. In any case, this "line of argument" does nothing, and we only have one left.

Under the current system "Not Every Vote Is Equal". This is the true reason Koza dislikes the Electoral College. It is also the reason he thinks the National Popular vote is preferable, because he thinks it will mean that all votes would be equal. Unfortunately, he again provides no reason whatsoever that this is a bad thing. He assumes that every person who values democracy in any form will see the obvious truth that every vote should count equally. He does recount evidence which shows that a vote in one state will count more than a vote in a different state, but again, I don't think anyone, including the founders, missed that fact. But repeating facts over and over doesn't establish whether those facts are good or bad.

I have already given many instances in our representative democracy where one person's vote doesn't count as much as another's, but where no one thinks that it makes the system unjust. Perhaps the nationwide election of the President is an exception, but we need to see an argument to that effect, not just question-begging emotional appeals. In fact, changing the Constitution to make the President elected by popular vote would be the first and only instance of direct democracy in our Federal system. It is not and never has been the norm. Furthermore, any argument will be hopelessly incomplete unless it addresses the issue of the vertical distribution of authority. There is a very good reason to have a Union of States, and not a single state.

If it weren't enough that Koza doesn't present a single decent argument for his position, his view seems to counter the very reason Hillary Clinton declares that we should end the Electoral College. She pointed out how we now have mass media. Exactly. Any American can go online and find out more about the various Presidential candidates than at any time in American history. To think that a voter cannot find out about a candidate unless that candidate comes to his state and advertises on his television and radio stations is absolute cluelessness. If anything, most everyone I know *complains* about the frequency of campaign television commercials at election time. No one I know worries that there isn't enough campaigning, and I live in California, which everyone knows will vote for the Democrat.

There were some various other reasons offered in the Forwards of Koza's book. They offer little more than emotional appeals, but they will serve to support many of the claims I have made and will make about leftists in general.

Independent John B. Anderson rails that the statewide winner-take-all system combined with the Electoral College "divided us on regional lines, undercuts accountability, dampens voter participation, and can trump the national popular vote. The system is not based on majority rule, and it fails to provide political equality". He also arrogantly thinks that the Founding Fathers had "a wildly mistaken understanding of the way our political system would evolve", and he adds that the system is "anti-democratic" because "there is no national incentive to spur turnout in a state and expand the franchise". I just note that he assumes that "democracy" requires incentives to voters to cast their votes, and that he seems to misunderstand what "franchise" means.

Democrat Birch Bayh writes that "the most compelling reason for directly electing our president and vice president is one of principle. In the United States every vote must count equally. One person, one vote is more than a clever phrase, it's the cornerstone of justice and equality". At least Bayh has tried to offer some kind of justification for the principle, unlike Koza does in the body of the book. Again, democrats make these kinds of appeals to direct democracy often. The question is whether they really live up to them. Will they, for example, want to get rid of the Supreme Court in favor of direct democracy when it comes to Constitutional interpretation?

Tom Campbell, a very moderate to leftist Republican from California, writes that "If a Third World country, coming into democratic principles out of tyranny, announced a scheme with some citizens worth 4 times as much as others in their governance, it would be told to try again. Indeed, America would tell it to try again!" What an arrogant attitude, made even more troublesome because of its blithe ignorance. First, our Founding Fathers created the very system he thinks we would boldly dismiss, but more importantly he seems to be unaware that his very words condemn *any* kind of representative democracy.

I don't get angry at people who reason poorly, or who are unable to support their opinions with anything but the most spurious and fallacious arguments, or even those who fail to consider deeply the reasons for their beliefs. It is very different when those same people are attempting to compel the rest of us to live according to their ill-considered opinions. I'm not even saying that it would be a bad idea to switch to a direct election of the President. I would only say that the Electoral College is consistent with our values of representative democracy, and that unless a good argument can be made to change it, we should keep it the way it is. I am also saying that Democrats and other leftists try to manipulate the public by using rhetoric appealing to direct democracy, even though they don't support direct democracy in general.

One political institution in our system which is incredibly non-"democratic", but which even very recently most Democrats vigorously argued to preserve, and even argued was sacrosanct, is the Senatorial filibuster. It strikes me as so odd that perhaps I must be overlooking something, but consider a situation where a minority of voters could prevent a majority from acting. Wouldn't we all call that non-democratic? Yet this is exactly what happens in a filibuster.

A filibuster is where a group of 41 Senators can prevent 59 Senators from enacting any piece of legislation. In 2005, a fight was brewing in the Senate over judicial filibusters. When the Senate was going to vote to confirm some of President Bush's judicial nominees, enough Senators supported a filibuster to prevent the confirmation vote from proceeding, effectively postponing indefinitely the confirmation.

Technically, the vote for cloture did not meet the supermajority of 60% required in the Senate in order to proceed.

One might think that the Democrats would argue vociferously to end the whole concept of the filibuster, as it is clearly undemocratic, but surprisingly, it was the Republicans who threatened to end the practice. Amazingly, most Democrats argued strongly that the filibuster should be retained. Eventually, in an extensive bout of political wrangling, Senator John McCain and the so-called "Gang of 14" came to an agreement where seven Republicans agreed to preserve the filibuster, and seven Democrats agreed to only filibuster judicial nominations in "extraordinary circumstances."

The vote to end a filibuster requires a supermajority to pass. A simple majority is achieved when more people vote for a measure than against it, 50.1%. A supermajority requires more than that, usually a two-thirds majority, but it could be set at any percentage above 50%. Supermajorities are non-democratic, at least on the basic definition. It clearly makes some votes count more than others.

And yet that is exactly what Democrats were supporting when they defended the right to filibuster. Since supermajorities are so contrary to one of the basic tenets of democracy, namely that of majority rule, one might think they would be extremely rare in our Constitution. You can judge for yourself. Here are the instances in the Constitution which call for super-majorities:

- Convicting an Impeachment (2/3 majority in the Senate - Article 1, Section 3)
- Expulsion of a member of one house of Congress (2/3 vote of the house in question - Article 1, Section 5)
- Override a Presidential Veto (2/3 majority in both the House and the Senate - Article 1, Section 7)
- Ratify a treaty (2/3 majority in the Senate - Article 2, Section 2)
- Passing of a Constitutional Amendment by Congress (2/3 majority in both the House and the Senate - Article 5)
- Calling for a Constitutional Convention (2/3 of the state legislatures - Article 5)
- Ratifying a Constitutional Amendment (3/4 of the states - Article 5)
- Restore the ability of certain rebels to serve in the government (2/3 majority in both the House and the Senate - 14th Amendment)

- Approval of removal of the President from his position after the Vice President and the Cabinet approve such removal and after the President contests the removal (2/3 majority in both the House and the Senate - 25th Amendment)

Shouldn't anyone who wants to eliminate the undemocratic Electoral College at least have considered whether all of these undemocratic supermajorities should have been eliminated as well? I should point out that many states have also adopted supermajority requirements, generally in regard to raising taxes.

There is also another supermajority requirement in our political system which I'm confident no Democrat would want to eliminate. Juries are a part of our political system. They usually require a unanimous vote. If one of the most basic principles of democracy is majority rule, what could be less democratic? Yet, no one seems to want to get rid of that anachronistic policy.

In fact, a little reflection indicates that most opponents of the Electoral College haven't really thought through their arguments. The entire institution of the Senate is as undemocratic as the Electoral College, if not more!

Ms. Guinier complains in the passage quoted earlier that under the Electoral College, some votes in the College represent more people than others. An elector from Wyoming can represent 71,000 citizens, while one elector in Florida can represent 238,000. Apparently, she thinks this gross inequality violates the democratic ideal of having every vote count equally.

One wonders if she considered the Senate for even one second. Since every state has two Senators, each Senator from California can be said to represent about 18,000,000 people, while each Senator from Wyoming represents around 260,000. This disparity is far greater than the one to which Ms. Guinier was objecting. Would she argue that we should get rid of the U.S. Senate? Would or has any democrat? I would think that anyone who called for the elimination of the Electoral College on these grounds would argue even more vociferously to get rid of the U.S. Senate, as well as numerous other institutions.

There are still other areas where Democrats don't seem to press for a "democratic" vote. Consider the Primaries and Caucuses for the nomination to be President. The Delegates to the Democratic Convention are selected by votes throughout the entire country. It is a simple observation that not every delegate will represent the exact same number of voters. Yet each delegate gets the same vote as every other. I don't recall any Democrat arguing to completely throw out the

Nominating Convention, and replace it with a national popular vote. Maybe I have overlooked someone.

An especially clear example of this disparity was made by the results of the Democratic Primary for the 2008 election. We didn't even need to wait until the convention to see the problem. The Democrats in Nevada award their delegates on the basis of each congressional district. So, let's say they have twenty districts, if one candidate receives the majority of the vote in every district, then they will win all twenty delegates. In general, some districts will have majorities voting for different candidates, so that the delegates will be split, but the size of the majorities makes a big difference.

That year, when one added up all the votes across Nevada, it turned out that Hillary Clinton received more votes. Yet, when the delegates were awarded, Barack Obama had actually won the majority of votes in more districts than did Mrs. Clinton. He was awarded thirteen delegates, whereas she received twelve delegates. The reason was that in districts where Obama won, the vote was very close, and those districts voting for Clinton had a wider vote margin.

The incident was reported by most news outlets, but the disparity between the popular vote and the delegate count was rarely commented upon. When it was, there was no hand-wringing, condemnation, or outrage. It was treated more like a curiosity than anything else. Yet, when we think about it, it is just as undemocratic as the Electoral College. What seems even more incredible is that to my knowledge, no Democrat of any prominence has proposed changing the primary in Nevada to make it more "democratic". Hillary Clinton continually pushed her popular vote count, but I don't recall her declaring that Nevada change its system, much less take any action which would push Nevadans in that direction. Nor has anyone commented on any of the other states which award delegates the same way, but which were lucky enough not to have the popular vote majority diverge with the majority of the delegates. *No one would need to amend the Constitution in order to change these policies.*

Here's another undemocratic institution within the Democratic Party. Interestingly, this one doesn't date back to the founding of the country or the party. I understand that it only goes back to the 1970's. It is the institution of superdelegates, who have the power of delegates, but are not elected.

Ordinary delegates are representatives to the Democratic Convention who are awarded on the basis of the elections or caucuses in the individual states and counties. They pledge to vote for the candidate that wins the relevant primary election or caucus. The Democratic Party awards 3,253 delegates in this way. But there are also

796 superdelegates. These people are able to vote for the Democratic nominee for President merely by virtue of their status in the Democratic Party. They can vote for whomever they want. At the beginning of the primary season for the last Presidential election, the large majority of superdelegates who had announced their position said they were going to vote for Hillary Clinton.[10]

The reason superdelegates became an issue this election cycle is that people began to realize that if the election was close between Barack Obama and Hillary Clinton, then there was a chance the superdelegates could push the election toward Clinton, even if Obama had more popular votes. Ouch. It sounds like the Electoral College all over again. But the superdelegate system was an institution created by Democrats only 40 years or so ago. No one can blame this undemocratic institution on the supposed shortsightedness or stupidity of the founding fathers.

The leaders of the Democratic Party could easily eliminate the provisions for superdelegates from their rules. They wouldn't need the permission of the Republican Party, or the Supreme Court, and they wouldn't need to get the States to approve a Constitutional amendment. I don't recall Mrs. Clinton urging the powerful people in her own party to end this "undemocratic" institution.

If you were wondering whether the Republicans have the same system, they do. They also have automatic unpledged voters. Yet, according to CNN, only 123 of them[11]. So, they have much less of an influence than in the Democratic Party. Besides that, as far as I can tell, Republicans don't use the rhetoric of direct democracy to try to fundamentally alter political structures or for political gain. Republicans may have their flaws, but I don't find them to be inconsistent on this score.

Just to make it clear, the institution of superdelegates was put in place as late as the 1970's, in order to *reduce* the power of the average democratic voter. It was put in place to shift some of the power for electing a nominee from individual Democratic voters to the people who held power within the Democratic Party. It was put in place to allow the people in power to have a veto over regular voters. It has no other function. It is clearly undemocratic, at least on the basic definition.

The Presidential veto power itself is undemocratic, as is any veto power. I am astounded as well at the infrequent, if not non-existent, Democratic criticism of the President's veto power. What institution could be less democratic than for one man to block the wishes of the majority of the representatives in Congress?

The truth is that our political system is riddled with undemocratic institutions, and the Democratic Party seems to be no better, or perhaps no worse. Perhaps we don't value "democracy" in the way some people think we do.

Perhaps Not Everyone Should Vote

One other aspect of democracy, whether direct or republican, is to respect the sanctity of the vote. Even if we recognize that direct democracy may not be an important aspect of our political system, or even that it doesn't matter at all, it still seems important that when someone is allowed to vote for a representative that they are able to do so. No governmental authority should interfere in the franchise of those people who are entitled to vote. If it did, then the people in power could misuse the electoral process to keep that power.

In fact, we don't think anyone should interfere in the ability of people to vote, whether they have governmental authority or not. We have rules against electioneering near polling places, and against bribing someone for their votes, and numerous other rules. We expect our state governments to ensure that these types of abuses do not occur, and if they don't or won't, then we expect the federal government to do so. We do not tolerate the disenfranchisement of voters. This also seems to be a core principle of democracy.

Yet, even here Democrats seem to want to push our country toward a "democratic" ideal which it has never held, and probably should never hold. It is one thing to put barriers in the way of a voter, but it is quite another to put pressure on people to cast their vote. While we can all agree that barriers to voting should go, many of us do not believe that it is important that we encourage all people to vote.

In the passages I quoted earlier, as well as in much Democratic rhetoric, one of the most important things that comes through is the importance of having *everyone* vote. I get the sense that Democrats think a voter who is so disgusted by politics that he stays home has been disenfranchised. Sean Combs, the rapper, said exactly that in an interview on election day in 2004 for CNN. When he was asked why he hadn't voted between 2000 and 2004, he said that he had been disenfranchised, just like younger people. The interviewer pressed him on how he had been disenfranchised, and Mr. Combs replied:

"Because politicians, they just didn't pay attention to us. We're part -- I call ourselves the forgotten ones, youth and minority voters. Their campaign trails don't come into our communities unless they go to the churches, and they don't stop and speak to us as young men and women, like we have power like veterans do or senior citizens, but that's all about to change....

You know, just the candidates not, you know, speaking to my needs, not coming in my community. I'm from Harlem, New York, from an inner-city community, and just going, seeing the school systems there not being taken care of, seeing the people having problems with health care, people having problems getting jobs. And you feel just like nobody cares about you. And your vote doesn't count."[12]

Taking Democrats rhetoric at face value, they are very interested in getting people to the polls regardless of the way the people are going to vote, even if the people are disinterested themselves. They do not seem to care so much that those voters are informed or are capable of making sound judgments, just that they go and cast a vote. Perhaps I have grown overly skeptical, but I've come to believe there is some ulterior motivation going on.

When people are casting a vote, it does matter how informed they are, certainly when they are actually casting a vote for a proposed law, but even when they are only casting a vote to select the person who will be representing them. In fact, the less informed a voter is, and the shallower their understanding of political philosophy, the easier it is to manipulate them into voting a certain way. If a person doesn't have the motivation to cast a vote unless they are dragged to the polls, what makes anyone think that they will be motivated enough to get informed, or learn about the issues, or develop a deep and consistent political philosophy. Yet, without these motivations, it seems like conceit to demand that we respect one's right to vote.

The right to vote, and to influence the course of our government and laws, should not be considered such a trivial thing. Do I want uninformed, disinterested people who can easily be manipulated to cast votes? Consider it this way. We're all in a car together, with each of us having a right to have one hand on the steering wheel. I'm looking ahead to see where we are going. Another person is sitting in the back seat, and not paying any attention at all. Would I want him to exercise his right to put one hand on the steering wheel? The emphatic answer is "No!"

Would I be glad that he didn't have his hand on the wheel? In a sense. My emotions would be mixed. I would hope he would look up and pay attention, and then I would be honored and glad for him to join me in steering, even if he didn't want to go in exactly the same direction as me. But, as long as he is not doing so, yes, in a way I am kinda glad that he is letting the rest of us do the steering.

If some of the people in the car didn't like the way we were going, and decided to use pressure to get even those disinterested, uninformed people to put their hand on the wheel, wouldn't you be suspicious? Wouldn't you worry that they would try to manipulate those who are not paying attention so that they will steer in the new direction, even if that went against their own interests and values? Wouldn't you remind people that they didn't have to put their hand on the wheel, and that they should probably start paying attention before doing so?

I would. I don't think anything good comes out of pushing people to exercise their right to vote. I just don't see that as a valuable thing. If there is an election, and only 20% of eligible voters casts a vote, it does make me a little disheartened that so many people were not that interested, but I also think that maybe I shouldn't judge others so harshly. If they are too busy with their own lives, and they don't have the time to squeeze in a trip to the polling booth, that's not the end of the world. Manipulating and lying to them telling them that their vote "counts" in some magical way, or making them feel bad about it seems a lot worse to me. And 20% of people voting, where each one of them is well-informed and knowledgeable about his own political values and the relevant issues seems a lot better to me than 100% of the people voting, where 90% of them had to be dragged there and don't know the issues, and pretty much vote the way the last commercial they saw urged them to vote.

If urging people to vote, or the fact that they actually decided to cast a vote, truly did motivate them to get involved and learn more, then perhaps one might be able to make the case that we should urge people to vote. Unless someone can show that this causal connection does exist, and that it outweighs the possible damage that can be done by large numbers of people casting uninformed votes, I remain confident that we should not put undue pressure on people to vote. We should welcome them in becoming educated and casting an informed vote, but just getting them to the polls seems not only wasteful, but also positively counter-productive.

Hopefully we can all still agree that direct impediments to voting, or trying to get some people's vote not counted is a bad thing, even if we continue to disagree about the sagaciousness of encouraging disinterested voters to get to the polls. I do take voter disenfranchisement seriously, which is why I don't want people to confuse disenfranchisement with voter apathy. I'm not so bothered by voter apathy, and sometimes think that it is a healthy response. But voter disenfranchisement is always a horrible thing.

The conventional wisdom seems to be that Democrats also care deeply about disenfranchised voters. They often criticize Republicans for using intimidation, lying, and all sorts of other tactics in order to intimidate voters. One of the most prominent examples was in the Florida election of 2000. Google "Florida voter disenfranchisement 2000" and you'll have about 60,000 web pages to sort through.

Looking through many of these pages, one gets the distinct impression that Republicans were behind much of the voter intimidation. None of the articles ever proves anything, but they often do a fantastic job of innuendo, so that most readers will come away from their reading with the distinct impression that Republicans were behind the problems. Some of them outright blame the Republicans, but these are usually obviously biased sources.

One also gets the distinct impression that something incredibly nefarious was going on. Many pages portray the story in a way which indicates that there is something more than just a tragedy going on. It is a tragedy that people are not able to cast their vote, but we need to be clear on what the problem is before we act. Are there people out there who are purposefully targeting certain voters (usually old people and minorities) for their own electoral advantage? There seems to be no evidence to indicate that there is.

In my own personal experience, I have heard many students just blurt out that the Republicans were behind the suppression of minority votes in Florida. They certainly weren't hearing this from Republicans. Over the years I have heard many Democrats cite the Florida example as proof of racist voter disenfranchisement, often citing the fact that the Governor and Secretary of State were Republicans. They obviously believe that the Democrats care deeply about ending voter disenfranchisement and also that Republicans care deeply about continuing voter disenfranchisement.

It seems much more likely to me that it is simply a case of poll workers who don't have much training or knowledge of election procedures. One can lament this fact, but I'm not sure what to do about it. Perhaps they should receive more training, or perhaps we should screen them better, but I believe that there are not enough of them already. Screening them so that we know they are familiar with every voting irregularity might mean that there are not enough of them to run the polls. Training them more would be more expensive.

In my own experience, I have had to correct poll workers on more than one occasion. But I'm knowledgeable about elections and the electoral process. I didn't interpret these events as people trying to disenfranchise voters. I just realized that they were honest, hard-working Americans trying to do their best for their country, who were simply mistaken.

In any case, I am more than happy to consider all the problems and consider solutions. I know the system is far from perfect, but unless we want to coerce well-informed and well-trained people to man the polls, no system will be perfect. And if there are any credible cases where there is prima facie evidence that any person or group intimidated voters in an illegal way, we should consider prosecuting them.

Obviously, I don't think it is true that only Democrats care about voter disenfranchisement. Nor, am I saying that the reality is the exact opposite, where Democrats don't care and everyone else does. What I am saying is that the issue is much more complicated than it is usually presented in the media. Democrats are not above trying to make it harder for some people to vote, and easier for others, and for the most part, they are attempting to gain electoral advantage when they do so.

First, I should point out that poorer people, minorities, and older people tend to vote Democratic. So, for Democrats to fight to ensure that their votes are counted supports the political ambitions of Democrats. I am not saying this to indicate that Democrats are only doing it for crass political advantage, but that it doesn't show that Democrats care about voter enfranchisement just for the sake of some democratic principle or ideal. If Republicans fought to ensure that these voters had their votes counted, that would positively demonstrate that Republicans care about principle over politic advantage.

So, in order to see whether Democrats are fighting for principle over politics, one would need to look at groups of voters who don't tend to vote for the Democrats. Have Democrats fought to ensure that these voters have their votes counted?

Sadly, it looks like in many cases they have not. One of the most famous cases was in the Florida election of 2000. There were 2411 ballots which were cast by military personnel which arrived shortly after the day of the election, or were rejected for some other reason. These ballots were not counted in the original election, but since Florida was engaged in a hand recount, in cases where a voter's intent could be determined, these ballots were being counted. Thirteen Democrats sued to have these ballots thrown out, but the District Court ruled against them, and the ruling was upheld by the 11th Circuit Court of Appeals.[13]

It was widely presumed that military members would tend to vote in favor of George Bush, which was confirmed in this case. Bush received 1,575 of the votes in question, while Gore received 836. There may be a legitimate debate about whether barring these votes would count as disenfranchisement, but my aim is not to settle that issue. The point I am trying to make is that it seems odd for members of a party dedicated to making every vote count suing to get some votes excluded, especially while the party fights strongly to include numerous other excluded votes. I conclude from this that Democrats aren't as worried about disenfranchising voters as they are about disenfranchising *Democratic voters*.

Anyone who doubts whether the Democratic Party or Democratic voters will attempt to disenfranchise non-Democratic voters should talk to Ralph Nader. Nader is despised today by many Democratic voters for allegedly spoiling the election in 2000. He ran in the Green Party, and arguably took just enough votes from Al Gore to throw the election to the Republicans.

Nader recently sued the Democratic Party over the 2004 election. As many readers will remember, many Democrats were still angry over the 2000 election, and strongly urged Nader not to run. He alleges in his lawsuit that they did much more. His lawsuit claims that Democratic "officials conspired to keep him from taking votes away from nominee John Kerry. The suit also alleges that the Democratic National Committee conspired to force Nader off the ballot in several states."[14]

The suit includes numerous allegations, according to Nader's lawyer Carl Mayer, including the following:

> 1. Democratic leaders, including the chairman of the DNC, members of the Kerry Presidential campaign, 53 law firms and over 90 lawyers, coordinated 24 "groundless and abusive" lawsuits against Ralph Nader's 2004 campaign, the majority of which were lost, as a concerted and conspiratorial effort to keep Ralph Nader off the ballot, or to drain him of resources and money.
>
> 2. Democratic leaders or their surrogates filed 5 complaints with the Federal Elections Commission, all of which were dismissed.
>
> 3. These same people and organizations directed people to call petition circulators for Ralph Nader, often at their homes, "informing" them that they could be charged with felonies for certain mistakes on the petitions. While these calls may be accurate, they are clearly attempts at intimidation and fear-mongering.
>
> 4. Certain Democratic operatives in Oregon packed a nominating convention, intending to crowd others out. Ralph Nader needed 1000 signatures to get his name on the ballot, but

since the Democrats wouldn't sign it, he failed to get the requisite number of signatures.

5.   The Service Employees International Union had a project, ACT, or Americans Coming Together, directed its employees to sign petitions for Ralph Nader in the wrong place, so as to void to entire petition.

6.   Toby Moffett, a former Democratic Congressman and president of The Ballot Project, a group apparently organized around keeping Nader off the ballot, admitted to the Guardian UK that "We had a role in the ballot challenges. We distracted him and drained him of resources. I'd be less than honest if I said it was all about the law. It was about stopping Bush from getting elected."[15]

Nader's lawsuit was dismissed by a lower court on the grounds that the actions of the Democratic Party fell under the protections of the First Amendment, which may be true, but this ruling would only seem to confirm that some forms of voter disenfranchisement are Constitutionally protected. We may never know for sure, since the Appeals court avoided answering the substance of the case and instead upheld the dismissal of the case on procedural grounds, namely that the statute of limitations had passed. Still, if even a quarter of what Nader alleges is true and even if these actions are legal, that would still show that Democrats do what they can to keep people who might politically hurt them off the ballot. They are willing to deny voters the ability to cast a vote for the candidate for whom they wish to vote. If that's not voter disenfranchisment, I don't know what is.

Separately from the court case, we can still confirm many of the claims in the lawsuit. The New York Times published a story in 2004, largely confirming the anti-democratic aims of the Ballot Project and other Democratic organizations.[16]

Furthermore, the Pittsburgh Post-Gazette printed a story which backs up the some of the substance of Nader's claims. The following excerpt speaks for itself:

"E-mail messages exchanged by top aides in the Democratic caucus starting in 2004 make clear that taxpayer-funded bonuses were given to legislative employees for their work on election campaigns.

The messages, obtained by the Post-Gazette, are a key component in an investigation by Attorney General Tom Corbett into the bonuses and whether they constituted an illegal use of state money for political work.

In startlingly blunt language, a group of aides, at points working under the direction of then-House Minority Whip Michael Veon, D-Beaver, rated the political work of state employees, sometimes adjusting the amounts of the bonuses based on time they spent in the field or, in one instance, in getting presidential candidate Ralph Nader off the Pennsylvania ballot."[17]

What we need to distinguish is illegal voter disenfranchisement from legal attempts to discourage one's political opponents from voting or from getting their votes counted. As far as I know, there are no widespread illegal attempts at voter disenfranchisement on either side of the political aisle. But I am sure that Democrats engage in numerous activities to discourage or block votes which would hurt them politically. Perhaps Republicans engage in the same political gamesmanship to a greater or lesser extent, but I haven't examined the evidence one way or another. But it is clear that Democrats don't care about voter disenfranchisement generally because of a noble adherence to political principles.

Another anti-democratic endeavor engaged in frequently by Democrats (as well as Republicans) is called gerrymandering. Gerrymandering is the process of elected officials manipulating voting districts to eliminate competition, generally by drawing lines in such a way to make their districts a lock for their own Party. If one Party can put a large majority of the other Party's voters into one district, they will lose that district. But they might be able to do so while ensuring that their Party has five other "safe" districts.

Gerrymanding is another anti-democratic process. It puts power into the hands of politicians and takes it out of the hands of voters. Yet, it's no wonder that nothing has really been done about it. After all, it works. Those politicians who have benefited from the practice are the ones who have the power to do something about it, and for some reason they don't seem to be too motivated to change anything. In fact, some of them brazenly brag about the clever way they can win their seats. In 2001, Democratic candidate Loretta Sanchez admitted as much to the Orange County Register:

"So Rep. Loretta Sanchez of Santa Ana said she and the rest of the Democratic congressional delegation went to Berman and made their own deal. Thirty of the 32 Democratic incumbents have paid Berman $20,000 each, she said, for an 'incumbent-protection plan.' 'Twenty thousand is nothing to keep your seat,' Sanchez said. 'I spend $2 million (campaigning) every election. If my colleagues are smart, they'll pay their $20,000, and Michael will draw the district they can win in. Those who have refused to pay? God help them.'"[18]

Michael Berman was the Democratic consultant hired by the Democratically-controlled legislature to draw up the new Congressional district lines. Far from being indicted for conspiracy charges, Rep. Sanchez still proudly serves in Congress.[19]

There was an effort in California to end the unfairness of gerrymandered districts. Governor Schwarzenegger supported Proposition 77 in 2005. It would take redistricting away from the Democratic controlled legislature and put it in the hands of retired judges. After enormous opposition from both Republican *and* Democratic incumbents, the proposition was defeated. So much for a more "democratic" system.

Two events in the recent primary race are especially noteworthy in considering whether Democrats truly oppose all forms of voter disenfranchisement. First, there was an especially contentious fight in Nevada about certain at-large voting caucuses.

The Nevada Democratic Party wanted to set up at-large caucuses along the Vegas Strip to accommodate hotel employees and other shift workers, who might otherwise have had a more difficult time getting to the traditional caucus sites. The reason they did this was apparently a desire to help certain voters cast their ballots. The teacher's union, largely a Democratic Party subsidiary, sued to prevent these caucuses from being held. The culinary workers union, many of whom work in the casinos, had endorsed Barack Obama, and it was thought that these caucuses would largely tilt toward him. The teacher's union backed Hillary Clinton (although there is no evidence that the Clinton campaign was directly involved the lawsuit), and so it would be in their interest to prevent casino workers from caucusing. Ultimately, a judge sided with the Democratic Party, and the at-large caucuses were held.[20]

Either way, one side of the issue argued that the other side took a position that disenfranchised voters. So much for the commitment to end disenfranchisement. Or maybe we should admit that the issue of disenfranchisement is a complicated issue, and we shouldn't use it as a political club with which to beat up our opponents.

The other issue from the 2008 primaries that highlights the Democrats association with disenfranchisement of voters is the decision of the DNC to strip Florida and Michigan of their delegates to their nominating convention. Democratic Party rules demand that only certain states, which have traditionally done so, may have their primaries or caucuses before February fifth. The political leaders in Florida and Michigan desperately wanted to influence the selection of the presidential nominees, however, and moved their primaries up to January.

The DNC couldn't stand by and allow those leaders to ignore party rules, and so they voted to punish the states. How? By punishing the voters in those states and disallowing all of their delegates their seats at the National Convention. Stripping voters of their vote, or at least from having their vote count in the nomination, was seen as the best way to punish the leaders of those states for disobedience. Wow.

For a party whose members sometimes argue that felons should still retain the right to vote to strip law-abiding citizens of the franchise seems a bit severe. Disenfranchising millions of voters because their leaders didn't obey the DNC seems, well, undemocratic.

Hillary Clinton argued to reseat the delegates, but since she stood to benefit from doing so (she was the only person with her name on the ballot in Michigan), it is difficult to believe that she did it out of principle. What is clear is that the Democratic Party was perfectly willing to disenfranchise voters in order to enforce their own rules, and it was likely political machinations and not principle that drove some Democrats to try to re-enfranchise those voters.

I'm not necessarily condemning Democrats here. I'm just recognizing that many of them put their own electoral interests above that of the "democratic" principle. Okay, that sounds like I'm condemning them. What I'm saying is that the Democrats engage in political machinations which go against "democratic" principles much as the rest of us do. They do what they can to ensure that they will win. If that means requiring officials to abide by the law, and in cases where the law is unclear, pushing for judges to interpret the laws in the way most favorable to them, then they are willing to do so, much as is everyone else, maybe even more strongly than others. They are willing to argue rhetorically for "democratic" ideals when it will help them politically, and they are willing to go against democracy when that will help them. The problem is that they seem oblivious to any kind of inconsistency in their rhetoric, and remember, I really hate intellectual inconsistency.

The resolution to the Florida/Michigan dilemma demonstrates my point. The Rules committee of the Democratic Party held a hearing to decide the issue. I believe that in this meeting they jettisoned two core "democratic" principles, with nary a peep in the media. The first is that they abandoned the one/man one vote principle. Instead they allowed each delegate from Michigan and Florida one half of a vote (Oh, except for the superdelegates, who got their full vote, even though many of them were involved in the decision to move the date of the primary in the first place). I guess they didn't really believe it was a core principle after all.

Secondly, with regard to Michigan, they decided to award votes to a person whose name wasn't even on the ballot. They basically said that they didn't like the results (even though they were the predictable result of their previous decisions), and so instead of apportioning delegates on the basis of the primary, they would substitute their best judgment on what the vote would have looked like *if* they hadn't made their earlier decision to disenfranchise the voters of Michigan. They basically looked at polls gathered on the day of the election, and instead used them to apportion delegates.

I know the Democrats and the media have some close relations, but this seems to give the media a little too much power. On this logic, it seems a waste to have elections at all. If polls were this reliable, we should just rely on them and save the hundreds of millions of dollars it costs to have nationwide elections. Seriously though, if a legislature made the exact same move, we would all recognize it as voter tampering.

I will readily concede that the Democrats believe that they have policies which will be best for the country, and they think their policies are best for those who are disadvantaged. And perhaps they believe that justifies their behavior. I don't think they need any kind of justification. They do what they can within the law to win elections. I don't know why that would need to be justified.

I do object to the reputation Democrats have gotten, though. They seem to have gotten the reputation of being the defenders of the downtrodden, riding out on a white horse to protect minority voters against the evil, rich, white Republicans who are trying to steal their votes away from them. When it comes down to it, Democrats are not above altering rules to make it harder for some people to vote when it helps them politically. It might be nice if they stood on principle here, and supported the principle of "democracy" even when it hurt them, but I can't really expect them to. After all, it's a flawed principle to begin with.

What I do expect of them is that they not use overblown rhetoric about the high ideals of democracy, including one man/one vote and majority rule, in trying to overturn the electoral college and other institutions, while at the same time ignoring those principles in their own Party rules and decisions.

Nor Should Anyone Accept the Principle of Direct Democracy

In the last section, I provided examples of how the Democrats don't in practice support the principle of direct democracy, or the basic principles of majority rule and one man/one vote tied to the basic concept of democracy. They retain and even support numerous anti-democratic policies in our governmental institutions, and even in their own rules. Yet, an insightful reader might still respond that the Democrats are only being hypocritical. That wouldn't prove that they were wrong when they espoused more direct democracy in their rhetoric. The fact that they don't live up to that rhetoric only shows that their actions are inconsistent with their principles, not that there is a problem with their principles.

All of this is true, but what I want to show in this section is that Democrats, and probably everyone reading my words, supports principles which are in direct conflict with the principles of direct democracy, or at least what we all rightfully expect from direct democracy. Let me put this as directly as I can: Anyone who believes in minority rights must reject the principles at the heart of direct democracy.

Should we follow the will of the people? The answer is that it depends. Every time the Supreme Court rules that a law is unconstitutional is for it to violate the will of the people (expressed through their representatives). Anytime someone argues that a law is unjust because it violate someone's rights is to reject the principle that the majority should rule. The unfortunate fact is that a system which allows majoritarian rule as its *highest* value is one which is doomed to severe injustice. Probably the simplest way to say it is that if we were to have pure majority rule, then there would be no such thing as rights of any kind. If our most basic political principle were simply democracy, then in every political struggle, the majority, whether of all the people or of their elected representatives, would have the right to do whatever it wanted with any minority group, whether racial, ethnic, ideological, or simply the minority who voted against the law.

Gone would be the concept of civil rights, personal rights, even human rights, only to be replaced by the principle that if the majority of the people decide something, then it is true. If the majority decides that an individual should act in one way, and that individual refuses, then the majority is justified in fining, imprisoning, and even possibly executing that individual.

The only reason we recognize rights is to place an activity outside the jurisdiction of majority rule, or any authority. My right to free speech is there to protect me from the majority when it doesn't like what I am saying. It says that even if the majority wanted to prevent me from speaking (within certain clearly defined limits), then it could not. At least, not justly. And our system is set up so that there are individuals in place who can protect me from that majority. That is one of the functions of the judicial branch of government.

Consider any number of situations: a majority of Americans decides to put Japanese Americans in internment camps, a majority of Americans decides to subject Muslims to additional security procedures before they board a plane, a majority of Americans votes to allow slavery, a majority of Americans wants to round up immigrants and send them home, a majority of Americans decides that American Indians should all live on reservations, a majority of Americans wants to make homosexuality illegal, a majority of Americans thinks it is permissible to insert the words "under God" in the pledge of allegiance, and have everyone else recite it.

Each one of these has either occurred historically, or else is plausible even today. If one truly believed in the concept of direct democratic majoritarian rule, then one would have to say that the majority should get its way in every one of these cases. One could not then consistently argue that each of these minority groups has rights, or should be treated decently, or even fairly. To try to go against the majority in any of these situations necessarily puts some certain value *above* the value of direct democracy and majority rule.

The majority of California voters not too long ago voted in favor of Proposition 187. It was a law which, among other things, would prevent the children of illegal immigrants from getting a free public education in America. Did Democrats sit back and say that the majority had ruled, and after all we are a democracy, so every should get one vote and have their votes counted? No. They went to a judge. One person. One person whose "vote" could overrule millions of voters. No one could call this "democratic" in the strict sense. Yet, even those who supported Proposition 187 should realize that there must be constitutional limits even on laws passed directly by a majority of citizens.

So, then, if democracy cannot be our highest value, what can be? And, why do we value democracy at all? For us in the United States, historically, the answer has been clear: Liberty. The United States was founded on the idea that government has as its mandate the protection of freedom. The guiding political principle upon which our country was founded was that of liberty, and the respect for the autonomy of all, and *not* majority rule. The highest value enshrined and embodied in our political institutions has been the principle that a person is entitled to act in any way he chooses as long as he does not infringe on another person's choices and autonomy, and that government is instituted to protect this entitlement.

A person has freedom when there is a lack of directly coercive measures being used to manipulate him into behaving or believing a certain way. A person's freedom is taken away when he has several legitimate choices (one's which do not infringe on the autonomous choices of others) open to him, and someone uses force or fraud to take one of those choices away.

Adopting the value of freedom has numerous related implications. It means that we will judge our political institutions by how well they promote the value of freedom. It means that if our political system takes away freedom instead of supporting it, we will find that system deficient, if not downright unjust. It also means that we cannot support direct democracy, since we are well aware through historical experience and common sense that in a direct democracy, freedom is too often sacrificed for security or for the moral sensibility of the majority.

So, if liberty is our guiding principle, what political system should we institute in order to preserve and maximize our liberty? There aren't a lot of alternatives. We could entrust liberty in no one's hands, so that each person could gain as much liberty as he has strength. Most of us don't think anarchy is the way to go. We could entrust our liberty into the hands of the majority of the popular vote, but as we have seen, this option might not be the best option. Another alternative is to entrust our liberty into the hands of one man. Thomas Hobbes wrote *Leviathan* long ago to advocate that this was the only rational position. Most of us, however, think that this solution leaves a lot to be desired. Dictatorship has not historically been associated with freedom.

The only other alternative is to entrust our liberty to groups of men. If it were a group of men who never changed, I suspect most of us would worry that we would become an oligarchy. Instead, we change our leaders often in order to prevent that from happening. It's not that we think our leaders will always be corrupted by power, although that is a concern, but more that if they are corrupted, it may be too late to change things unless we already have a system in place. Plus, we are confident that there are many people in our country who are competent enough to wield power, and we think we should spread it around a bit.

We also know that many people in power will want to continue holding on to that power, and so we need something besides just frequent elections to prevent that. Here, we don't hold out hope that all of our leaders will be purely idealistic, but adopt a system that works even when some people want to overreach the power they think they have. When one leader goes too far, we have others leaders to reign him in. If they are all vying for power, then they will keep each other in check, so that we don't have to. That's the beauty of having power distributed among many people.

We also ingeniously distribute power horizontally among different branches of government, each with their own job, responsibilities, and limits. The executive, legislative, and judicial branches of government accomplish this horizontal distribution. Each branch will naturally think itself the most important, and want to become more powerful than the others, but that's why we give each of them power over the others in a system called checks and balances. One branch of government can override what another branch is doing. The President can veto Congress, and the Supreme Court can override laws. The President can commute sentences, and he decides when to ignore violations of a law as well. The Congress can begin the process to amend the Constitution and override the President's veto. It's kind of like a game of rock, paper, scissors, but with the real world at stake.

We also divide political authority vertically, by having several layers of political authority, with each layer having different purposes and jurisdictions. Thus, we have the federal government, state governments, and various county, or city governments as well. Each layer has its own limits to its authority, and the other layers have recourse to prevent any layer from gaining excessive power, although often they must rely on one of the branches of the federal government.

Having set terms for elected officials is also an essential feature of a good political system. Terms themselves put limits on the majority. Many people think that the only purpose of set terms is to get rid of politicians after a given time, but an equal function is to *keep* them in office longer than people might want them there. Imagine a system where we could remove an official from office just by an internet vote. On any given day, if a majority of the people who logged on and voted wanted to remove a government official from office, they would immediately be removed from office. I know many of us feel an intuitive pinch that this would be a great device. It would ensure that all of these governmental officials would govern in accordance with the wishes of the majority. Yet, that is exactly the point I have been trying to demonstrate. We should recognize that sometimes we want our officials to govern in direct opposition to what the majority would want. Often, we consider these leaders to be the most courageous and honorable. Consider Martin Luther King, Jr.: Did he just go with the flow, or did he fight to overturn the sentiments of the majority and dignify our nation.

Even though every official obtains his office and will lose it because the majority of the people want it to be so, we realize that we must in some way insulate these officials from immediate retaliation. Presumably, some of these officials will have to decide matters in favor of our primary value, liberty, over the implicit or expressed will of the majority, and we wouldn't want the majority to immediately take it out against these officials by removing them from office.

Our Constitution is the document that sets these limits on authority. It puts self-imposed limits on how far any majority can push any minority. The Constitution enshrines our values and principles, and puts a system in place whereby the majority knows its will can be frustrated by single officials. We realize that a majority of the people can sometimes act in a shortsighted and impetuous manner, which is part of the reason why we have a representative democracy in the first place. This realization also leads us to put in writing our highest principles, and then put people in place who will help us live up to those principles even when we don't feel like it.

Ideally, we decide on constitutional principles and rights in calm, reflective moments which offer the greatest protection of freedom, so that when we are in less reflective moments a majority of the people cannot simply force its will on any minority. Our highest political value is not democracy, per se, but liberty, but we recognize that a democracy is the best way to achieve it. Not a direct democracy, of course, but a constitutional republic, or representative democracy, with power and authority distributed horizontally and vertically, and plenty of checks and balances.

Truth, Justice, and the American Way. All societies must value truth and justice, but only America values freedom as an inherent good and the highest political value. Furthermore, the American understanding of justice depends on its value of liberty. Justice must be practiced by any functioning society, but what counts as just or unjust is a function of what amount of liberty each person is recognized to have. In America, we have traditionally understood each person to have a maximal amount of liberty, which means we have understood any attempt by the government to dictate to Americans how to live their lives to be unjust.

When it comes to the issue of supermajorities, the whole point is to shield minority groups from the capricious decisions of the majority, especially a bare majority. One can often entice a majority with pure rhetoric and emotional manipulation. We presume that to convince a supermajority requires more substantive persuasive devices. To persuade a supermajority requires that one have a good reason to enact some governmental policy. No one who has a good reason on his side should be afraid of having to entice a supermajority to enact legislation.

I hope it is clear at this point that the heart of constitutional democracy, or perhaps its brain, is that the majority does not, and *should not*, always get what it wants. One of the most basic checks in a constitutional representative democracy is *on* the majority, which is just as it should be.

I would be open to arguments that the Electoral College is not necessary for us to live up to the ideals of American democracy, but these arguments should not be capricious and emotional and based upon disappointment over an electoral outcome. They should also take seriously the checks and balances inherent in the horizontal and vertical distribution of governmental authority.

If one appeals to the principle of one-man one-vote to support your choice for president, or for pulling out of Iraq, for example, then I expect the same person to adhere to that principle when it comes to what our country should do with illegal aliens, and when it comes to gay marriage. One who appeals to the voice of the people when it comes to universal healthcare must also accept it when it comes to prayer in schools.

One should not, however, demand that we accept the will of the people when the majority agrees with one's viewpoint, and then attack those who disagree for being undemocratic. Not while at the same time arguing that judges should strike down any law which the majority supports because one finds it Constitutionally objectionable. Either accept majoritarianism, or don't. But don't try to have it both ways. Recognize that strict majority rule without any check has never been one of the values of the United States, and that supporting one's policies and laws merely by pointing to popular agreement only betrays that one cannot support those policies and laws by using reason and argument.

Final Thoughts

Perhaps there is a kind of conservative point to supermajority requirements. It tends to mitigate against unreflective, hasty changes, and that would fit at least one definition for "conservative." But if so, then we are all conservatives in that sense, and that is a good thing.

What prevents me from being a Democrat, even in this regard, is their hypocritical use of the majority. On the one hand, they will treat it as sacred, in such a way that preventing it from obtaining its will is tantamount to fascism. Then, in other cases they will unreflectively attack that same majority as wrong-headed and irrelevant to obtaining the "true" democratic paradise they know is always just around the corner, which can only be obtained by judicial fiat.

I can overlook a lot, and if either Democratic regulars, or their Democratic leaders knew about this hypocritical tendency, and spoke against it, criticizing it and trying to ameliorate it, then this tendency alone would not prevent me from being a Democrat. But it seems to me that the hypocrisy is strewn throughout all levels of Democrats, and that their leaders use it rhetorically in speeches, intensifying and solidifying it among Democratic regulars who already lean in the same direction.

The truth is that the minority should sometimes get what it wants and sometimes the majority should not, and the republic we have created allows that to happen. Democracy, in terms of majority rule and the idea of each person having an equal say, has never been for us an intrinsic value. It is only an instrumental value, worthy only because it provides for the maximum amount of liberty possible. Once democracy starts to tread on liberty, we should recognize it as failing, and should take steps to correct it. If one recognizes that this is the way it should be, then one should never make an unreflective appeal to majority rule or democracy in the simple sense.

As for democracy in the broad sense, as a system of government which recognizes strong civil rights and freedoms, these are fantastic values which I support. Yet, I must note that there is nothing "democratic" about them, which is why I am a Liberal, but not a Democrat. If that doesn't make any sense to you, make sure you read the last chapter.

I might be able to overlook what I take to be hypocrisy in this regard, if it were my only concern. The truth is that I have many other reasons, probably the most serious of which is that I believe that Democratic ideology is strewn with racism, as I will argue in the next chapter.

CHAPTER TWO

The Democratic Party: Racist Then, Racist Now

I have a dream that my four little children will one live in a nation where they will not be judged by the color of their skin, but by the content of their character.
—Martin Luther King, Jr.

A Cold Winter Day in January

In celebration of Martin Luther King, Jr. Day in 2003, Hillary Clinton made the following comments:

> "Yes, we want to be judged by the content of our character and not the color of our skin. But what makes up character? If we don't take race as part of our character, then we are kidding ourselves."

Later in the day she expressed the same basic idea in the following way:

> "Well, of course [we want to be judged by our character], but what is character? The sum total of who you are. The color of your skin and how you deal with it is part of your character."

I have very strong feelings regarding these comments, but I will wait to address them until the end of this chapter.

Do Republicans tend to be racists? I suspect most Democrats will say that they do, or at the very least that Republicans tend to be more racist than Democrats tend to be. This is an important issue for me. If this view is correct, then it would give me a strong impetus to become a Democrat. Even if the leaders and structures of the Republican Party were not racist, but only rank and file Republicans were, or vice versa, then I suspect I would still quickly join the Democratic Party.

I'm not convinced. Take the issue of Affirmative Action. Democrats, by and large, want to treat minorities differently, and Republicans, by and large, don't. Republicans sometimes say that Democrats are racist because of the Democrat's view in favor of

Affirmative Action, and Democrats often accuse Republicans of racism precisely because they are opposed to it. They can't both be right.

As a philosopher, I know that when people are in a disagreement like this, it is important to take a step back and define one's terms. It won't always settle the issue, but it can be a start. Before we do that, however, we should settle an issue where I think all of us would agree: in the past, there were large numbers of virulently racist Americans. And in order to avoid making any mistakes in the future, it is important to fully understand the past. With that in mind, I ask you to take the following survey.

A Quick Survey

Answer the following questions for yourself. The answer is either Democrat or Republican for each question. Don't read ahead until you've honestly attempted to answer each one.

1. Which political party pushed to end slavery?
2. Which political party enacted Jim Crow laws to prevent black people from voting?
3. Which political party first supported civil rights laws?
4. Which political party supports affirmative action?
5. Members of which political party fought to ensure that schools remained segregated?

Don't read on until you answer the questions above.

Answers:

The Democratic Party is the answer to questions 2, 4, and 5, and the Republican Party is the answer for questions 1 and 3. I would hope that every American responding to this brief survey would get every answer correct, but I have watched Jay Leno's "Jaywalking" segment often enough to know better.

I recently gave this survey to some of my own junior college classes, although I let them answer using any political party and not just Democrats and Republicans. Here are the results from my classes:

Question 1: Republican 42% (correct); Democrat 27%; other 31%; (58% wrong)

Question 2: Democrat 36% (correct); Republican 40%; other 24%; (64% wrong)

Question 3: Republican 26% (correct); Democrat 53%; other 21%; (74% wrong)

Question 4: Democrat 62% (correct); Republican 32%; other 6%; (38% wrong)

Question 5: Democrat 21% (correct); Republican 63%; other 17%; (79% wrong)

As one can see, they didn't do very well. The only question the majority got correct was the one about affirmative action. I don't blame them as much as I blame our school system. The job of the schools is to inform students and give them the knowledge they need to be responsible adults, and in this area, I think the results speak for themselves.

What seems especially troubling is that Democrats get far more credit for progress on civil rights than they deserve. These results say quite a bit about my student's knowledge of history, as well as their attitude toward and understanding of the Democratic Party.

Regardless of the current state of affairs, I think it is important to have a solid background in history. Forming one's opinions cannot be as complete, and will often be completely skewed, unless those opinions are informed by knowledge of the past. Most of you reading this will no doubt think that the Democratic Party is the leader in terms of racial issues and racial equality, but you cannot let that belief write a new history for the Party. If the Democratic Party is the more progressive party on race, it is *in spite* of its history, and not a continuation of its history.

The Ugly History of the Democratic Party

The Democratic Party was formed out of the older Democratic-Republican party which fought with the Federalists at the beginning of political parties in America. From the very beginning, the Party had its strongest support in the Southern states. One of the first Democrats was Andrew Jackson, who incidentally greatly expanded the "spoils-system" of paying off political allies with government positions.

The Republican Party is much younger, and was formed shortly before the Civil War by disaffected Whigs and Democrats with the express purpose of halting the expansion of slavery. It was associated with the anti-slavery North, and its second Presidential nominee was Abraham Lincoln.

Even before the Civil War, the Democrats were behind some pretty vile pieces of legislation. They supported the Kansas-Nebraska Act of 1854, which rescinded the Missouri Compromise, allowing slavery to extend north of latitude 36°30'. This Act led to bloodshed in Kansas, and was part of the impetus for the formation of the Republican Party. Democrats also supported the Fugitive Slave Law of 1850, which included various provisions to ensure that fugitive slaves were returned, and to punish anyone, like Harriet Tubman, who helped slaves escape.

When the Southern states seceded, beginning in 1860, the Democrats who remained in the North no longer had the support of their Southern contingent, and the Republicans basically ran the Federal government for the next ten years. Republicans retained the Senate for almost twenty.

When Abraham Lincoln issued the Emancipation Proclamation in 1862, freeing all slaves in the Southern states, it was Democrats, both Southern and Northern (known as Copperheads), who opposed it. Perhaps analogously to their modern brethren, many of the Copperheads wanted Lincoln to end the war and withdraw from the South. They believed that the South could not be beaten, and resented the fact that they thought the war was being continued in order to end slavery.

Republicans in the Senate were pushing to end slavery throughout the entire Union by passing the Thirteenth Amendment even before the Civil War was over. The more moderate House of Representatives prevented it. In the elections of 1864, Abraham Lincoln, in a politically astute move, chose Andrew Johnson, a southern Democrat, for his Vice-President. Lincoln was reelected, and perhaps feeling more secure, he finally asked the House to pass the amendment to end slavery, which it then did.[21]

Just to demonstrate the size of the difference between the parties on the issue, all 86 Republican Representatives of Congress voted to end slavery, with none being absent. Of the 72 Democrats in the House, only ten voted to end slavery with 8 not voting.[22] The end of the war came a few months after Congress passed this amendment.

Although he supported the Thirteenth Amendment, which he knew would infuriate Southerners and most Democrats, Lincoln was otherwise in favor of an amicable Reconstruction. Many northern Republicans, however, wanted to punish the South, and to forcefully remove all vestiges of Southern privilege.

When he was assassinated, the Republicans were concerned that Johnson would pursue Lincoln's amicable strategy. They were right to be concerned. Johnson, a Democrat, also thought that issues of how ex-slaves were to be handled should be left to the individual states to decide, a policy which would have left many of them little better than they were as slaves.

In response, the Republicans attempted to pass a Civil Rights Bill, along with other legislation, all of which Johnson routinely vetoed. The Congress overrode the President's veto of the Civil Rights Bill, which then conferred citizenship on all black people, overriding the Dred Scot Decision, and guaranteed civil rights for all. Doubts about the Constitutionality of the measure, however, led some members of Congress to introduce the Fourteenth Amendment. As you can imagine, Republicans voted overwhelmingly in favor of it, and Democrats against.

The issue of voting had remained unresolved, even though Lincoln and other Republicans had brought it up. In fact, it was likely the reason Booth decided to assassinate Lincoln instead of just kidnapping him. One problem was that slaves had originally been counted as three-fifths of a person for the issue of apportionment, or for assigning representatives. If black people would then count as one person without being able to vote, all of a sudden, the South would have a dramatic boost in their representatives, threatening to overturn everything won in the Civil War.

The easy solution was to ensure that one's race could not be used by the States to exclude people from voting. The right to vote was the final piece of legislation to bring black people to anywhere near having equal rights in America. I'm sure that at this point, no reader would be too surprised to read that every Congressman who voted in favor of the Fifteenth Amendment was a Republican, and every single Democrat voted against it.[23]

The South, mostly, though not exclusively Democratic, did not take all this lying down. They were pressured into accepting the Fifteenth Amendment because they would not be readmitted to the Union until they had, but they did everything they could to make sure that equality was postponed. According to the non-partisan Reader's Digest Association:

> "Some say Reconstruction failed because it was not carried far enough; others insist corruption and white Southern resistance to Negro equality doomed it from the start. Whatever the answer, Reconstruction's failure recoiled upon the unfortunate Negroes when Southern whites [mostly Democrats] again assumed full power. In addition, Southern bitterness generated by loss of the war and dislike of

Republican control during Reconstruction helped create a solid bloc of Democratic votes upon which the party could count, regardless of its programs, for more than a hundred years."[24]

The Democratic response to the growing power of anti-slavery activists was to form the KKK, according to PBS' "American Experience", which was later used to intimidate Republicans and others. When Democrats gained control of the House in 1876, they put a stop to all Civil Rights legislation, and in 1892, when they gained control of all three branches of government, they repealed all the civil rights protections they could. Then their fellow Democrats in the Southern State's governments set about instituting Jim Crow laws and Poll taxes.

This is the history of the Democratic Party, and it is pretty disgusting. Many readers may be protesting that this history is long gone, and the Democratic Party has grown quite a bit from its vile, racist past. They would certainly be correct that the Democratic Party has changed. I do still wonder how anyone could be a member of a party with such a sordid past. Couldn't Democrats change the name of the party, or form a new party, or do something to firmly and unequivocally repudiate its racist history? Besides just ignoring or forgetting it, that is.

In the early part of the 20th century Southern Democrats continued to institute and protect segregation and Jim Crow laws, and the dominance of the Democratic Party in Washington meant that the federal government failed to come down on them. In fact, the nonpartisan Dirksen Congressional Center reports that "In the twenty-six major civil rights votes since 1933, a majority of Democrats opposed civil rights legislation in over 80% of the votes. By contrast, the Republican majority favored civil rights in over 96% of the votes."[25]

Yet, there was a clear split in the Democratic Party, which began at some point in the early twentieth century. When Civil Rights finally made it to the legislative agenda in the sixties, there was a large contingent of Democrats, mainly from the North and West, who supported Civil Rights for all. When it came to the Civil Rights Act of 1964, fully 63% of Democrats supported the bill. That's not very close to the Republican 80% who supported it, but it still shows that there was significant change in the Democratic Party.

I do have to say that I believe that some portions of the Civil Rights Act may be unconstitutional and unjust, but I will leave that for the chapter on liberalism. Suffice it to say that when good men do something unjust as an overreaction to not-so-good people doing something unjust, they can still be considered good men.

The Democratic Party Today

Although it is well-established that the history of the Democratic Party is filled with racism and bigotry, I don't mean to imply that nothing has changed. As many readers have no doubt already considered, it is not fair to criticize the Democratic Party today for what it did fifty years ago and more. This is of course true, but it is not what I have been doing. So far, I have only condemned the Democratic Party for what it did fifty years ago. No one should think that the racist past of the Democratic Party necessarily means that the Democratic Party is racist today, but nor should anyone forget that history. Nor should anyone distort the past and think that the Democratic Party of the past fought for civil rights or struggled to free slaves, when it in fact did the exact opposite.

In order to judge the Democratic Party today, we need to examine the present, and its positions and attitudes today. As we will see, I believe that the available evidence reveals that in opposition to what most Americans expect, the Democratic Party is just as racist as it has ever been. It is true that the animosity of the past has largely dissipated, but racism goes beyond animosity. Racial hatred is only the outward sign of a much deeper sickness. Before examining any evidence, first we need to investigate what it means to be a racist.

Defining Terms

I think that when most people think about racism, they associate it with animosity toward people in a particular race. A racist is a person who hates people in a race other than his own.

I have no doubt that a person who hates people in another race should be classified as racist. My question is whether anyone else can be a racist. It is true that Democrats today are no longer full of the hatred and bigotry that their forbears had, but I submit that one can be racist in other ways. Racism is not just hatred; in fact, it is primarily something else.

I think I can demonstrate this point by considering a hypothetical passage. What would we all say about a person who made this speech:

"I love all people, especially those in the African-American community. They have such a vibrant culture which is so interesting. It just so happens that in America in the past, African-Americans were horribly mistreated and discriminated against, and so today they are not as intelligent nor as able as white people. And I'm not sure they will ever be. That's why we white people have to give them affirmative action. We, being smarter and more able, have to take care of them, just like able-bodied family members should take care of children who are developmentally disabled."

I take it that we would all consider this person to be a racist. Yet, there is not a hint of animosity or hatred in the passage. If you agree that this person is a racist, then you cannot consistently believe that one must have hate in order to be a racist. One important consequence of this fact is that one cannot defend oneself from a charge of racism by saying "but I don't hate anyone." Hatred is not a necessary component of racism.

Another way to see the same point is to consider the power of the word "racist." It is not an idle criticism to be lightly tossed around. It is not like calling someone a "hater," which is a negative label. Saying that someone hates another person might be a criticism, but it is nowhere near calling them a racist. Calling someone a racist indicates that you think he *is* a racist, which is a deep moral flaw. It may not be as bad as murder, but I suspect many of us think it is worse than some commonly recognized crimes. Consider this: would you rather have your parents think you are a racist, or a shoplifter?

So, racism goes beyond just hatred, and there must be something else which gives the term the power that it has. Hating one individual because of the things he has done might be justifiable, and I don't think that alone could ever make someone a racist. Hating someone simply because of the color of his skin, that is what makes a person a racist. But what exactly is the difference, and why does the difference matter so much?

I hope the answer to these questions will become clear by considering several other possible definitions for "racism". Here they are.

A racist is someone who:

1) hates all people in another race.
2) discriminates against people in another race.
3) believes they are a member of a superior race.

4) makes race-based generalizations about people.

5) doubts, diminishes, or questions whether black people have it harder in our society than others.

6) believes that a there are inherent differences among people in different races.

As we have seen, the first definition is too narrow. It doesn't capture the essence of what is wrong with being racist. The second definition seems to be a bit better, but still faces an insurmountable obstacle: someone can be racist even if he never actually discriminates against anyone. One can be racist in thought only, which would be impossible if we defined racism purely in terms of actual discrimination. We need a definition which encompasses beliefs, attitudes, or behavior, and the second definition doesn't work.

Of course, one's racist attitude will often be revealed in one's behavior, and we can't judge a person's opinion's unless he shares them with us. So, often our only evidence for a person's racism will be his behavior, but our definition must apply to one's opinions if it is going to match the actual use of the term in our conversations. Thus, racial discrimination might be evidence that a person is a racist, but it is not the definition of racism.

The third definition might seem promising, but suffers the same problem as the first two definitions. People who believe they are a member of a superior race are no doubt racist, but is every racist a person who believes he is a member of a superior race. Imagine a person who thinks he is a member of an inferior race, someone who truly believes that there were superior and inferior races, but that he happened to be born into the inferior one. I would classify such a person as a racist. So, the third definition is also deficient.

Perhaps the fourth definition is what we have had in mind all along. Certainly a person who hates the members of a certain race will make race-based generalizations, and one who discriminates against others or thinks he is in a superior (or inferior) race will make racial generalizations. In this way, the fourth definition can subsume the other definitions under it. That makes it a much better candidate for a successful definition. It does a better job than any of the other definitions at capturing what we think is truly wrong with racism.

Unfortunately, I don't think it will work either. Here, I think the problem is that the definition is too broad. It will include people who are not racists.

Stereotypes are generalizations about people, so this definition in effect says that anyone who engages in racial stereotyping is a racist.

Perhaps many readers will find that this is an acceptable definition, but careful examination reveals that it is not. A person who is not a racist can engage in racial stereotyping, and a few considerations will show this to be true.

If no generalizations could ever be made about race, then sociologists would be out of a job. Truthfully, they would still be able to collect data on gender and other differences (until we consider feminism, perhaps), but a large part of what they do would be morally wrong. Sociologists make racial generalizations all the time, when they present statistics on the differences between people of different races.

For one to say that black people make less money on average than white people is a racial generalization. I would hope that no one would consider it to be morally wrong to say so. There are numerous ways in which the Hispanic population differs from other racial groups. The field of sociology takes pride in finding and cataloging these differences. To recognize that these differences exist is not racism, it's not even morally wrong.

Don't think that I just said that there is nothing wrong with any kind of stereotyping. My point is that drawing racial generalizations about people is not always wrong, and so it would not be a good way to define racism. There still may be plenty wrong with stereotyping.

One problem with most forms of stereotyping is that it is done on the basis of too small of a sample. To jump from the experiences one has with a group of people to make conclusions about every member of that group is wrong. But this is an intellectual error, and it applies whether we are talking about people and races, or cell phones and call zones. To make hasty generalizations is a flawed form of reasoning, no matter what we are talking about. Perhaps it is especially wrong when considering the diversity of human beings, but it is still an intellectual error, and not a moral one.

Racism is a deep moral flaw, and not a simple intellectual problem. If racism were simple fallacious reasoning, then the criticism could not carry the weight that we give it.

If you still aren't convinced, just consider the comparable weights of these criticisms:

A: You drew a hasty generalization.
B: You are a racist.

There seems to be no comparison. Being a racist must mean more than simply engaging in basic fallacious reasoning. We don't morally condemn someone who is guilty only of reasoning poorly.

Besides this, notice how easily it is to move from thinking statistically about populations, to thinking intrinsically. Sociologists rarely make any assertions about *all* members of a population. They only claim to achieve a measure of the differing variability among different groups.

Imagine someone asserts that white people are taller than Hispanic people. Would this alone make them racist? I don't see how. If the person asserting it meant that every white person was taller than every Hispanic person, even then I don't see how that by itself makes him a racist, but we do seem to be getting closer. If, in his experience, every Hispanic person had been shorter than every white person, we might fault him for his lack of experience, or we might fault him for generalizing too hastily over people outside his own experience, but this wouldn't even get us close to the moral condemnation inherent in a charge of racism.

Moreover, he may not even be asserting than all white people are taller than all Hispanic people. He quite possibly was asserting that most white people are taller than most Hispanic people, or that white people were taller, on average, than Hispanic people. These are not claims that would make him a racist, and they may very well be true. I might worry about the person if he made this assertion even in the face of contrary evidence. If he asserted that white people were taller, even though everything he saw should convince him otherwise, I would think that maybe he has adopted a racist view, and that explains why he is engaging in poor critical thinking. But the racist view would be primary, and only be confirmed by his assertions. It wouldn't consist solely in his assertions.

In fact, I am far less likely to think that someone who makes ambiguous generalizations is racist, than I am to think that someone who always interprets generalizations as universal generalizations is a racist. Consider the following example.

Imagine someone says that white people are morally better than black people. The case is exactly the same as it is with the example of being taller. Our analysis shouldn't change simply because now we are dealing with a description which carries judgmental import. I generally worry more about the person who lashes out at someone who says this that I do the person who actually says it. A person who automatically understood this statement to mean "Every white person is morally better than every black person" is far more prone to thinking in a racist way than a person who actually meant "White people are on average more moral than black people."

Don't get me wrong, please. I'm not saying that this claim is true or false, and I'm not saying that someone who says it cannot be a racist.

I'm only saying that if someone meant the statement the second way, this fact by itself isn't anywhere near enough to convict him of being a racist.

If we really wanted to know whether he was a racist, wouldn't we at least have to ask why he believes it? He could respond with any number of things which we would take to confirm that he is a racist. He could say that he hates all black people, or that black people have a gene which makes them evil. But the question is whether he could say anything which would not be racist. I think the answer is yes.

He could say that black people commit more crime than white people on a proportional basis. Most murderers are white people, but statistically, far more black people kill unjustly than white people. These pieces of information would point toward the given conclusion. If they were true, they would count as evidence that white people are more moral than black people. He could be wrong in any number of ways, but the person would be demonstrating some basic reasoning.

I realize that many people will strongly disagree, but I firmly believe that any disagreement is purely emotional and not thought out. Perhaps some confusion will arise out of the idea that no one can be morally better than any other individual, and I will address that issue when I discuss relativism. Given the common sense view that some individuals can be more moral than others, it follows that some groups can be more moral than others, from a statistical standpoint.

One might question the statistics, to be sure, and also the standards being used. Perhaps one might want to focus on church attendance, or giving to charity, or some other standard to establish morality. Or one might insist that morality just includes too much, and while it might make sense to say that someone is more honest than another person, it is too vague to ascribe superior morality, in a general way, to someone. Such criticisms can certainly be made, but none of them point to the racism of the person making the claim. Again, these are epistemological questions about the role of evidence in our decisions, and not moral failings.

I want to be absolutely clear about the conclusions I am making. A person who is making racial generalizations which are statistical, even when it comes to properties we might think indicate superiority of some kind, and who does so on the basis of good evidence has done nothing wrong at all. Since the word "racist" denotes wrongdoing, such a person should not be considered a racist. Furthermore, even if one accepts the belief without good evidence it doesn't seem like this fact could be what makes someone a racist. It must lie in some other characteristic, and so the fourth definition fails.

Before I proceed, I want to briefly consider the fifth definition. I have come to believe more and more that many people are using this definition in their arguments. Too often I have seen someone decried as a racist for nothing more than the fact that he questioned the level of racism present in America. Go into a college classroom today, say that there is almost no racial discrimination going on in America today, and a significant number of students will go home believing you are a racist.

I hope my preceding discussion also makes it clear why a person who denies the existence of discrimination cannot, because of that fact alone, be considered a racist. One might be ignorant of facts, or blind, or unaware of what is going on, but those do not make one racist.

Certainly, a racist might say that there is no or little discrimination, but the mistake of people who understand racism as in definition five is to think that *only* a racist could say anything like this. So, not only will definition five not work as a definition, but it fails on its own as even evidence for racism.

Earlier it seemed as if the closest we got to finding racism was for someone to make a universal generalization about race. Thinking that every member of a racial group has a certain characteristic is much harder to justify than making a claim about a majority of them, or a higher percentage than some other group.

How could anyone possibly think that every member of a racial group has anything in common? Perhaps my mind is limited, but I can only imagine two ways. First, someone could have a very limited exposure to people of that race, and an inability to think critically. Perhaps they really have only had exposure to people in that race who had a certain characteristic, and the person generalized inappropriately without thinking very hard. As I have explained, I don't see how we could call this racism.

The second way is for someone to think that human characteristics are determined by race, that there are some characteristics one has which are inherent in one's nature as a member of a race. There would be no other way for every member of one race to be better in some characteristic than every other member of another race. It seems to me that this is what we mean when we say that something is racist. Seeing people in this way is to put one's race above one's individuality. It is to ignore the fact that each individual is unique and forms his own identity, and instead substitute a racial cookie-cutter model. It is deeply morally wrong because it fails to respect persons for who they are. It doesn't respect the infinite worth of each human being, but instead diminishes them, treating them as simple cogs in life's drama. To put it simply, it is dehumanizing.

I must restate that I do not believe that there are any personality characteristics or abilities for which every member of one race is better than every member of another race. It may be possible that some physical differences are universally true. For example, I think that I've heard that only Irish people have red hair. Even so, these are the exception, as most physical differences are only statistically true. Certainly, if there are personality differences among races, they are only statistically true. This does not mean at all that those differences are caused by something within our different genes. Indeed, they may be purely coincidental, or more likely, caused by differences in culture.

Perhaps it is true that there are some minor differences, or some tendencies in ability or personality, which are caused by differences in race alone. The moral issue comes into play, however, when one ignores the reality of each individual. It is racist to confine an individual to the borders of his race. It is to disallow one's individual nature to shine through, and instead to impose racial shackles on people. It is to think that the person one becomes is defined by one's race.

It is nearly certainly true that someone who believes that any particular race is better in a universal way than any other is a racist, but the only reason this is true is because they must believe that personality traits and abilities are racially determined. This is why being a racist is such a morally bad thing. It is not just a general failure to think properly, which might be excused at least in part. Instead, being racist is to fail to respect the individual nature of personhood; it is a particularly disgusting way to dehumanize people.

Ultimately, I would define racism as that mindset which considers individual characteristics to be mapped onto racial heritage, instead of being, well, individual characteristics. Racism is to ignore one's individual talents, abilities, or identity, and instead insist that one must have certain characteristics because of one's race. That's racism, and I believe it is wrong. Deeply, fundamentally, wrong.

I must point out a particularly egregious example of racism. I have focused on personality characteristics and abilities until now, both of which theoretically might have some basis in genetics, which might be traceable in some way to one's race. To immediately assume that one individual therefore has a certain characteristic as a result of one's race is still problematic, since one could have been a member of that race and still not had the characteristic. In any case, one should treat every person as their own person. I just wanted to leave room for a theoretically possible way that abilities and some personality characteristics could be influenced by one's genetic background in a statistical sense, although I would still insist that one should never assert any difference unless one has some strong form of evidence, and not just anecdotal stories.

For one to go beyond even those, and insist that even one's beliefs are tied in some inherent way to one's race, is a particularly disgusting form of dehumanizing racism. For one to say that an athlete is fast and tall because he is black, might be excusable, even though morally and intellectually problematic if it is based on nothing but speculation, but to say that someone holds a belief to be true because of the race he was born with, that goes beyond excuse. How one forms beliefs is indeed a complicated thing which we do not fully understand, but to think that one can explain the fact that someone believes something even in part because of his race is the height of racism.

Of course it might be true that proportionately more black people have a certain belief than Asian people, but only a racist would jump to the conclusion that somehow race must play an inherent role in belief formation. It is to assume that people are born within confining boundaries, prescribed by their race, and it is especially repulsive.

How the Democratic Party is Racist Today

Although I have spent a good deal of time demonstrating that the Democratic Party has had a tremendously racist past, one of which we all should be ashamed, I would be remiss if I didn't recognize that some things have changed. No one can think that the Democratic Party of today still harbors the intense racial animosity which was one of its hallmarks in the past. There has been a great reformation in the Democratic Party, and no one should forget that.

Yet, that reformation doesn't necessarily mean that the Democratic Party is not racist. Yes, the Party has largely abandoned the racial hatred which it had a hundred years ago, but as we have seen, racism cannot be simply equated with racial animus. When determining whether the Democratic Party of today is racist, we must turn off our preconceptions about what is true which are based upon who knows what (almost certainly propaganda and innuendo). Instead we should apply the definition as we have just now come to understand it. When we use this more sophisticated definition, we will see that the Democratic Party is just as racist as ever, if not more. This is indeed a controversial claim, but that is exactly why I spent so much time trying to figure out exactly what we mean by the term "racist".

One way to understand how racist assumptions still pervade the Democratic Party is to look back at how the perception of the two parties changed so radically. Why is it that now people look at the Democratic Party as being very supportive of minorities, and the Republican Party as being, let's face it, racist? (I'll let the Republicans defend themselves from such charges.)

Franklin Delano Roosevelt's policies might have gotten the ball rolling. This gave the impression that Democrats cared about poor people, as did policies such as welfare, and social security. And certainly, John F. Kennedy calling Martin Luther King Jr.'s family while King was in jail had a big impact. Yet, perhaps what sealed the deal, and moved the black vote to Democrats on the order of 90%, was Democratic support for Affirmative Action.

Republicans actually supported the 1964 Civil Rights Act and the 1965 Voting Rights Act in higher proportions than Democrats. So, it would be odd to say that this support is what drove black people into the arms of the Democrats. It should also be pointed out that Richard Nixon supported some of the first Affirmative Action programs. Yet, when the debate about affirmative action solidified, it was Democrats who supported it, and Republicans who fought against it. Perhaps no other issue contributed to the incredible partisan reversal among black voters.

Not every Democrat supports affirmative action, just as not every Republican is opposed to it. Yet, Democrats tend to be for it, and Republicans opposed to it. Even more important for our purposes, affirmative action is called for in the platform of the Democratic Party[26]. It is certainly the case that one can join a party while disagreeing with some of the planks endorsed by that party, yet when one considers one of the planks to be racist, then it makes it much more difficult, if not impossible.

Unfortunately, I have not found a definition of affirmative action in any Democratic platform. Yet, I think misunderstanding the definition of affirmative action leads to a great deal of the confusion here. Affirmative Action is not when one hires people based on qualifications alone. A person who only hired white people even when other more qualified applicants applied would almost certainly be a racist. Asking him to fairly consider minority applicants is not to ask him to engage in affirmative action, but to abandon his racist views. Perhaps some people have defined affirmative action in this way for emotional effect, but we can't take it seriously. Hiring people based solely on their qualifications, regardless of their racial, ethnic, or other background, is just basic decency, and not affirmative action.

In order for a policy to count as "affirmative action," it must go beyond what we recognize as simple decency. If I am hiring 20 employees, and I declare that I will hire ten minority candidates and ten white males, so that qualifications are secondary, we would all recognize this as a form of affirmative action. If a university admits only candidates with a score over 700, on whatever standard they are using, but adds 40 points to the score of every minority, they are engaging in an affirmative action policy.

Non-discrimination is not affirmative action. Affirmative action requires race-based discrimination. Otherwise, it is just being non-discriminatory, which is our moral obligation in the first place. Affirmative action is when one goes beyond examining qualifications alone, and instead bases hiring, staffing, or admission decisions in some manner on an applicant's race. It is not to treat everyone equally based upon their merit or talents, but to go beyond equal treatment, for the sake of some purportedly higher value. It is necessarily to treat people differently based upon their race.

Any person or organization which supports affirmative action is faced with a dilemma. Either they must say that affirmative action is not racist, or they must say that sometimes racism is morally acceptable. On a simplistic definition of racism as racial animosity, the solution would be easy. Affirmative action does not involve racism, and presumably racism is always wrong. But if racism means something more that just racial animosity, as we have argued that it does, where do we stand?

It would seem undeniable that affirmative action is racist using our definition. Specifically, Affirmative Action rewards people based solely upon their race. It does not look at their individual situation whatsoever. What qualifies people (if that is the right word) to receive benefits under affirmative action is their race, and their race alone. This presupposes that there is something inherently the same among all members of a race which we should consider important. It is to ignore the individual characteristics the person holds, and instead focus on their race. Affirmative action treats people of different races as being different "in kind" and not merely different (at least potentially) "in degree".

This, as we have seen, is exactly what racism entails, and what makes racism wrong in the first place. What makes racism wrong is that it groups people into separate categories based on an accidental feature, and by doing so sanctions treating them differently. If there were inherent differences between the races, as racists hold, and affirmative action seems to require, then it would make perfect sense to treat white people and black people differently. It is not reasonable to treat black people and white people differently precisely because there are no inherent differences between them.

Yet, if this is the right way to understand racism, then there seems to be no way to adopt a moderate position on race. If affirmative action is indeed racist, it will not suffice to argue that it is one of the "good" kinds of racism. Our duty to respect the individuality of each person is constant, and cannot be tossed aside for lesser values. One might argue that treating people in different races for an ignoble reason, like hate, is not the same as treating them differently for a noble reason, like a misguided desire for equality (I'll explain equality in another chapter.) However, they are both guilty of prejudging a person, and they both involve rejecting the consideration of them as individuals. It is as if they treat people not as individuals, but merely pieces of the race to which they belong. This is precisely what makes both justifications racist in nature.

The Democratic Party has had a sordid past on race. Yes, that era is thankfully gone, but the leaders of the Democratic Party over the years have completely misdiagnosed the root problem. They didn't accept the words of Martin Luther King, Jr., but instead adopted the apparently more publicly palatable racism which still exists today. They didn't realize what was truly wrong with racism, as did Martin Luther King, Jr. They instead thought that the wrong of racism was simply the animosity involved. They didn't understand that the hatred was bad, but wasn't what made racism such a bad thing. They mistook the thing itself with one of its accidental features. The thing about racism which is wrong has always been and still remains its grounding principle, which allows hatred to be focused on a particular group. It is the idea that race is an essential characteristic of who one is. This principle, as is shown in its support for affirmative action, is still dearly held by a large number of Democrats, most importantly its leaders who are defining what being a Democrat means.

Lest one think that there is only one way in which the Democratic Party is racist, namely in its insistence for affirmative action, it would be a practical impossibility for this viewpoint not to impact other areas. The subverted racism of Democrats plays out in numerous other ways, from their explanations of certain social phenomena to their reactions to events to their tolerance of racist comments when those comments are made by Democrats.

My aim here is not to cause pain. I have no doubt that many Democrats sincerely believe that they are not racist. After considering carefully the definition of the term, and the policies and practices of a great many Democrats, I must conclude that many of them are mistaken. I am not indicting every Democrat. Yet, if anyone, Democrat or not, engages in any of the practices outlined below, or supports them at all, I must advise him to do some intense soul-searching. I believe that all of these practices betray a racist mindset. Yes, it may be painful to admit that one is engaging in racist practices, but facing that pain is the only way to overcome it.

Other Racist Practices and Positions

Democrats are certainly not the only ones to support things like "Black History month", but they are generally the most supporting of them. I have to admit that some of the people who are opposed to such things as "Black history month" do so out of racist hatred for black people. If one hates black people, they probably will be opposed to any attempt to honor black people. Unfortunately, as I see it, *every* person who supports "Black History month" is a racist. Yes, I wrote exactly what I meant. If you support "Black History month" or any of the myriad similar recent creations, then I think that you are a racist, and unless you find a flaw in our definition of racist, then I argue that you think you are a racist as well.

To insist that there is a different history for black people as a people is to say that black people are different from and separable from people generally. Students don't study "white" history for a reason. Teachers of history are supposed to take the most important events and people of the past, and teach their students about them, and they shouldn't care to what race those people belonged. Of course, if their race affected what people said about them, or how they treated them, that should be mentioned, but as far as history goes, there is only one history.

If anyone objects to the selections that history teachers and historians have made, and think that they are excluding people who are significant, whether because of a charge of racism or whatever, then one should argue with those historians and try to convince them that their judgments are mistaken. To make *Ad Hominem* circumstantial charges will not suffice. If one thinks that someone has made a contribution to history and he has been overlooked, then teach others about the contribution that person has made.

I can understand classes in a history department focusing on specific groups as occasions for study, although I'm not sure what I think about demarcating "black people" as a group, or even "African-American" when used as anything other than a placeholder for those who immigrated from Africa, or those whose parents or maybe grandparents immigrated from Africa. But that would include white people as well, as long as they immigrated from Africa. And it wouldn't include black people from England, for example.

We could focus on oppressed people, or people who made contributions which were overlooked, or other such groups, and still not be racist. It would not be racist to study descendants of slaves, even if all slaves were black people. That study still is predicated on an actual personal characteristic that all such people have in common. It is not predicated solely on race as a category to divide people.

To mark a month as "Black history month" smacks of an obsession with race and dividing people up by racial categories. It is to try to create division where it need not be. Again, to me it bespeaks a racist attitude, which holds that one's race is what makes one the person one becomes.

Even the often-used, seemingly innocuous phrase "black community" makes me cringe when I hear it. The concept screams out to me a racist principle: that all black people somehow make up a community or a unified whole separate from other people. It says that one of my black students has more in common with some nameless other black person on the other side of the country whom he has never met than he or she does with the Hispanic or white students sitting next to him.

There are communities of people who come together and share ideas or values; I deny, however, that an entire race can ever be a community. To me, it sounds exactly like saying "the community of people over six feet tall". Such people have one thing, and only one thing, in common. To presume otherwise would be to overlook each person's individual nature, just as it would be to speak of "the black community", both of which would be equally immoral.

To react to what I just said by responding that height is disanalogous to race because there are things that all black people have in common *is* racism. It doesn't matter whether hatred is involved, or whether one feels superior or inferior. What matters is that when one thinks in such a racist way, one cannot help but overlook the individual nature of the members of that group. You can argue that race has a strong social significance which height doesn't have, and I would agree, but only in a qualified sense. Short people are certainly treated more poorly in our society than tall people, but I don't want to quibble. It is true that in the past (largely due to Democrats) people who were black, however that is defined, were treated worse than other people. But so what. The fact that racist people think of black people as different in kind from white people doesn't mean we have to agree with them, and it certainly doesn't justify our accepting this racist principle.

This is such an important point, I better say something more. I fail to see how the fact that people have suffered, even if they have suffered in the same way for the same reason, makes them a community. People must commune together in some way in order to be a community. Having the same skin color and being treated in similar ways by others does not satisfy the conditions for being a community, so there can be no such thing as a black community which encompasses all black people, unless all black people somehow commune together in a way that they don't with others. I know some people who would say that they do, that by the very nature of their skin, or the way that they are treated because of their skin, they are connected in ways that no one else is. I call these people racists.

I am completely aware of the fact that these sorts of racial set-asides were in part pushed through because those who would oppose them were afraid of being called racists. I consider this a supreme and scary irony. I believe we are living on the other side of the looking glass, and can only hope that pointing out that things are backwards will help us find our way back.

Just as there is no such thing as a "black community", there is no such thing as a "black experience". This is another term which I can only understand as being racist, but which many people who don't think of themselves as racist still use. Either I am mistaken, or many more people are racist than would admit it (I know leftists would say that this claim is true, but they usually mean it about people other than themselves).

What could it possibly mean for someone to have a "black experience"? That they have been discriminated against, or looked down upon because of their race. If so, why on Earth is this called a "black experience". These things have happened to people in every possibly identifiable race. To label this, or anything else, a "black experience", makes about as much sense as thinking that discriminating against someone else is a "white experience". Of course, no one would do that. No one would try to distill the complex and diverse experiences of white people down into a single descriptive term and call it a "white experience". We recognize that no white person has the same experience as every other white person, because they are all different, and that to do so would be dehumanizing and wrong. Yet, somehow to do the same thing to black people is not regarded as wrong, and indeed is considered to be acceptable, or even morally obligatory, by numerous people on the left side of the political spectrum. I refuse to refrain from recognizing something as racist merely because it is politically correct.

It doesn't happen as much today, but I still recall a strong push among Democrats to reconsider standardized tests because they were "culturally insensitive." The point, as I remember it, was that the tests were organized and written from the perspective of the dominant white majority, and that this supposed fact was taken to explain why many members of minority races didn't do as well on them. Instead of explaining the performance of these students based upon their abilities, interests, and values, the different results between students of different races was supposed to be racial discrimination.

I do not deny that there are different cultures. I only deny that there are cultures which are racially based. There is no such thing as a racially-hispanic culture, or a black culture. One might consider Hispanic culture, if one wants to focus on the practices of people throughout Central and South America, but this is geographically based, and not genetically or racially based.

Minority students, as I understand from the sociologists, do not do as well in school as white students (although Asians often outperform white students). There must be numerous explanations for this phenomenon. Whatever else they may be, I deny that it has anything to do with a student's race. Perhaps the student's culture might be a factor, but this is exactly my point. In my view, only a racist could believe that culture is determined *by* race.

I have heard too many Democrats speaking as if a person's race is the most important thing in the formation of a person for me to overlook it. The appeal to race as an explanation for behavior, especially failure, is made so routinely, that any other explanation is crowded out, such as an attitude among many families, of all stripes, that education doesn't matter.

As a community college professor, I know many students who have to fight against pressures from their family and community in order to continue their education, mostly Hispanic women and black people of all ages and genders. It's as if some people have already decided what and who my students are or can be just based upon what race they accidentally have. I cannot believe that focusing on race as an explanation is the solution to this problem, but in fact only makes it worse. Actually, it is a part of the very problem which needs to be fixed.

It can only be counterproductive to tell a failing student that his failure is due even in part to his race. Shouldn't I tell that student that his failure is due to his own dedication or lack thereof? If his family and others inculcated in him values which are not conducive to a good life, then it is up to him to change those values. It is not one's race that makes one disvalue education, it is one's environment.

And that is the very problem here. When one adopts the mindset that allows race to be considered a defining characteristic of who one is, real solutions are often not even allowed to enter one's consciousness. It is not the fact that one belongs to a particular race that makes one value education or not, it is how one is raised. But to say so, and to recognize that many Hispanic and black children do not value education, is necessarily to say that many of their parents are not doing a good enough job raising them. And that is one thing Democrats are clear that no one should ever do: say that certain minorities are, statistically speaking, doing a poor job raising their children. That would involve making a judgment, and would certainly risk a loss of a large number of votes. But I will get to the non-judgmentalism of Democrats in another chapter.

Another policy which I think is driven by the racism I am discussing is "hate crime" legislation. The term is actually euphemistic, because it doesn't really refer to all crimes based on hate. If I hate my neighbor because he's a rude bastard, and I go up to him and punch him in the face, I have committed a crime, but it is apparently not a "hate crime". It is only a "hate crime" if I commit a crime while hating another person because he is a member of a particular group, whether racial, ethnic, or some other protected class. I'm not sure whether an assault on a clown because of hatred toward clowns would count as a hate crime, but I'm not sure why not.

Again, the focus here is on hatred for a group, and not hatred for an individual. Somehow, a crime against a person based on hatred for that person is not supposed to be as serious or egregious as a crime against a person based on hatred for a group to which that person belongs. I just don't understand it.

It seems to me that it goes back to this idea that black people and other minorities are not individuals, but are instead merely pieces of a whole which we call the black race, or in other instances, the Hispanic race, or whatever other groups are protected. Again, it goes back to the basic racism held by many Democrats even today.

Any time people engage in a racial double standard, where they do not hold members of minority races up to the same standards they hold white people up to simply because they are a member of that race, that is a sure sign of racism. Of course, in many cases it is difficult to assess whether the double standard is purely based on race, but in some cases it seems an inescapable conclusion.

For example, Michael Moore, the video polemicist, recently appeared on Larry King's interview program. Moore is a prominent Democrat, who is lauded by the Democratic Party. Michael Moore tries to justify the double standard, but in my view only confirms that he is a racist. Here is a portion of the transcript[27].

Asked to comment on the Jeremiah Wright controversy, Michael Moore responded:

MOORE: Yes, I'm a white guy. And I think -- I think -- I've got to tell you something. If you were black in this country, especially if you are of his age, of his era or even -- or times before that or even kids today, when you look at the situation in our inner city schools, I mean, you have to ask yourself, Larry, what's it like to be black in America? And what kind of rage would you feel? And if you did feel that rage, what kind of things would you say that, at times, would be outrageous, crazy even, because you've had to live through this for so long.

And I do not believe, as a white guy, that I am in any position to judge a black man who has had to live through that. …That's what we should be talking about and not what an elderly black man is saying because he's upset on how he's been treated.

King later wondered whether John McCain had [legitimate?] gripes, since he had given his body for the country, and because at his age he might have a very difficult time finding a job.

KING: So they all can have gripes?
MOORE: Well, no, not me because...
KING: You have no gripes?
MOORE: Well, I'm not -- I can't -- no. I have no gripe about the fact that I'm a 50-year-old white guy because we've been running the show for a long time. And it's time to open it up, I think, and let some other people run this show.

Michael Moore's racism is evident in two places. First, there is the double standard involved in judging people. He believes he cannot judge a black man because of what the black man has gone through. I would have to ask him, what if a white man were racist because he had been mistreated by black people all of his life? Would Michael Moore feel like he could judge that man, *because* he is white. White people can judge white people and black people can judge black people, but not vice versa. Or has Mr. Moore fully stepped through the looking glass, and would take the position that anyone can judge white people, but no one can judge black people?

The racism seethes throughout Mr. Moore's entire worldview. He also seems to believe that people in a certain race all share a metaphysical connection, which is not shared by anyone else. In the second section, he says that he cannot have any gripes because "we've been running the show." Does he mean Larry King and Michael Moore? No. He means white men. Old white men in particular. So, if a group of white men are in charge, apparently that personal characteristic can leech over this metaphysical connection so that all white men can be said to be in charge. After all, we're not individuals. We are all members of one racial heritage, and that means that if you're white, then you share all the guilt for any white man, and if you are black, then you are shielded from criticism because of any burden placed on any black man.

Ridiculous.

The saddest thing is that it is not ridiculed. Michael Moore is an icon in Democratic circles. Democrats generally do not ridicule Mr. Moore's mindset because they share it. Democrats and leftists in general will bend over backwards to give some people, generally minorities, the benefit of the doubt, but will twist other people's words to make them sound racist, when the speakers had no such intention. When minorities say racist things, they generally get a pass from Democrats (and often in the mainstream media), while white people, especially Republicans, who say things that aren't racist, but sound racist, they are pounced upon and calls are made for them to step down from whatever positions they hold.

There was the time Cruz Bustamante, then the Democratic Lieutenant Governor of California, use the word "nigger" in a speech. It was apparently a slip of the tongue, where he misspoke and substituted the word "nigger" for "negro", which would probably be taboo as well, except that he was naming a civil rights group which had that word in their title. According to an article in Jet,[28] "While some Black officials criticized him for allegedly knowing exactly what he was saying, most have supported Bustamante, who has been an advocate for maintaining affirmative action and other civil rights causes."

Apparently, some people think supporting racist policies insulates one from charges of racism. Okay, they don't recognize the racism inherent in affirmative action, but the irony is hard for me to miss. The point is that as I recall, the burden of proof for most Democrats seemed to be on the side which thought Bustamante was racist. Nevermind that he had been a member of a nationalistic organization largely recognized as racist, which he never condemned.

Mecha, the Movimeiento Estudiantil Chicano de Aztlan, still counts as one of its historical documents a racist screed titled "El Plan Espiritual de Aztlan." Interestingly, although it is listed on their website, it is not linked to the actual document. For that, one must look elsewhere, although many local Mecha chapters have have obliged by putting it online.

Here is a passage from that document:

> In the spirit of a new people that is conscious not only of its proud historical heritage but also of the brutal "gringo" invasion of our territories, *we,* the Chicano inhabitants and civilizers of the northern land of Aztlan ... *declare* that the call of our blood is our power, our responsibility, and our inevitable destiny. ...Brotherhood unites us, and love for our brothers makes us a people whose time has come and who struggles against the foreigner "gabacho" who exploits our riches and destroys our culture. With our heart in our hands and our hands in the soil, we declare the independence of our mestizo nation. We are a bronze people with a bronze culture. Before the world, before all of North America, before all our brothers in the bronze continent, we are a nation, we are a union of free pueblos, we are *Aztlán.*
>
> *Por La Raza todo. Fuera de La Raza nada.*

The Spanish sentence at the end means "For the race everything, for those outside the race nothing." Interestingly, those on the political left don't run such groups off the campus, but instead welcome them. They don't reject politicians associated with such groups, but instead defend them against charges of racism.

In another case, Charles Barron, who was a New York City Council member at the time, said to a crowd supporting reparations that he'd like to walk up to a white man and slap him, for the crime of not understanding the plight of black men. It sounds fantastic for a politician to say, but here is the quote: "I want to go up to the closest white person and say, 'You can't understand this, it's a black thing' and then slap him, just for my mental health."[29]

Thankfully, some people even on the left condemned the remark, but he still seemingly has a future in politics, though there are hopeful signs that his support may be diminishing.[30] It is inconceivable that a local New York white Republican politician could say something similar and not be excoriated from coast to coast and immediately drummed out of office.

Donna Brazile was the first black woman to run a Presidential campaign. She ran Al Gore's unsuccessful 2000 race. In an interview with the Washington Post on November 16, 1999, she also said that she will not let the "white boys" win. Out of context, of course it sounds like she could be talking about Republicans in their bid for the Presidency. But at least one leftist media watchdog group[31] rightly pointed out that the comment was taken out of context. Her racist comment did not point to the Republican Party, it was directed at all white men. How refreshing. Her comment wasn't partisan, it was just out and out racist.

Why would a media watchdog, even an extremely partisan one, reduce its credibility by using a red herring in an underhanded defense of her comment. Maybe they didn't think it was racist, as they insisted on presenting Brazile's full quote from the Post, which added: "And that's not a description of 'gender or race, it's an attitude. A white-boy attitude is "I must exclude, denigrate and leave behind," Brazile says." They even emphasized that section by putting it in bold.

Imagine a white campaign manager for a Republican saying "I'm not gonna let those niggers in New Orleans be harmed by government bureaucracy. And that's not a race thing, it's an attitude. It's an attitude that says I'm going to wait for the government to come take care of me instead of solving problems for myself and for my community." Now imagine a Democrat taking the statement out of context. Then imagine a conservative watchdog group accepting that pitiful and inconsistent explanation, and instead criticizing the Democrat who misquoted the comment. Now you're about where I am when I consider the Donna Brazile comment.

I'm not saying that "white boy" is an equal insult as "nigger." There is a qualitative difference between the two. But both are racially divisive, and the point is that the explanation Brazile offers, that her term is not racist because it's about an attitude, would never be accepted if offered by a conservative Republican, not even from most Republicans.

The most amazing thing to me is that *she stayed on* as Gore's campaign manager. He did not have the moral fiber to ask her to resign or fire her. Also, it's pretty amazing to me that millions of Americans still voted for him, even though his campaign advisor had made racist comments, and not just on one occasion, as we will see in a bit. I can excuse many of them for not being aware of the comments, but certainly many of those who voted for him knew about the comments. In my view, that should be enough to disqualify someone for public office, but apparently not in theirs.

It is often reported that Jesse Jackson used the term "hymie" to refer to Jews, and "Hymie-town" to refer to New York[32]. He did apologize for the remark, but his influence in politics seems to be undiminished. When some people apologize, such as Trent Lott, as we will see, it only seems to feed the frenzy.

Willie Brown, a veteran politician in California, after winning the 1995 election said, "The white boys got taken fair and square,"[33] and has apparently used the term "white boy" to denigrate others.[34] He is still respected in Democratic circles in California.

U.S. Representative from Florida Corrine Brown, a Democrat, sat in on a briefing in early 2004 about what the Bush Administration was doing in regard to Haiti. She said that the President and his administration were "racist" and "a bunch of white men." Apparently, Assistant Secretary of State Roger Noriega, who is of Mexican ancestry, said that he resented being called a racist and a white man. Brown then told him "you all look alike to me."[35] The incident was widely reported. She is still in Congress.

Perhaps she doesn't belong on this list, since she is not directly involved in politics, but commentator Dr. Julianne Malveaux has said many racist things, including "There's no great, white bigot; there's just about 200 million little white bigots out there."[36] She is now the President of Bennett College for women, and has her columns appear in USA Today.

None of this is intended to convey the impression that Republican politicians and policymakers do not say racist things. Who can forget George Allen's "Machaca" comment? Nor am I saying that Republicans do not sometimes go easier on Republicans. It would be refreshing for both sides to treat comparable cases comparably.

It's just that the Democratic Party and its members seem to want to hold themselves up as the moral authority on racist incidents, and yet it seems to tolerate and excuse racism in its ranks, particularly when it is minorities making racist statements. That's a big problem for me. The sanctimonious way that Democrats sometimes hypocritically twist Republican comments to make them sound racist is also a big problem for me.

One situation I have in mind is an incident involving William Bennett. He told his radio show audience that "If you wanted to reduce crime, you could -- if that were your sole purpose -- you could abort every black baby in this country and your crime rate would go down."[37] Bennett was decried as a racist all over the place. Perhaps I'm blind, and I'm sure some will say I must be racist, but I can't see a hint of racism in his words. He was relying on the well-known fact that the crime rate among people who are considered black is higher than most other groups. There are a lot of factors that go into it, such as living in communities with poverty, and having fewer fathers in the home, and all sorts of things. But it seems to me undisputed that it is true.

He didn't say that black people are inherently criminal in their genetic makeup. That would be racist, and he didn't say it. So, he is attacked for something he didn't say, while Democratic racists who actually say racist things are mollycoddled. [I'm not really sure where that word comes from. I hope it's not some racist slur.]

To make things clear, Bennett immediately added: "That would be an impossibly ridiculous and morally reprehensible thing to do, but your crime rate would go down." He was making the point that the ends do not justify the means. Perhaps Democrats disagree with his assertion, but that doesn't make his statements racist.

Then there was the whole Trent Lott controversy. Trent Lott, in praising Senator Strom Thurman, said that "I want to say this about my state: When Strom Thurmond ran for president, we voted for him. We're proud of it. And if the rest of the country had followed our lead, we wouldn't have had all these problems over all these years, either."[38] Anyone has to admit, it doesn't sound great, if you know the history. Strom Thurmond ran on the breakaway State's Rights Democratic ticket, which had segregation as one of its main platforms, along with state's rights. They were often referred to as Dixiecrats. Obviously, one can interpret Trent Lott as saying he wished that segregation had continued.

The question is whether he really did. Democrats may not have twisted his words, but they certainly interpreted them in the worst possible light. There were 8 planks in the State's Rights Democratic Party, and most of them were concerned with state's rights, strict construction of the Constitution, and the rejection of a police state.[39] Certainly, the emphasis on State's rights was founded on the belief that it would allow the States to continue segregation, but there are other important reasons to support state's rights.

Does anyone really think that Lott meant that he wanted to bring back segregation? He is a member of the Republican Party, many of whose members would have ended segregation back in the 1880's, if they weren't blocked by Democrats. It's just silly to think that he meant we would be better today with segregation.

Was he saying that we should have kept segregation for longer than we did in our history? That is also doubtful. He does not believe in segregation now, but he does still believe in state's rights and a strict interpretation of the Constitution. Could he have had those things in mind? Did he realize that Thurmond had changed his views on segregation over time, and think that he might have made a great

President even if he had supported segregation at the time? What were "all the problems" Lott was concerned with?

Unfortunately, we might never know. After he was attacked, he clammed up about what he meant, and instead made *mea culpa* speeches. If someone had approached him with a little courtesy and asked him, maybe he would have felt comfortable enough to explain. But under fire from every angle, there was no way he was going to reveal anything which might be interpreted badly. He was pressured to resign his position as Majority Leader, although he did remain in Congress.

What I find especially sad is that a short time later Senator Chris Dodd, a Democrat, said something very similar about Senator Robert Byrd, who had been a member of the KKK. If you didn't know, the KKK stood for things a lot worse than segregation. To be fair, Byrd has repudiated his former views. Here is what Dodd said: "[Byrd] would have been a great senator at any moment. He would have been right at the founding of this country. He would have been in the leadership crafting this Constitution. He would have been right during the great conflict of Civil War in this nation."[40]

Democrats were not disturbed by this comment at all, but instead defended it, and pointed out that it was not analogous to Lott's comments. Now, I think it's clear that interpreted charitably, or even reasonably, neither man's comments betrayed any hint of racism, and uncharitably, they both did. I just wish that more people, on both sides of the aisle, wouldn't let partisanship color their viewpoints.

I can't help but point out one of the most inconsistent Democrats at the time. In the same New York Times article I quoted above, Al Gore put in his two cents. Remember, the same Al Gore who wouldn't fire Donna Brazile for her racially divisive comments. Al Gore finds Lott's words to be racist. You won't believe what he said to justify his stance: "Trent Lott made a statement that I think is a racist statement, yes. That's why I think he should withdraw those comments or I think the United States Senate should undertake a censure of those comments. It is not a small thing ... to say that our problems are caused by integration and that we should have had a segregationist candidate. That is divisive and it is divisive along racial lines. That's the definition of a racist comment."

The blatant inconsistency is hard to miss, but don't overlook the fact that Gore had to twist Lott's words in the process. Perhaps Gore doesn't think that criticizing people for their "white boy attitude" is divisive along racial lines.

Perhaps all of these examples do not show that most Democrats are generally racist in the racial animus sense. It just shows that some of them are, and others seem to overlook or excuse racism when it comes from minorities. As I see it, this proves that many leading Democrats are racist in the basic sense of racism. I'm not even saying we should be so sensitive about such remarks. I can even overlook the fact that Byrd used the term "white niggers" in an interview with Fox News[41], and I wouldn't consider him a racist on the basis of just that phrase. What astounds me is the lack of consistency I see from many Democrats. If a statement is racist, what does it matter who makes it?

Here is what I'm getting at: if it were just about ideology, I could dismiss it as partisan gamesmanship for political advantage, but there seems to be something more to it. In 2008, Geraldine Ferraro said that Senator Barack Obama was lucky to be a black man today:

> If Obama was a white man, he would not be in this position, and if he was a woman (of any color) he would not be in this position. He happens to be very lucky to be who he is. And the country is caught up in the concept.[42]

Ferraro was lambasted in most Democratic circles, where people said this was a racist statement, even many people who supported Hillary Clinton. So, the difference seems not to be a political one, but the fact the Geraldine Ferraro is white. I have no doubt that if a black person had said the same thing, then no one would have said anything at all in criticism.

Bill Clinton has also said a few things during the last Presidential election that have been criticized as racist. So, apparently, it is possible for a Democrat to accuse another Democrat of being racist, as long as he is white. Unfortunately, this just makes me think charges of racism are more than just political games for electoral advantage, and are actually deep-seated racism. Only a racist could have lower moral standards for black people or other minorities than they do for white people.

I have not yet included some of the worst comments, because they tell me that the racism in the Democratic Party is so deep, that it even includes ideological purity. Prominent Democrats, well-respected in Democratic circles, say things which imply that they believe that one's race is so overpowering, that it should define one's beliefs and values. This explanation is the only way I can understand some of the most disgustingly racist attacks which are hurled at black conservative thinkers or politicians. For example, Maureen Dowd, a columnist for the New York Times, wrote in her column of June 25, 2003 regarding Clarence Thomas that "It makes him crazy that people think he is where he is because of his race, but he is where he is because of his race." I'll overlook the fact that this comment sounds an awful lot like Geraldine Ferraro's, and that Democrats did not seem to criticize Maureen Dowd's comment at all, and I will focus on what she is saying.

It sounds to me like what she is saying is that no black man could get into any high positions unless he is given affirmative action. Apparently, for her it's not possible for a black man to be intelligent or talented, or reasonable, or maybe just that no white person would be able to recognize it. Either way, her comment reveals racist assumptions. The truth is that Clarence Thomas was and always has been an extraordinarily brilliant man. As Jan Crawford Greenburg, the author of *Supreme Conflict: The Inside Story of the Struggle for Control of the United States Supreme Court* puts it in an interview with Amazon.com,

> "Clarence Thomas has been the most maligned justice in modern history--and also the most misunderstood and mischaracterized. I found conclusive evidence that far from being Antonin Scalia's intellectual understudy, Thomas has had a substantial role in shaping the direction of the Court-- from his very first week on the bench. The early storyline on Thomas was that he was just following Scalia's direction, or as one columnist at the time wrote, 'Thomas Walks in Scalia's Shoes.' That is patently false, as the documents and notes in the Blackmun papers unquestionably show. If any justice was changing his vote to join the other that first year, it was Scalia joining Thomas, not the other way around."[43]

Yet, in the eyes of many Democrats, Clarence Thomas is a lackey to white men. Maureen Dowd's comments, though revealing, are nowhere near the worst. Jeff Jacoby, a columnist for the Boston Globe, catalogs a few examples in a column from the end of 1996.[44] Among his examples is the fact that Ward Connerly, who advocated against affirmative action, was called an "Uncle Tom" and a "traitor". State Senator Diane Watson said "He's married to a white woman. He wants to be white." She went on to add "He wants a colorless society. He has no ethnic pride. He doesn't want to be black." When asked about the remark, she didn't apologize, but added "That's right. I said that."[45]

Jacoby also adds that "The Oakland Tribune depicted [Connerly] in a cartoon as the proprietor of 'Connerly & Co./ Ethnic Cleansers' -- with a Klansman's robe hanging in the window." And there is plenty more. "On the cover of its November issue, Emerge, a liberal black magazine, portrayed 'Uncle Thomas' as a 'Lawn Jockey for the Far Right.' Inside, a grinning Thomas crouched at Justice Antonin Scalia's feet, shining his shoes."

When Michael Steele appeared in a gubernatorial debate in 2002 in Maryland, students handed out oreo cookies, and a few may have been thrown in the air, according to Kevin Martin, who was there.[46] There was also an incident where an image of Michael Steele was made to look like Sambo, and put online. For my part, I'm not very sensitive to racial diatribe, and the fact that students used oreos to ridicule a black conservative, I can actually see the humor in it. It's sophomoric humor, but we can all be a little sophomoric sometimes. I don't think I see any humor though, in the caricature of Mr. Steele as Sambo.

It's not the words themselves, or the language anyone uses that bothers me. In fact, many comedians often seem to me to be the least racist people, even though they use the most "racist" language. No, it's the presumption that if someone is black, his "natural" place is on the Democratic side. There seems to be this general consensus among Democrats that a black conservative or Republican is a sellout, and I can only surmise that there is this implicit assumption that "All black people are supposed to think a certain way." The implication is that black people should all "tow the party line" simply because of their race. They should support affirmative action, generous welfare programs, and all the rest, and if they don't, then it is permissible to ridicule them in ways one would never ridicule a black person who was "on the plantation."

I can't say I have ever seen Republicans engage in such a disgusting racial double standard. Nor do I see them defending truly racist comments, whether by Republicans or Democrats. It reminds me of the position that only white people can be racist. I've heard of silly things before, but this seems to be right up there.

The position has been asserted by all sorts of people, although as far as I know, no high-ranking public officials. It has always been asserted by leftists, though. Perhaps I'm being a little sloppy in connecting Democrats to the political left, but people in general don't offer their political affiliation offhand. I can recognize their views as being on the left, but I don't always have conclusive proof that the person putting forward the view is a Democrat. But I don't think it's that much of a stretch either. It is clear that leftists saturate the Democratic Party, and the leftist ideas are often triumphed by Democratic politicians.

One author who asserts this position is Derald Wing Sue, a psychologist, in his book *Overcoming Our Racism*[47] though he is by no means the only one. It was apparently fairly widespread on the left, judging by references online. In Sue's view, racism necessarily involves having the power to put one's discriminatory attitude into practice, and since only white people have this power, only white people can be racist. A related view is that if there is any racial discrimination on the part of black people and other minorities, it is only a reaction to oppression of the white overlords. Still another view is that not only is it true that only white people are racist, it is also true that all white people are racists.

My view is that any scholar who asserts this theory, and anyone else who repeats it, is only twisting definitions in order to support their own racist viewpoint. In ordinary conversation, people never use the term "racist" to refer to this specialized definition. There is no distinction made between racism in one's mind, and racism acted out, although it is often assumed that the former will lead to the latter. Perhaps that is why no distinction is made. I agree that this might be a useful distinction to make, I just don't think the way to make it is by twisting the definition of "racism". One can of course make up a definition of a word and use it in a specialized academic context, but to pretend that one is capturing the meaning of the term as it is used in general conversation is ridiculous.

And like I said, it is more than that. If the reason that academics and others have created this persuasive definition of racism is to protect black people from criticism, I really think that something more is going on. It seems to me that there is this motivation some people on the left have to refrain from criticism of black people. This definition is just one example. Another example is when people explain white criminal's behavior by their choices, and black criminal's behavior by their living situations.

Some people will tolerate certain behavior by black people and other minorities which they would never tolerate in white people. Do I have to bring up Mayor Marion Barry[48]? Or how about the fact that black rappers can routinely use racist, misogynist language which country singers would never get away with? This smacks to me of a condescending racial double standard. It is to assume that minorities do not have it in their nature to act according to the same standards that educated white people are routinely expected to follow.

We will truly have made progress in this country when everyone feels comfortable condemning a black man, or a Hispanic lesbian, in the same terms and for the same behavior as anyone else. Those who currently cannot bring themselves to do so suffer from a condescending attitude toward minorities. And like it or not, this condescending attitude is a form of racism. It is an example of treating minorities as if they are inherently different, and in this case lesser, than others.

It is the same attitude that I see inherent in favoring affirmative action. It is to hold that minorities are incapable of competing with white people, and since the assumption is made that every member of every minority is in the same category in this respect, it is a racist attitude. Affirmative action simply categorizes people by race, and doesn't look any further into how and why they do not measure up to other individuals. That's what makes it racist.

All of this goes back to the comment by Hillary Clinton with which I started the chapter. Let me refresh your memory:

> "Yes, we want to be judged by the content of our character and not the color of our skin. But what makes up character? If we don't take race as part of our character, then we are kidding ourselves."

These words prove that Hillary Clinton is a racist, in the basic sense of the word. If you don't believe me, consider what Martin Luther King, Jr. actually said:

> "I have a dream that my four children will one day live in a nation where they will not be judged by the color of their skin, but by the content of their characters."

In order to see my point, all you need to do is rephrase Dr. King's words by adding to them what Hillary Clinton said. According to Mrs. Clinton, we should understand Dr. King to be saying this:

> "I have a dream that my four children will one day live in a nation where they will not be judged by the color of their skin, but by the content of their characters, which includes their skin color."

This Clintonian revision would reduce Dr. King's majestic call for equality to an inept and inconsistent platitude. Regardless of whether you agree with Mrs. Clinton, or with Dr. King, what is unmistakeably clear is that they are saying two different things. Dr. King is calling for us to ignore skin color and treat people independently of that skin color, and instead by their character. Mrs. Clinton is exhorting us to treat people differently depending on their skin color, and she disingenuously and shamelessly argues that doing so *is* treating them according to their character.

If this is what she means, and I don't see how we can interpret her words in any other way, then I contend that Mrs. Clinton is a racist, as is anyone who shares a similar view. In light of this fact, the only thing more astounding than Mrs. Clinton's hubris, insensitivity, and misunderstanding is the fact that there was little public outrage about her ridiculous comments. If any prominent Republican were to declare publicly that Dr. Martin Luther King was "kidding" himself, he would have rightly been raked over the coals. But, Mrs. Clinton received little opprobrium, and it doesn't seem to have hurt her political prospects in the slightest.

In fact, her prospects in the Democratic Party have only risen since then, as shown by her very nearly capturing the Democratic nomination for President. Her words, far from being a slip of the tongue, accurately represent her thought-out views. She speaks them several times, reformulating them, but presenting the same view repeatedly. Moreover, they reflect her positions on issues regarding race, in particular affirmative action. And, they reflect the position of the Democratic Party and I take it, the majority of Democrats, considering the large number of Democrats willing to vote for her.

On a day intended to honor Dr. Martin Luther King, Jr., Mrs. Clinton spits in his face, twists his words into the exact opposite of what he intended, and self-righteously demands that we accept her version as his own. She is directly contradicting his viewpoint, in effect, rejecting his brilliant and honorable viewpoint in favor of a childish, simplistic, racist approach. Dr. King's courageous and inspiring words were degraded and defiled, turned into pathetic gibberish. I know these are very strong words, but I have been very careful in choosing them.

I constantly hear Republicans being berated for their racist views and attitudes, but I have come to realize that most Republicans agree with Dr. Martin Luther King, while most Democrats agree with Hillary Clinton. How on Earth does our television and print media frame the debate in ways which make it seem like Republicans are racist and not Democrats. If you don't believe me, then think back to your reaction to the title of this chapter. If your reaction was incredulousness, then I would argue that you have bought into the party line of most of the mass media.

I wouldn't mind joining a political party. I'm a little tired of being an independent and not having much of an effect on the political system. But I cannot join a party which would support a woman who would so obliviously state such blatantly racist things.

Empirical Evidence

If my reasoning thus far has been unpersuasive, let me share with you a study that I found in conducting my research. Earlier I considered defining racism as any dismissal of the racism which exists in America today. I rejected defining racism in this way, but perhaps one might still argue that even if it isn't racism, it is still ignorant to dismiss the prevalence of racial discrimination in America today. If that's the way you feel, this study is going to confirm a lot of your beliefs, but it will come at a price.

Professor Shanto Iyengar, director of Stanford University's Political Communication Lab and Richard Morin, director of Washington Post polling, wanted to investigate what they call "implicit" racial bias. People don't admit to being racist and discriminating against minorities, but Iyengar and Morin wanted to see how people acted when they didn't know they were being tested for racism.

They presented subjects who clicked on a link on the Washington Post website a story about a Katrina victim, and then asked to answer a questionnaire involving how much money the Federal government should give the victim, and for how long. They received responses from about 2300 people, and they gathered information about the participants. They were mostly white (85%), highly educated, and most of them self-identified as liberal or Democrat. Only 12% identified themselves as Republican.

It is clear that this sample cannot be extended to all Americans with any high degree of certainty, but it seems a reasonable sample size to draw conclusions about highly educated white people, especially Democrats and independents.

In order to test for racial bias, some of the participants were shown a darkened face, and sometimes a lighter one. In some cases, the face was the same person, just with the face digitally altered. To many, the results will not be surprising. On average, considering the monthly amount and the number of months of payments, these educated white people were willing to give a white victim about $1,000 more than a darker-skinned or black victim. As Iyengar and Morin wrote in the Washington Post, these differences are powerful "testimony to the persistent and primordial power of racial imagery in American life."[49]

Not so fast, however. Once the data was examined more carefully, a more specific finding occurred. It turned out that the Party affiliation of the subject made a difference in the results. Richard Morin noted in a follow-up column that "Democrats were willing to give whites about $1,500 more than they chose to give to a black or other minority."[50] According to Iyengar, Republican "responses to the assistance questions are relatively invariant across the different media conditions." In other words, Republicans gave roughly the same amount regardless of race.

Iyengar preferred to call Democrats "unprincipled" instead of bigoted, but he did add that these results match perfectly with the results of an earlier study on race and crime which he conducted with Franklin D. Gilliam Jr. of UCLA. As he puts it, "Republicans supported tough treatment of criminals no matter what they encountered in the news. Others were more elastic in their position, coming to support more harsh measures when the criminal suspect they encountered was non-white."

I won't be so coy. Democrats are racist. It is evident in their positions, their double standards, and even in their behavior. It's time we all recognized it.

Final Thoughts

If someone asked me to join a political organization which had a virulently racist history, like the Democratic Party had, I suspect that would generally be enough to prevent me from joining. If this person pointed out that the organization had changed its fundamental beliefs so that it no longer harbored hatred toward other races, I suspect I might consider joining it, presuming he was right, and it was the only group which stood for other principles which I supported. But if I found out that, although it had abandoned hatred toward other races, it still harbored the racist assumptions underlying its hatred, I couldn't possibly become a member.

What makes me even more disinclined to join the Democratic Party is that prominent Democrats generally seem to have it exactly backwards. They seem to allow that race can be determinative of personal characteristics, but absolutely deny that one's gender or sex can be, whereas I believe that race tells us nothing about a person, but gender often does.

In any case, I consider this issue much more important than the issue of direct democracy. On that issue, I could consider rhetorical flourishes to be just that, and probably overlook it. Here I see a deep ideological issue, one which I would have a hard time ignoring. I will not join the Democratic Party until either they change their ideology, or else someone can convince me that I am wrong, and that the Democratic Party is not full of racism.

CHAPTER THREE
Force-feeding Morality

The only part of the conduct of anyone, for which he is amenable to society, is that which concerns others. In the part which merely concerns himself, his independence is, of right, absolute. Over himself, over his own body and mind, the individual is sovereign.

—John Stuart Mill

*I*f you have had experiences similar to mine, then you have witnessed this sort of dialogue on numerous occasions.

Uncertain Voter: I would vote for the Democrat, but I am against abortion.

Democrat: Don't you know that we live in a country where people get to make their own moral decisions? You might think it's wrong because of your religion, but in America we have freedom of religion.

Uncertain Voter: That's true, but I'm not against abortion just because I'm religious. I think it's morally wrong.

Democrat: I can respect that. But still, you think it's immoral, and maybe I think it's immoral, but there are a lot of people who don't have a moral problem with it. They think it is morally permissible. You wouldn't want to force your moral view on them, would you? Democrats respect the freedom of choice on abortion, which is why you should vote for them.

Uncertain Voter: Are you saying I should allow something to occur even though I think it is morally wrong?

Democrat: Of course. That's the whole basis for America. You can't legislate morality, even if you tried. Even though you think abortion is wrong, and so you would never get an abortion, other people disagree. We live in a pluralistic society, and in order to get along, we have to allow people to make their own moral decisions. Republicans would take away that freedom, which is why you should vote Democrat.

Uncertain Voter: Well, I don't want to force my morality on others like those Republicans do. I guess I should vote Democratic after all.

I may have presented my interlocutors as being more courteous than I have ever witnessed in real life, but I have seen more bombastic or antagonistic versions of this argument more times than I can remember. I suspect most of us have. Democrats seem to take great pride in being the party which does not legislate morality, and they harshly criticize Republicans for imposing their moral perspective on people who have different moral views.

There is a fundamental ambiguity which must be straightened out before we proceed. When some people say that we can't legislate morality, what they mean is that no matter what laws we pass, we will not turn people away from immorality. All we can do is make it harder for immoral people to gain from their immoral ways. Even if an immoral person doesn't engage in an immoral act because it is illegal, they aren't really doing it for a moral reason. So, no legislation can make people adopt the right values.

On this view, the claim that we can't legislate morality has nothing to do with whether any laws are appropriate. Unless a person is an anarchist, he believes we should have some laws. The question is what laws are appropriate to have, and the question of whether laws will turn people into good people is a red herring. Laws were never meant to inculcate goodness into people, which must be done in other ways, if at all. So, in deciding what laws are proper and which are improper, we must turn to the other meaning.

The problem is that the other understanding of the phrase is not literally true. When people say you can't legislate morality, what they actually mean is not that one *can't* make laws forbidding immoral behavior, but that one *shouldn't*. In fact, they often use this phrase to criticize a law which is already on the books. People who criticize anti-sodomy laws, for example, will often use the phrase. People have legislated against moral issues, which proves that they can. The question is whether they should.

I enjoy when complex ideas or issues are simplified. It helps me to understand them, and organize my thoughts, so that I can continue to explore those issues in a more fruitful way. I suspect that I'm not alone in this. What I don't do is think that because an idea can be presented in a simplified way, that the issue is not complex. There can be incredible complexity, even in a simple idea, or a simple dichotomy.

I also try to avoid presenting ideas in a simplistic way. To oversimplify an issue, so that it doesn't even resemble the original idea, is to distort reality in an unacceptable way. For example, thinking that we should not legislate morality. This idea is so simplistic that it is literally ridiculous.

Consider murder. I think all my readers would agree that murdering someone is morally wrong. Go ahead, answer this question and see:

Do you think that murder is immoral? If you answered "No," I think you've got a lot more problems than I can handle here.

So, if we all agree that murder is immoral, and we adopt the principle that one cannot legislate morality, then it follows that we cannot make murder illegal. It's basic logic. It's so basic, that it makes me think that anyone who asserts that we cannot legislate morality cannot have thought about the issue one iota, and so is probably not worth listening to. But that would be judgmental. It's a good thing for me that we can't legislate against being judgmental. (Or can we?)

Of course we can and should legislate moral issues, and to deny it is to live in a childish fantasy world. The only question is which things that we think are immoral are the ones which we should make illegal? Torture, rape, theft, murder, arson; these acts I think we would all agree are immoral, and also that they are acts which we should make illegal. Anyone care to disagree?

Yet, I think we would all agree that there are some things which each of us thinks are immoral, and yet we would not want the legislature to make illegal. At least those of us in America who like to think of it as a free country. Perhaps adultery is one issue. I think most of us agree that it is immoral, and yet very few of us would want to make it a crime punishable by the state.

Fortunately, we live in a society which recognizes this distinction. Not all people throughout history have been so lucky. In fact, we are likely in the vast minority of people who have ever existed. The vast majority of governing bodies throughout history made no distinction between what was immoral and what could be prohibited by law. That doesn't mean that they would necessarily outlaw everything they considered immoral, but they didn't think that they were precluded from doing so.

Before we continue, it may help us to clarify several terms I will be using throughout the rest of this chapter, and the rest of the book.

Defining terms

Legal Moralism: the viewpoint that legislative bodies are empowered to outlaw any behavior which they deem to be immoral.

Conservatism: the viewpoint that legislative bodies can only outlaw any behavior which they consider to be destructive of society, or its cohesiveness.

Liberalism: the viewpoint that legislative bodies are empowered to prohibit only behavior where an identifiable person is harmed or infringed upon against his will.

Anarchism: the viewpoint that no legislative body has any authority to enact any legislation whatsoever.

Paternalism: the viewpoint that legislative bodies are empowered to discourage, through coercive means, each person from causing harm to himself (imposing fines or imprisonment, for example).

These five views are not the only political philosophies, but they cover a broad range of views. The first four are mutually exclusive positions along a spectrum of viewpoints, with Legal Moralism at one extreme and Anarchism at the other. It is not possible to adopt more than one of them, at least not consistently. Paternalism is theoretically consistent with any other view except Anarchism, but there does seem to be some tension between Liberalism as defined here and Paternalism.

A Legal Moralist is one who says that the fact that an act is immoral is enough to make that act illegal. In somewhat technical terms, it holds that "an act's being immoral" is a sufficient condition to justify a law against that act. Most Americans are strongly opposed to Legal Moralism, at least in concept. I think a lot of Democrats suspect that Legal Moralism is the default position of most Republicans, or at least those Republicans on the religious right. I hear this criticism in many of the attacks they aim at the Republican Party.

There may be some disagreement about what Conservatism is, but I believe the definition I've given really captures something people associate with it. The view I identify as Conservatism holds that not everything which is immoral should be illegal, but that there is a class of actions they would take to be immoral which should be legally proscribed. These acts are the ones which are bad for society, where "bad" is usually not defined very clearly. Sometimes something more specific is said, such as they are beneath the dignity of a human being, or some other criterion. For example, someone who wants to ban the viewing of pornography might be appealing to this standard. It may be a victimless crime, in some sense, but it might somehow contribute to some negative development to society at large. This view is less stringent than legal moralism, in that not every immoral thing will be illegal. It will only legislate against those things which might be said to harm society in general, even if they do no specifiable harm to any particular person (or perhaps something some people would not consider harmful).

It seems to me that when I hear people who are called conservatives articulate their views, this is the point at which they and I disagree, so I have a predilection to call this the conservative position. I think that most of the people who are called "conservative" in America today would accept this principle, though I'm open to being disproven. As I see it, the conservative position holds that "being for the good of society" is a sufficient condition to justify a law. This would mean that if banning an act is good for society, in some more or less defined sort of way, the conservative would agree that this fact by itself justifies banning that act.

One last position I want to define is that of liberalism as it was understood throughout history before the mid-twentieth century in America, and as it is still known throughout the rest of the world besides America. In this sense, a liberal is one who generally accepts John Stuart Mill's Harm Principle. Mill stated that "the only purpose for which power can be rightfully exercised over any member of a civilized community, against his will, is to prevent harm to others."[51] Under this principle, the only way a law can be justified is if it is tailored to prevent someone from harming another, or in general, from infringing on that person's rights. So, liberals believe that harming someone, or violating one's [negative] rights, is a necessary condition to justify a law.

An anarchist believes that no government is ever justified. No group of men, whether chosen by God or elected by others, can presume any authority to dictate to other men how they should behave, at least not under the force of law. Anarchists do not believe that any government can claim any justifiable authority, and that every man should be free to do whatever he wishes. Although anarchism is sometimes associated with the left, such as in the protests against the WTO, I find that many people who call themselves anarchists would be happy with a socialistic government, and so perhaps are not really anarchists. I don't associate the Democratic Party with anarchism at all, and will not address anarchism any further.

Finally, a paternalist believes that individuals should not be able to decide for themselves what is good for them, but instead society in general should. A paternalist would say that if a person is causing harm to himself in the view of society, then society can and should interfere in his freedom so as to discourage him from his actions. Paternalism is independent logically from the first three viewpoints, in that it can be added to or left out of them. A conservative could be a paternalist, or not, for example.

As I said earlier, if you ask most Democrats where they would put other Democrats, or the Democratic Party in general, I suspect that there would be widespread agreement. Most Democrats are liberals, they would say. Furthermore, I don't suspect that they would consider themselves Paternalists. They would also say that more Republicans are Legal Moralists, or at the very least conservative. That is one big complaint that is made against Republicans: on issues such as abortion or homosexuality, Republicans want to force their (usually religious) morality down every else's throats.

Let me be clear. I am a liberal, and I am not a paternalist. I think it is an intolerable injustice to force another human being to abide by any moral code beyond refraining from harming others, or violating their rights. I will add more about liberalism in another chapter. Here I am only examining the claim that it is Republicans who want to impose their moral views on the rest of the country, and not Democrats. When it comes to morality, who is the bigger bully?

Here's what I propose. Let's make a list of things that Democrats, and the left in general, think are morally wrong, and then we'll make a list of things which Republicans, or members of the political right, think are morally wrong. Then, we'll see who wants to make more of their list illegal, or regulated through taxation, or some other means. If Democrats are correct, then we should find numerous areas where Republicans attempt to legislate morality, and presumably very few areas where Democrats want to impose their moral views. Republicans should adopt a conservative or legal moralist position, and Democrats should adopt a liberal viewpoint, unless something very odd is going on.

There is no way to make an absolutely definitive list, but I think we can do a passing job of it. I will attempt to be fair and honest in making this list, but there will no doubt be areas where each of us will disagree. I am confident that anyone who also fairly attempts to create their own list will still obtain comparable conclusions as me. Here it is:

Issue	Left's Position	Right's Position
Murder, Rape, Theft, Assault, etc.	Immoral	Immoral
Abortion	Generally moral	Generally immoral
Euthanasia	Tends toward moral	Active euthanasia is immoral
Stem-cell research	Moral	Immoral
Animal experimentation	Tends toward immoral	Moral
Global Warming [environment]	Immoral to ignore	Moral to ignore now

Issue	Left's Position	Right's Position
Homosexuality	Moral	Immoral
Gay marriage	Tends toward moral	Immoral
War	Tends toward immoral	Moral, at times
Capital punishment	Immoral	Moral
Affirmative action	Moral	Immoral
Paying someone too little	Immoral	Tends toward immoral
Homosexual discrimination	Immoral	Tends toward moral
Using racist language	Immoral	Immoral
Allowing others to go hungry	Immoral	Immoral
Inequality in general	Immoral	Moral
Unlimited money in campaigning	Immoral	Moral
Pornography	Moral	Immoral
Drugs	Tends toward moral	Immoral
Gambling	Moral	Immoral
Premarital sex	Moral	Immoral
Divorce	Moral	Tends toward immoral
Tattoos	Moral	Tends toward immoral
Wearing revealing clothing	Moral	Immoral
Women in the workplace	Moral	Probably moral
Hunting	Tends toward immoral	Moral
Owning a gun	Tends toward immoral	Moral
Smoking	Tends toward immoral	Moral
Torturing terrorists	Immoral	Moral
Being intolerant of others	Immoral	Immoral, but not always
Failing to wear a seatbelt	Irrational	Irrational

Obviously, these descriptions are only very rough generalizations. If I thought there was an issue where it would be grossly unfair to label one side as being moral or immoral, but there were substantial factions on that side which fell clearly on moral or immoral, I put "tends toward". It may be that a firm judgment would only be held by the far right or far left, or that there was a split, but still a large majority would lean one way.

Every reader will have to decide whether I have overly simplified an issue and the stances of the left and right on that issue. You will also have to decide whether I have selected a balanced range of issues, or if I have chosen in some sort of biased way. I think that even if you disagree with a few examples, that overall sound generalizations can still be made. Before I make any of those, however, we should go issue by issue and see what Democrats say about each one.

Murder, Rape, Theft, Assault, etc.

Democrats and Republicans alike condemn murder, assault, stealing, and a whole host of acts as immoral, and also support keeping them illegal. All this tells us, however, is that they are not anarchists. As far as we can tell by their support of these issues they could be liberals, conservatives, or legal moralists. Killing someone unjustly does cause someone else harm, which means it violates Mill's harm principle, and thus can be legally prohibited even by a Liberal. We don't learn much about the deeper philosophy of Democrats by looking at these issues.

Abortion

Obviously, abortion is a very complex issue, and we can consider numerous fine points about which circumstances make for morally permissible abortions. I think almost everyone agrees that removing a fetus growing in a woman's fallopian tube (an ectopic pregnancy), where the mother would have no chance of surviving even long enough to remove a viable fetus, is morally permissible. So, almost everyone thinks that abortion should be morally permissible in at least some cases. Still, it is pretty clear that the Democrats are the ones who hold that abortion is generally morally permissible, and Republicans tend to say that abortion is generally morally wrong. Of course, what I am saying won't apply to everyone in either political party, but I believe it applies to most people in each respective party, and even more so for the leaders of those parties.

It also seems more than clear that the Democratic Party is the one fighting to ensure that abortion remains legally available in as many circumstances as possible. The Republican Party might be a little more divided, but still would restrict abortion in numerous ways, ultimately making it available in only a few restricted cases (when the mother's life is at stake, and perhaps pregnancies due to incest or rape).

To be even more specific, it seems that Republicans, when they believe an abortion is immoral, do want to make it illegal, and when an abortion is morally permissible, Republicans want it to be legally available. Perhaps the generally held view, that Republicans are legal moralists, is correct. For particular Democrats, it seems that even when they might believe a particular instance of abortion is morally wrong, they would still allow it to be legally available. It sounds like liberalism to me, though I will argue shortly that this appearance is deceptive.

Euthanasia

Euthanasia is also a complicated, gut-wrenching issue. One of the simpler distinctions which can be made is the difference between active and passive euthanasia. Passive euthanasia is when a terminally ill patient intentionally refuses treatment which might prolong his or her life. Most everyone agrees that passive euthanasia is moral, at least generally. So, the real issue is active euthanasia, where someone actually gives a terminally ill person a shot which will end his life artificially and immediately. I think active euthanasia is still considered immoral by a great number of people in both parties, but it also seems true that if there is a side which would consider it morally permissible, it would be the left. Perhaps this is one case where it is really the far left which believes it to be permissible morally.

It seems to me though, that whoever believes it to be immoral, also thinks it should be illegal, whatever political party to which they belong. Those who believe it to be morally permissible, also think it should be legally available. We are less likely to find many people who say that it is morally wrong, but still should be legally available, which would clearly indicate the liberal position. I am assuming here that no one is harmed or has their rights violated by active euthanasia. It seems to me difficult to maintain that anyone is harmed, when they knowingly and willingly make the decision to end their own lives. The case where one person decides to end another person's life, however, as in the case of Terri Schiavo, is at least a little more problematic.

Stem-cell research

Democrats in general support stem-cell research, and find nothing wrong with it morally. Republicans are probably a little more diverse in their thinking, but there are large numbers of Republicans who think it is morally wrong. Obviously, those Democrats who find it moral will also want it to be legally allowed, but what I find more interesting is that they are quite often also in favor of using tax dollars to pay for it. In effect, they are willing to take money from people who find an activity immoral, and use that money to engage in the activity. Talk about forcing your moral viewpoint on others!

In contrast, it seems that most, or at least many, Republicans are willing to allow stem-cell research to continue, even though they find it to be immoral. They are certainly against having the research funded by forced taxation, but that seems to be in line with liberal principles. It seems that at best the general Democratic position is best classified as conservative. They believe that society is better off with such research and the cures such research promises, and that this justifies forcing people to contribute their money in order to bring such research about.

Animal experimentation

We could say a lot about animals and whether they have rights, but I think we should focus on one aspect of that debate. Should we experiment on animals? Interestingly, the positions here seem to be reversed from those of stem-cell research. Some leftist Democrats are strongly opposed to all animal research, condemning it as grossly immoral, while more moderate Democrats tend to consider it morally permissible, at least in some cases. Republicans, and those on the right, seem to more uniformly consider it morally permissible.

It seems to me that most Democrats want some animal experimentation to be illegal, and that when asked where to draw the line, it would for the most part cleave along the moral dividing line. That research they consider immoral would be the research they would want to ban. There are probably some Democrats who want some research to be legal even though they find it immoral, but I suspect they are in the minority. These considerations lead me to conclude that Democrats are often legal moralists on the issue of animal experimentation.

In the wake of the allegations against NFL Quarterback Michael Vick, it also seems appropriate in this section to discuss animal fighting, such as cock-fighting, dog fighting, and bull-fighting. It seems that most Democrats would say that it is immoral, and they would also want it to be illegal. Consider that no person is harmed during such contests (usually) seems to make this a variety of legal moralism, although most Republicans would probably also be in the same boat on this issue.

Environment/Global Warming

I'm not really sure how to phrase this issue, since "the environment" is not an activity which can be immoral. One way to get at the issue is to think about global warming. Those on the left would certainly say that big businesses which are profiting off despoiling the environment are doing something immoral. They also would like to pass regulation and laws to prevent such businesses from doing so. Thus, it looks like legal moralism in this case.

This conclusion, however, may be a little premature. One way of looking at it is to say that if the global temperature were being raised by pollution in the atmosphere, then it is a case of people being harmed. If right, then this situation would fall squarely under the harm principle, and would comport with liberalism. Then legislation such as the Kyoto Protocol, which would cost billions of dollars to implement, could be justified.

I have to say that I think such arguments are tenuous at best. The heart of liberalism is about non-interference in people's lives. It demands that for government to intervene and regulate people's lives, there should be substantial proof that what they are doing is directly harmful. It just doesn't strike me to be very liberal to take a theory about what might occur which has no conclusive proof to it, and use it to make enormous public policy changes which will negatively affect hundreds of millions of people's lives. Argue all you want that global warming is real, there is no substantial scientific evidence which conclusively shows that human activity is anything more than a marginal factor, at least none which isn't contradicted by evidence of equal weight.

It seems to me that I'd have to classify the Democratic position on global warming and how we should respond to it as conservative, or possibly even legal moralism directly.

Homosexuality

Thank God for homosexuality. The issue, I mean. It's much less complicated than most of these issues are. Those on the left generally believe that homosexuality is morally permitted, and those on the right generally believe that it is not. What's nice is that there is near universal agreement that homosexuality should be legally allowed, at least in first and second world countries. (or whatever the politically correct term for these is now). Sure, there are a few far right ideologues who are legal moralists on this issue, but in America they are very few and far between, thankfully.

So, it's pretty clear that in terms of political philosophy, those on the right (generally Republicans) are liberal, at least those who find homosexuality to be immoral. Unfortunately, it doesn't really tell us anything about those on the left. They think homosexuality is morally permissible, and so whatever philosophical position they adopt, they would not want to see it legally prohibited.

Gay Marriage

The issue of whether the state should recognize marriage between individuals with the same gender (or for those more p.c., sex, or with the same genitalia), is more complicated. Republicans seem to be more uniformly against it, even those Republicans who find nothing wrong with homosexuality morally. Democrats seem to be more split.

Honestly, I'm not sure how to classify positions on gay marriage with the political philosophies defined earlier. It seems to me that all that liberalism would require is that homosexuals are allowed to live together as they see fit. A marriage contract seems to go beyond that. A marriage contract is an explicit endorsement, if not encouragement, of a practice. I can certainly understand why gay people would want the government to endorse their lifestyle, but I don't see why it would be right to force people who believe that homosexuality is wrong to endorse the practice.

It is true that no one is forced to be gay or to enter into a marriage with a person of the same sex, but having a marriage contract endorsed by the state does force people to endorse the moral viewpoint that homosexuality is morally permissible. Some of you may say, yes, absolutely, we should force intolerant homophobic bigots to accept that homosexuality is morally permissible, but no one can ignore the fact that it does force a certain moral viewpoint on others. And no one can deny that it is overwhelmingly the Democratic left which is trying to do so.

War

The right is hawkish, and the left is dovish. That's just the way it is. It's true that individual Democrats will at times take a more hawkish position, but in general, it will be the Democrats who want to avoid war, and when war has commenced will be the first ones to want to pull out.

The issue of war is in one important way like the issue of gay marriage. It doesn't involve simply the behavior of individual citizens, but public policy decisions. It seems that either way, whoever wants to enact their public policy position will be forcing its morality on others. Think about it. If some people think a particular war is immoral, and move to try to end the war, they are attempting to force their moral view on others. Those on the right might argue that they are not forcing anyone to go to war, since we don't have a draft, but since our wars are funded by taxpayer dollars, they will be forcing others to pay for something they find to be immoral.

Unfortunately, when it comes to war, there seems to be no way to avoid imposing a moral perspective on others. Unless someone said that war was immoral, but never argued against starting or in favor of ending a war, but there seems to be very few of those people around. So, it will not help us to distinguish which of the five political philosophies most people have.

Capital Punishment

Capital punishment is also a public policy choice, so perhaps it doesn't tell us much about what one's political philosophy is, at least not along the spectrum we are considering here. Again, whatever side gets its way will be forcing its morality on everyone else. If one thinks capital punishment is immoral, then it would seem to be anti-liberal to require others to refrain from capital punishment by law. Perhaps one can argue that the death penalty actually does harm people, but I don't really see how that will help. After all, doesn't throwing someone in prison harm him? It cannot be that liberalism prohibits us from punishing any one ever. So, it must be permissible to harm people in some sense, as a just form of punishment.

Perhaps one can say that putting an innocent man to death would be harming him or her. It seems that this might make sense for people who oppose capital punishment for practical reasons, but not for those who are opposed to it on principle alone. Those who are opposed to capital punishment even when we know that someone is a vicious, unrepentant murderer cannot claim that we are harming such a person in the same sort of way. And even so, it still seems that they are trying to force other people to follow their moral perspective.

On the other hand, those who believe in capital punishment don't want to force anyone to commit an execution who doesn't want to. Those who actually commit executions seem to find them morally permissible; at least I don't think it would be hard to find people in criminal justice who would find it morally permissible. Still, I suppose that those who are morally opposed to capital punishment will feel like having society engage in an action they find immoral still compels them in some way. They might oppose funding the executions with their own tax money as well.

Affirmative Action

As I've already said, I believe affirmative action is immorally racist. I do not want my country to engage in racist, immoral behavior in my name. That's the trouble in a democracy. In a way, everything my country does is in my name. Can we say that it would engage in the policy not in my name? Perhaps if I don't vote for the policy in question? I don't think that this is a fruitful approach. After all, we've agreed to the political system in our country, so doesn't that mean that in some way everything it does, as long as it acts according to the rules, is done in the name of me and every other citizen.

When it comes to private businesses, the situation is a little more clear. The right generally says that a business should be free to voluntarily engage in affirmative action if its owners want. This position would fit with classical liberalism. I would have to say that the left is not quite as tolerant. It is true that many on the left would not force businesses to engage in affirmative action, but if there is force on the issue, it is from the Democratic left. Jesse Jackson is proud of his efforts to pressure corporations into adopting affirmative action policies.

Furthermore, it is the left which would violently assault anyone who wanted to hire only white people, using the force of law, of course. This is just the issue of fairness in hiring, or equal opportunity. Most Republicans would agree, but it seems to be more of a Democratic issue. There is absolutely no question that forcing someone to be fair in this sense is a matter of forcing one's moral viewpoint on others. Perhaps we should force them to do so, but it still seems like a case of legal moralism.

Paying someone too little

As a generalization, it is Democrats who support minimum wage laws, and sometimes even "living wage" laws. Ask them why, and they will say that it is wrong to pay someone too little for the work they do: everyone deserves a wage where they can pay for life's necessities, at the very least. Republicans are far more likely to say that it is morally permissible to offer any amount for labor.

So, where are the Democrats who say that, even though it is immoral to pay someone too little, people should be free to act according to their moral intuitions, and not those of the majority? Where are the Democrats who take a principled, liberal stance against minimum wage laws? Where are the Democrats who argue for "choice" when it comes to paying the minimum wage? If you know any, please introduce them to me, because I can't recall a single one.

On the issue of minimum wage, Democrats are legal moralists.

Discriminating against homosexuals

If we allowed people to freely decide whether to hire homosexuals, or to rent rooms to them, etc., we all know that many people would refuse to work or live with them. The Democratic left has been on the forefront of eliminating discrimination against homosexuals and everyone else. Perhaps you applaud what they have done, but if you don't recognize that you are forcing your moral perspective on others, then you are the metaphorical ostrich.

Again, I can't help wondering why there are no Democrats who say that of course it is morally wrong to discriminate against homosexuals, but my God, it would be worse to force my morality on others. At least none that I can recall. Why are Democrats so comfortable in enacting legislation to forbid others from this kind of discrimination? Is it just because they feel so strongly about it? But many people on the right feel just as strongly that homosexuality itself is morally wrong. Shouldn't we all object if those on the right wanted to force legislation outlawing homosexuality? Those of us who consider ourselves liberals should.

Using racist and other offensive language

It is true that Don Imus was removed because of social pressure alone; no government entity threatened to imprison the owners of his radio station. Although there was talk about fines from the FCC, I don't believe any of that discussion came from the FCC. If we listen to the media, it would seem that only Republicans engage in censorship, but the truth is far different. While the right does insist on censoring nudity and foul language, it is only the left which wants to censor language based on ideological content.

Have you ever heard of political correctness? Political correctness is the idea that being correct or right in the sense of true is not as important as being unoffensive. It is the idea that if someone has ideas which don't fit in with the orthodox viewpoint of mainstream society, then they should remain silent or face scorn, ridicule, or worse. It doesn't matter whether they are true, or what evidence one has that they are true, or how carefully one presents them. What matters is whether the people in power like them, and that they comport with an idealized view of the world where everyone is equal and no one is ever offended.

Think about Lawrence Summers, who was the President of Harvard. In a speech, he dared to question the orthodoxy that women are equally as capable as men when it comes to mathematics. He could not have been more circumspect in his assertion. First, he argued that the main reason that there are differences between the number of men and the number of women in high-profile positions was legitimate family choices, and that in science and engineering fields there were also aptitude differences between men and women, and also that less importantly were issues of socialization and discrimination. He then added "I would like nothing better than to be proved wrong, because I would like nothing better than for these problems to be addressable simply by everybody understanding what they are, and working very hard to address them."[52]

Apparently his reluctance was insufficient to protect him from demands for his resignation. Fortunately, politically correct advocates have not used government power to restrict speech in our houses, but they feel they have the right to restrict speech most everywhere else. Some universities have instituted speech codes which do place limits on what their students can say. Democrats have pushed for widely interpreted sexual harassment policies, where what someone says can cost them millions of dollars.

Let's not pretend that this isn't a case of some people on the left trying to force others to live according to the leftist moral viewpoint.

Allowing others to go hungry

What should happen when someone doesn't have enough money to feed himself? Let me put it a different way: do you think each of us has a moral obligation to share some of our food to help feed him? If you say "yes", then you think it is immoral to allow others to go hungry. It may surprise you, but there are moral codes which say otherwise. You might not like it, but if you support welfare given by the government through forced taxation, then you do support forcing your moral perspective on others.

Let me see. Which side is it that supports welfare? Oh, both major political parties. But you'd be ignorant if you didn't think that the Democratic left is far more in favor of generous welfare programs than the Republican right.

Inequality in general

When was the last time you heard a Republican bemoaning the fact that the gap between the rich and poor was increasing? Never, I suspect. It is only Democrats and people on the left who worry about this, and consider a society with inequality to be immoral. Are there any Democrats who take the liberal view, and say that although they find it immoral, they don't want to pass laws and regulations to impose their morality on others?

If they exist, they seem to be in the vast minority, and they have no influence within the Democratic Party. We've already covered some of the policies leftists propose to reduce inequality, including minimum wage and welfare programs. Progressive taxation is another, as is the inheritance tax. So, as far as political philosophies go, the Democratic left is clearly on the conservative/legal moralist side of this issue.

Unlimited money in Campaigning

Another area where Democrats want to reduce the inequality they abhor is in campaign donations. This inequality is their ostensible reason for putting limits on campaign donations. Answer for me just a few simple questions to see if you want to force your moral views on others. Do you think it is wrong that rich people can give any amount of money they want to anyone's electoral campaign? If you said "yes", then answer question number two: Do you want to have laws limiting the amount of money people can give to such campaigns?

If you answered "yes" to both questions then welcome to hyper-conservatism! Maybe I should use this term instead of "legal moralism," which just doesn't have the rhetorical force which I think is appropriate.

Pornography

Let's see if I can get this straight. The right supports pornography, right? And the left thinks it is immoral. Oh yeah, I got that backwards. So, the right wants to crack down on pornography and make it illegal then. Since they supposedly want to force their moral view on everyone else, wouldn't they have to?

Okay, there probably are some Republicans who would outlaw pornography, and all of us should worry about its prevalence and the ease with which it has become available. But most Republicans are pretty clear that although they think it is immoral, they wouldn't make it illegal, although they do support some regulations. Yet, even many Democrats who think that pornography per se is moral still want to see it regulated, at least as to where it can be displayed.

On a related issue, most people on both sides of the political divide think prostitution is immoral, and most people want to keep it illegal. Of course, I've never understood why someone can film themselves having sex with a stranger, put it on tape, and sell the tape, and yet not get arrested on prostitution charges. Maybe those convicted of prostitution should just call themselves pornographers, and sell videos of their activities. Do you think that would change what people say about it?

Drugs

Is it immoral to smoke marijuana? It is certainly an interesting question. I wish I could be inside your brains when you mull it over. If it is immoral, and that is why we want to make it illegal, then we are clearly being legal moralists. If it is not immoral, then on what basis are we going to make it illegal? Maybe it would just be better for society if we made it illegal. Ah, but then we are conservatives. It seems like the left might be in support of legalizing marijuana, but almost no politicians have called for legalization.

Perhaps this is a case of paternalism. We, as a society, just have a moral responsibility to take care of those people who are not smart enough to take care of themselves. Unfortunately for us if this is our position and we think we are liberals; it seems that this position too will force one moral view on everyone in society, and so is anti-liberal.

Although Republicans sometimes tar leftists with the "pot-smoking" label, the Democratic Party has not called for legalization of marijuana or any other drug. As for using marijuana for medicinal purposes, it would seem to be a decision between a person and his or her healthcare professional. Unless we want to force not only morality on others, but our opinion about medical care as well.

Gambling

Gambling doesn't seem to come up as much as an issue any more. Earlier in our history there was a strong antagonism toward gambling on moral/religious grounds, but somehow it seems to have abated. In any case, I still would say that if anyone would call gambling immoral, it would be the right. Inasmuch as anyone on the right who thinks gambling is immoral, but would still allow it legally, with regulation no doubt, that person is adopting a liberal political philosophy.

Since those on the left are, I think, more likely to say that gambling, in itself, is not immoral, it won't tell us where the left stands politically.

Premarital sex

This one is absolutely clear. The left thinks it is moral, and should be legal, and in fact probably encouraged. So, in terms of political philosophy, this issue is equivocal. The right thinks that it is immoral, but that it should remain legal, if highly discouraged. It doesn't get much more liberal than that.

Divorce

There have been people who have wanted to make divorce illegal, but almost all of them have been dead a long while. But there are still people who think it is immoral. And they are all on the right, I believe. The Roman Catholic Church does not recognize divorce for its members, but it doesn't prevent people from getting divorced civilly, nor is it trying to take away that right for others.

The left doesn't want to make divorce illegal, of course, but those on the left don't believe divorce is immoral.

Tattoos

Tattoos seem to be almost mainstream in today's America. I think most people who refrain from getting tattoos just think they're kind of dumb. Why mark one's body permanently, when we know we often change our views on things? But there are those Americans (on the right, I would say) who think that tattoos are immoral on religious grounds. I don't know of any who would want to make them illegal.

Those on the left seem to consider tattoos perfectly moral. In fact, if anything, the left wants to punish people who discriminate against people with tattoos. They haven't passed such legislation yet, but it wouldn't surprise me if it came soon.

Women working outside the home

Let's run a test. If I think it is morally proper for women to work outside the home, and act on my morality by hiring women for open employment positions, will I run afoul of any laws? Unlikely. If I think it is morally proper for women to be mothers only, and work in the home, and act on my morality by only hiring men, will I run afoul of any laws? You bet your bleep I will.

Again, the left wants to force one moral perspective on everyone else. As I said before, they certainly believe that their ethical perspective is correct, and that every other conflicting moral perspective is wrong, and they think that justifies the legal enforcement of their moral views on everyone else. But isn't that what everyone would say? Isn't that exactly what a legal moralist would say?

Hunting

I would have to say that those on the right think hunting is morally permissible, and of course should remain legally permissible, subject to some restrictions perhaps. There are some people, exclusively on the left, who would say that hunting is immoral, and I suspect many of them would want to outlaw hunting, but they are generally in the minority. I don't think that most Democrats feel that way.

So, on the issue of hunting, both political parties would say it is moral and should be legally permissible.

Owning a gun

Here, I think the issue is a little more complex. On the right, I think you'd be hard-pressed to find anyone who would say that owning a gun is morally wrong, and they are more in favor of legal ownership of guns. We all think there should be some restrictions, such as keeping guns away from convicted felons, but the right is in favor of as few restrictions as possible.

Those on the left are much more in favor of strong restrictions on gun-ownership, a few going so far as to want to outlaw all handguns. There seems to be consensus among most on the left that rifles should be accessible to hunters, but also that owning a handgun in a home for protection is a bad idea. Perhaps the left can argue that we would all as a society be better off if there were fewer or no guns available, but to use public policy to coerce others to live in accordance with this ideal is at the very least a conservative political philosophy.

Smoking

It is the left which has been behind the drive to eliminate smoking from restaurants and every other building. Not too long ago, people were free for themselves to decide when and where to smoke. Not so now. In some states, if you own a bar or restaurant and you want to allow people to smoke if they want, you still legally can't. Again, it may be better for society, but putting legal restrictions on smoking seems to be a matter of some people imposing one moralistic outlook on everyone else in society, and it's not people who are on the right.

Torturing terrorists

Some people think it is morally permissible, or even morally required to torture a terrorist to get information which might save someone's life. Some people think it's morally wrong, for any reason. And of course, everyone wants to let each person decide for himself, and at according to his own moral conscience, right? Wrong. The left wants to legally bar soldiers and other government workers from engaging in torture.

The right thing, so you say. Okay, but just don't deny that you want to use the law to compel other people to follow your moral viewpoint.

Being intolerant of others

We all want to be tolerant of others who are different from us, don't we? Maybe my perspective is a little skewed. After all, I work in the academy. Still, it would seem that being tolerant of others is a virtuous endeavor. So, I would say that in many cases, being intolerant is immoral. But the question is whether we want to use the force of government to force everyone to be tolerant of others.

If anything, it is Democrats who want to force others to be tolerant of others, at least when it comes to homosexuality, trans-gender issues, and others.

Wearing a seatbelt

For most of us, it's difficult to think of wearing a seatbelt as a moral issue. Yet, if we consider it as a question of a conflict of values, it can be seen as a moral issue. Even so, most of us would consider it irrational not to wear a seatbelt. After all, it can only help to save one's life, at the cost of a minor inconvenience. Only an irrational person would refuse to wear a seatbelt.

Yet, we still need to ask, should we force people to be rational? I think this is a very dangerous area on which to tread. I don't know if the issue can tell us anything about whether someone is liberal or conservative, but anyone who supports seatbelt laws is certainly being paternalistic. I'm not sure how Democrats fare with comparison to Republicans on the issue of seatbelt laws, but Democrats largely support them.

Analysis

I know I have made only the briefest comments about each of these issues, and relied on my background knowledge and my memories of what people have said and what I expect them to say in order to analyze them. I have attempted to be as fair and accurate as I can, however, and think that we can draw some pretty firm conclusions. Here is the table again, with political philosophies indicated.

Issue	Democratic Position	Republican Position
Murder, Rape, Theft, etc.	Inconclusive	Inconclusive
Abortion	Liberal (arguably)	Inconclusive
Euthanasia	Conservative (mostly)	Conservative/Legal Moralist
Stem-cell research	Conservative (monetarily)	Liberal (mostly)
Animal experimentation	Conservative/Legal Moralist	Inconclusive
Global Warming [environment]	Conservative/Legal Moralist	Liberal
Homosexuality	Inconclusive	Liberal
Gay Marriage	Inconclusive	Inconclusive
War	Inconclusive	Inconclusive
Capital Punishment	Inconclusive	Inconclusive
Affirmative Action	Conservative/Legal Moralist	Liberal (probably)
paying someone too little	Conservative/Legal Moralist	Conservative/Legal Moralist
Homosexual discrimination	Conservative/Legal Moralist	Probably inconsistent
using racist/offensive language	Conservative/Legal Moralist	Liberal
allowing others to go hungry	Conservative (monetarily)	Conservative (mostly)

Issue	Democratic Position	Republican Position
Inequality in general	Conservative/Legal Moralist	Inconclusive
Unlimited money in campaigning	Conservative/Legal Moralist	Inconclusive
Pornography	Inconclusive	Liberal
Drugs	Paternalist	Paternalist
Gambling	Inconclusive	Mixed, mostly Paternalist
Premarital sex	Inconclusive	Liberal
Divorce	Inconclusive	Inconclusive, for some Liberal
Tattoos	Inconclusive	Inconclusive, for some Liberal
wearing revealing clothing	Inconclusive	Inconclusive
Women in the workplace	Conservative/Legal Moralist	Conservative/Legal Moralist
Hunting	Inconclusive	Inconclusive
Owning a gun	Conservative/Legal Moralist	Liberal
Smoking	Conservative/Legal Moralist	Liberal
torturing terrorists	Conservative/Legal Moralist	Liberal
being intolerant of others	Conservative/Legal Moralist	Liberal (mostly)
Wearing a seatbelt	Paternalist	Paternalist (mostly)

As I crunch the data, I get the following results:

Democrats are liberal in some respects perhaps on the issue of abortion.

Democrats are clearly conservative or legal moralists in 13 cases.

Democrats are conservative in a monetary sense in at least two issues, where they are more than happy to take money from people and then use it in ways those people think are immoral.

Democrats are paternalistic at best on the issue of drugs and seatbelts.

Democrats are probably somewhat conservative on the issue of euthanasia.

Since legal moralists, conservatives, and arguably paternalists want to use the force of law to require people to act according to a certain moral code, when we really look closely, it is clear that Democrats want to force their moral views on others in 18 out of nineteen issues upon which we have been able to judge, and I think the issues we have examined are a fair collection to examine, i.e. they haven't been selected in a biased way to make Democrats look more conservative. The one issue where they might be said to be liberal is the issue of abortion, and I will examine that issue more closely at the end of this chapter. Republicans may be legal moralists on some issues, such as euthanasia, but they are also clearly liberal on many issues, such as homosexuality, pornography, and premarital sex.

This is so far out of line with the common expectation that I think something must have gone very wrong. Either I have made mistake after mistake in the analysis I just made, or something really problematic has occurred in our common understanding of political parties. I think I have argued fairly carefully so far, so I think the problem must be elsewhere.

In the minds of most people, especially young people, the Democratic Party is considered to be the one which allows people to live freely according to their own moral vision, and the Republican Party wants to force morality on others. As we have seen (though the reader must make his own judgment), the truth is almost the exact opposite. In America, the general zeitgeist is that forcing morality on others is just about the worst thing the government can do. So, it would be in the interest of every party to try to claim the liberal position, i.e. that they do not want to force their moral views on others.

I can only conclude that there is a more or less willful effort to try to confuse people for political gain. Democratic politicians support policies which force their moral viewpoints on others, but they use deceitful rhetoric in order to convince people otherwise. In fact, they seem to have convinced people generally that the Republican Party is much worse than they are in this respect, in direct opposition to reality. Don't believe it? Then consider this thought experiment. What would happen to the Democratic Party if you had its candidates argue in this manner:

"We have a bold new moral outlook, and we believe that the moral views of many Americans are just plain backwards. Vote for us, and we will ensure that all those people with archaic moral views will be legally forced to act according to our new morality. We will change the tax structure, provide repressive regulation, and just outright ban activity that we believe is wrong. After all, if we can't convince people to act morally through persuasion, then the only way we have left is through the law."

I believe that this speech would be fully accurate and truthful, and yet I could not imagine anyone possibly voting for such candidates. I am sure that if any candidate explained his moral outlook, and made it clear that it included tolerance for homosexuality and other things, then many more people would bite the bullet and vote for him, saying that some aspects of morality should be imposed, but I can't believe any such honest candidate could get elected.

My point is that Democrats know how to campaign. They are never going to say that they want to force morality on anyone, even when that is exactly what they want to do. And for a multitude of reasons no one in the media seems to call them on it. It makes sense that many people would have a hard time seeing it.

There are many intellectually honest people on the left who realize it. They refuse to call themselves "liberal", because they recognize that it would be a lie. They do not want people to live according to their own moral lights, but instead want the government to impose, through coercive measures, their own view of how people should behave and what the world should look like. They call themselves "progressives". I applaud their intellectual honesty, but I can't go along with the term. It just smacks of persuasive manipulation. Who in America could oppose "progress"? It is just such an emotionally loaded term that I think it is used rhetorically to fool people. It too strongly connotes that anyone who goes against it is "regressive".

I'm not sure what term would be more appropriate, but at least it is clear that they are legal moralists, no bones about it. I would have a lot more intellectual respect for the Democratic Party and Democrats in general if they too accepted that they are not in favor of freedom for people to act in the way their own morality tells them, but instead want to impose a morality on everyone.

The Issue of Abortion

I can't help reconsidering the issue of abortion. I have a colleague who vociferously argues that the only public policy choice we could make in a free country is to allow those who want to obtain an abortion to do so. I will address this question head-on in another chapter, but I want to address here only the issue of which position is imposing its own moral view on others.

The quickest way to see my point is to look back at the harm principle. The harm principle says that every person should be free to do what they want to do, as long as they are not harming anyone else. This principle is considered by many to be the core value of liberalism. Of course, in considering whether a liberal must allow abortions to occur, the question naturally arises "Is anyone being harmed?" It is obvious that a person who thinks that a fetus is a person and has the right to exist would think that killing the fetus does harm a person.

So, a liberal who believed this fact would be required *by his very liberal values* to outlaw abortion. Of course, a liberal who did not believe that fetuses are persons would think that liberalism would require him to allow abortions even if he thought they were immoral. Liberalism by itself is consistent with laws restricting or allowing abortion, and even Republicans who strongly favor laws outlawing abortion can possibly be liberals.

Also, while many people who want to outlaw abortion (at least some abortions) are criticized for wanting to force their moral view on others, which is true, it is equally clear to me that those who want to allow women to obtain abortions want to force their moral views on others. I know this will be controversial, so I will take it slowly.

Imagine that I am walking down the street, and I see a man beating up a woman. What would you say morality requires me to do? I suspect that we will get quite a few different answers. Some people will say I have no moral obligation, and should just walk away. Some will say I do have the moral obligation to do something, but calling the police is all that is required. I also think that some people would say that the right thing for me to do would be to intervene and stop it from happening.

What if the government said that for me to intervene to stop the man from beating the woman was illegal, and they threw me in jail because of it? It seems clear to me in this case that the government would be forcing me to act according to a particular moral view.

Let's up the ante. I have a gun for personal protection in my home, and the man is assaulting the woman right in front of my house. He leaves her lying in a heap on the floor and returns to his car. I went and got the gun when I first saw him, mostly because I was afraid for myself. I am quite relieved, though, when I see him returning to his car.

That relief evaporates, however, when I see him emerge from his vehicle with a big knife. He starts toward the woman. Somehow I find it within myself to shout at him to leave her alone. He looks at me and says to go back inside or I'm next.

I refuse, and tell him that I've already called the cops, who are on their way, and I have his license plate number. He continues toward the woman. I tell him that I have a gun, but he still continues toward the woman. I shout that if he doesn't leave, I will shoot him, and it does nothing. I even fire into the ground to startle him and let him know I am serious, but he just reaches down, grabs her hair, and pulls her head up, placing the knife against her throat.

Finally, I shoot him. I am a trained shot, and I aim at his shoulder from about thirty feet away. The woman was still far enough down that she was not in any appreciable danger, at least not from the gun in my hand. The man goes down, I run over, kick the knife away, and hold the gun on him until the police arrive.

Now, here's the kicker. When the police arrive, they arrest me. They say I've done something wrong, and when I think about it, can I blame them? I am standing with a gun in my hand, pointed down at a man whom I've just shot. I think if I was a cop, that's the first thing I would do, too: arrest anyone I found in that situation.

I try to explain what happened, but they don't really want to listen to my story. But they do listen to the woman, who explains exactly what happened. Her boyfriend was about to kill her because he caught her cheating on him, and I shot him right before he was about to kill her. She even has the cut on her throat to prove it.

Now, what if the police said that this information just confirms that I had done something wrong. Her testimony proves that I killed a man, and I'm going to prison. Would you be more than a little confused? I think we would all say that I had done pretty much exactly the right thing. Yes, I had used deadly force, but in the situation, where a person was going to be killed, I should have used deadly force to protect that person. Morality may not have required it, but certainly it would not prohibit my actions.

Let me be absolutely clear. If the government refused to force any moral viewpoint on anyone, then of course the government could not prevent or punish someone from getting an abortion. But neither could it prevent or punish someone for killing an abortion doctor. In the mind of a person who believes that a fetus is a person, that person would be justified by our basic moral codes in using force to prevent a doctor from aborting any fetus. If we permit him to act on our common morality, along with his basic belief about what constitutes a person, then he would be fully justified morally in using force to make doctors give up the abortion business. And if the government were to allow everyone to act according to their own moral lights, it could not punish him.

Think about it this way. For the government to say that doctors can perform abortions, and no one can stop them from doing so, is to adopt a moral viewpoint as the governing law of the land. It is to adopt the view that a fetus does not count as a person. But outlawing abortion would also be to impose a moral viewpoint on others, namely that the fetus is a person.

If we refused to impose any moral view on people, then we would have to allow people who believe the fetus is a person to act on their moral view, and we would have to allow them to act in defense of any fetus being aborted, even if they had to use force. To legally prevent me from acting upon my belief that a human person is unjustly being killed by using force against me is to impose a moral view on me.

Sure, we might argue that anyone can *hold* whatever moral view they want to hold, but we will just require them to behave as if they held the opposite moral view, specifically in this case that the fetus is not a person. Yet, wouldn't that be like saying "sure, any man can be attracted to any man and think homosexuality is moral, but we will just require him to behave as if homosexuality was immoral and refrain from behaving homosexually."

My point is that on the issue of abortion, we cannot let everyone act according to whatever moral viewpoint they so desire. Doing so would be too chaotic and dangerous. Ultimately, who counts as a person will have to be decided by society, and then everyone will be forced to follow this moral stance through the force of law.

Let me again be very clear. I did not argue that people should kill abortion doctors. All I argued was that if government truly decided not to impose any moral perspective on anyone regarding the issue of abortion, then it could not punish anyone for killing an abortion doctor. All this means is that both sides of the abortion debate want to have society impose its moral perspective on everyone in society, and that for better or worse, we must adopt one perspective. We cannot allow every person to act according to his own moral lights.

What this means is that any support for the abortion rights perspective which depended on the idea that only anti-abortion groups want to impose their views on others has completely evaporated. Liberals can be on both sides of the issue. I will argue about abortion itself in a later chapter.

Final Thoughts

I really don't understand how anyone can think that Democrats are not trying to impose their moral views on the rest of society (and largely succeeding). Conservatives consider more activities to be immoral, but recognize that there is a wide span between activities which are immoral and those which should be illegal. Democrats, on the other hand, don't think that as many things are immoral, but don't seem to have much distance at all between what they consider immoral and what should be illegal. It is as if they think that being wrong in their eyes is enough to make something illegal.

If any of my readers want to convince me to be a Democrat, the one thing you can't do is to say that the Democratic Party is the party of freedom, or the party that allows people to act on their own morality. Don't tell me that it is the party of "choice." As a party, they generally do not want people to choose to follow whatever morality they want to follow, but instead a morality which is, in the most favorable terminology, based upon openness, toleration, and equality.

Don't get me wrong, I want people to be tolerant and open, but this is a question about the proper role of government. I will try to convince people to be open and tolerant by the force of argument and persuasion, but not by the force of law.

In one way, I can't really fault Democrats for wanting to force individuals to obey a certain code of conduct. As I've already pointed out, on some issues, like abortion, and perhaps gay marriage, it is simply impossible to refrain from enforcing some morality. And no one balks at enforcing certain moral standards, such as murder, rape, assault, and many, many other unquestionably immoral actions.

My real problem is that Democrats try to make people think that only Republicans want to force people to behave morally, while they reinforce the idea that Democrats don't. Ultimately, this is a silly position, as every government must enforce some moral standards. The only question is which ones will be enforced, and perhaps more importantly, which ones won't. On this question, I disagree in large measure with the Democrats, even if I often agree with them about morality.

Ultimately, to convince me to become a Democrat, you must convince me that the morality the Democrats want to coerce other people to follow is the right morality, and more importantly that it would be just for us to use force to get others to abide by it.

CHAPTER FOUR
Organic Veggies, Maybe; Organic State, Never

Protecting the rights of even the least individual among us is basically the only excuse the government has for even existing.

—Ronald Reagan

There is a concept in Confucianism called the five great relationships. Confucius held that we are all ultimately and essentially parts of the relationships to which we belong, most of which are unchosen. The primary relationship is the relationship between parent and child. In this relationship, the parent is the superior, and the child the subordinate. The superior position in the relationship has duties toward the subordinate, such as the duty to care for and educate his children. Correspondingly, the subordinate, in this case the child, has duties toward the superior, primarily obedience.

All the other relationships have this hierarchical character, and have analogous duties. The other relationships are husband to wife, elder brother to younger brother, friend to friend (which is generally more reciprocal, but often can still be hierarchical if there is a large age or other difference), and ruler to subject.

In the Confucian view, these "relationships are just as real as any visible object. Human beings are not individuals, but interwoven threads of relationships with many people. To a great extent, in Confucian thinking, human beings *are* their relationships."[53] To Confucians, the individual is a foreign concept. Individual desires are looked upon as discordant, since they can lead to disagreements between people. In this worldview, the group is what really matters, and the individuals within the society have value only inasmuch as they support the group. As one scholar puts it, "The Confucian vision is that society will be in maximum harmony if individuals mute their individualistic desires [in order] to conform to the dictates of the Five Hierarchical Relationships."[54]

I bring up Confucianism because it offers a glimpse at a possible understanding of the state, and how one might conceptualize the state. What one takes the state to be, and what are the obligations and limits of the state, will depend in great measure on how one thinks the state should be conceptualized. For Confucians, the state is conceptualized as similar to the relationship between a father and son. So, the functions of the state, and its obligations and limits, will generally parallel those of a father to his son, and vice versa.

Everyone will conceive of the obligations of a parent to his children differently, but we can probably agree on a few general things. Parents must care for their children and protect them, feed them, clothe them, and take care of them. Parents also have a strong authority over their children, such that the parent can discipline the child for anything which the parent deems reasonable. Children don't get a say in what is right or wrong, and have the duty of obedience. Children should obey their parents. Some of us would allow for exceptions, such as when a parent commands his child to do something clearly immoral, although it would be hard to fault a child for obeying even an immoral command.

As you have no doubt realized, Confucianism strongly supports a paternalistic political philosophy. Depending on one's view of the parent-child relationship, it might support much more. This worldview also seems inconsistent with a liberal political philosophy, as defined earlier, and one who held a Confucian conception of the state would be inclined toward conservatism or even legal moralism. In an economic sphere, this conception would support socialistic policies, which in this context could be seen as an extreme form of paternalism.

Obviously, very few Democrats would consider themselves to be Confucians, but as we will see, it seems to me that Democrats generally accept a model of government which is much closer to this view than the one I have, which is one more reason why I am not a member of the Democratic Party. Before we get there, we should look at another model of society which is similar to the Confucian ideal.

In Plato's *Republic*, Socrates is portrayed as defending the view that one should always be just. In doing so, he presents an analogy between the soul of an individual and a state. He holds that just as the soul is composed of three principles (reason, appetite and spirit), a well-ordered society is composed of three classes of people (guardians/rulers, warriors, and merchants/producers). He also relates the parts, so that reason corresponds to the rulers, appetite to the merchants, and spirit to the warriors.

As Socrates sees it, one would never want one's soul to be controlled by one's appetite or spirit, but always by one's reason. Similarly, in a society, it should be the rulers who make the decisions, and not the merchants or the military or anyone else. To have any other system would be unjust, he says.

Since Plato, and perhaps before, many people have used similar analogies to understand political systems, and often they are further used to argue for one particular view or policy over another. According to David G. Hale, writing for the Dictionary of the History of Ideas at the University of Virginia, this analogy of the state to a body, often called organicism, can be found as far back as the first Hindu religious texts, the *Rig-Veda* and *Mahabharata*. Greeks besides Plato also made use of the analogy, and the Romans followed suit. The Roman Stoics explicitly stated that it was necessary for the desires of the individual to be subordinated to the well-being of the state, just as in a body every cell must cooperate in order for the body to live. Cicero made similar comparisons, arguing that just as for any part of the body to appropriate the role of the others would mean ill health or even death, for individuals to appropriate the role of the others would be to destroy the state. (*De officiis* III, 22).

Christians and Muslims also made use of these kinds of analogies, from the time of Augustine through the Middle Ages. Some of the comparisons during this period could be quite detailed. During the renaissance and beyond, the organicist analogy was beginning to be questioned in the western world, but was still used by some. The Elizabethan *Homily Against Disobedience* claimed that a subject judging a ruler is analogous to the foot judging the head. The very creative *Dialogue between Pole and Lupset*, by Thomas Starkey, uses medical theories about imbalances in the four humours of the body to diagnose and propose remedies for political difficulties.

Interestingly, Thomas Hobbes uses a modified version of the organic analogy, saying that the state was nothing but "an artificial man, though of greater stature and strength than the natural, for whose protection and defence it was intended."[55] Hobbes continues the analogy, saying that sovereignty is like the soul, magistrates are like joints, rewards and punishments are like nerves, wealth and riches are like strength, and equity and laws are like reason and will. He also says that concord is health, sedition is disease, and civil war is death. Although Hobbes makes use of the organic analogy, he does modify it by insisting that it is an artificial construction, one which is put together by men for their own benefit. I will say more about Hobbes' view in a moment.

Even after modernism made the organic analogy seem quaint, Herbert Spencer very creatively merged it with the modern theory of evolution. In *The Principles of Sociology*, Spencer extends the analogy to the evolution of species, arguing that just as simple forms of life evolve into larger ones, primitive societies evolve into modern nation-states.

Edmund Burke, an Irish politician of the eighteenth century, is often associated with organicism, but he made it clear that he thought the analogy was purely illustrative, and should not be used to derive or argue for any properties of the state. Burke is also commonly referred to as a conservative.

There were still uses of the analogy even into the twentieth century. One major political figure of the early twentieth century wrote regarding the state and man's role in it, that "man is viewed in his immanent relation to a higher law, endowed with an objective will transcending the individual and raising him to conscious membership in a spiritual society... Man is man only by virtue of the spiritual process to which he contributes as a member of the family, the social group, the nation." He adds that his conception of the state "stresses the importance of the State and accepts the individual only in so far as his interests coincide with those of the State."[56]

Another political figure writes that he is "able to imagine a State only to be the living organism of a nationality, but which, by a further training of its spiritual and ideal abilities, leads it to the highest freedom."[57] These quotations rely on the organicist analogy, but since the 1950's the analogy seems to have fallen into disrepute, at least when explicitly made. I will argue that conceptually it still plays a prevalent role in the view of leftist philosophy generally.

For most people during this period, then, new ideas about the proper limited role of government emerging out of liberalism and the renaissance made it more and more plain that the organic analogy really supported a government which was much too powerful for modern comfort. It was more appropriate to feudal lords and kings and absolute monarchs ruling over peasants.

David Hale, in the *Dictionary of the History of Ideas*, points out that for those states whose leaders adopt the organic analogy, they are generally "hierarchical and authoritarian and the ideas being supported are conservative, stressing social order and obedience."[58] As we have seen, the organic analogy supports the idea that each member of society has a proper role to play, and that no members should co-opt the role or duties of the others. Specifically, as the function of the care and management of the body should be left to the mind, decisions about what each member in a society should do are to be made by the leaders of society, and ideally, they should be immediately obeyed. Imagine what would occur if the spleen decided to ignore the commands it receives from the brain. Okay, I don't know about the function of the spleen, but if the heart thought it could decide for itself when it should pump and how much blood it wanted to pump, based upon its own interests, the result could very well be the death of the entire body.

Phil Washburn uses the term "relationalism" to refer to the political philosophy encompassing organicism. In his topical introductory textbook to philosophy, which I use in my courses, he uses the term "relationalism" to refer to the broad political philosophy which emphasizes the connections between people over the individual. He includes six positions under the heading of relationalism: organicism, paternalism, egalitarianism, socialism, internationalism, and essentialism. He recognizes, and I agree, that a relationalist can adopt an organic analogy of society, and that there is a close tie between the two views.

You should be able to see why I started this chapter with an overview of Confucianism. If the relationships between people are real and primary, then an individual does not get to make decisions for himself. He must be required to consider the relationships he is in, and cannot be allowed to act in his own benefit, unless it comports with the benefit of others. In many circumstances, he may have to forgo his own benefit for the sake of the whole, as one must when one is in a relationship. We often take pain on ourselves in order to protect the other partner in the relationship. Or, as in the organicist analogy, one body part may be called into action for the benefit of another, without regard to the first body part's wishes, risk, or damage. Sometimes one body part must be sacrificed for the whole to survive.

Hopefully, my readers will see why Washburn categorizes positions as he does. Organicism, again, emphasizes that the individual is less important than the whole. Paternalism says that the government has the right to decide what is best for individuals, and can and should force them to act accordingly. This impulse lies behind seatbelt and helmet laws. If people are too stupid to take care of themselves, then the government should do it for them. Clearly, this fits well with the organicist model, where the brain is the decision making organ, and other organs are supposed to obey. How would the liver know what is good for it?

It might be harder to see why Egalitarianism falls under Relationalism. An egalitarian holds that no person is better than any other person, that fundamentally, all people are equal. Now, how could anyone ever object to the principle that people are equal? The answer is that it depends on what we mean by equality. Do we mean equal in terms of how each person has equal freedom to value or disvalue whatever they want, and make decisions for themselves? Or do we mean that each person should have the same amount of material goods? Is it wrong for one individual to be rich while someone else starves?

It should be clearer now why the egalitarian is classified as a relationalist. He insists that there should be no distinction between rich and poor, not even the distinction of being rich or poor. Everyone is entitled to the same goods as everyone else. I won't go through the problems with such a philosophy here, I am only pointing out that the only way to implement such a philosophy is to adopt an organicist or relational model of society. The alternative view, which I shall introduce shortly, simply will not do it.

Socialism (and its cousin communism) is clearly an organicist philosophy. It holds that all goods, or more carefully all productive goods or businesses, are shared in common by the whole society. Whether individual private property is recognized divides socialist views and communist ones. Either way, these philosophies believe that the society is paramount and primary. The individual matters only because he is a part of a society.

Internationalism is the view that all varieties of nationalism are misguided or wrong. An Internationalist thinks that nation-states, if they exist at all, should be subordinate to a world-wide authority. Nationalists identify in very strong way with their own nation, and would not want any of their nation's sovereignty transferred to any super-national entity. I'm not sure that the connection is as clear here, but we could say that internationalists are more relationalists, as they push for even more centralized, absolute authority. They almost go beyond seeing a state as an organism, and see all human beings as simply aspects of a single great organism.

Essentialism is the view that race is an essential characteristic of one's identity. It defines a person and limits his choices, personality, ideas, and possibilities. It is the view that people in the same race share some metaphysical property that distinguishes them from all other people. In short, essentialism is the view I identified in chapter two as racism. A nonessentialist believes that race is an incidental characteristic, and that by itself, it does not distinguish individuals in any substantive way. It should be clear that essentialists are relationalists, and non-essentialists are individualistic. Essentialists subvert the individual, ignoring his individuality and elevating his connection to a certain group of individuals above his individual choices.

I should point out that the term relationalism is not common in political philosophy, but it seems to be very close to another political philosophy: communitarianism. The hallmark of this philosophy is the emphasis that each individual lives in a community, and therefore must circumscribe his behavior to conform to what is expected by the community, or what is beneficial to the community. It seems to be very similar, if not the same, as relationalism, and thus also fits well with the organicist model.

Many Democratic Policies Only Make Sense within an Organic Philosophy

Before I comment on why I prefer a different model for political organization, let me first try to argue that the Democratic Party, although not explicitly adopting the organic analogy, does support policies which can only be supported by an organic analogy, or by some kind of forced relationalism.

Let's first consider the idea of taxes. It's pretty clear that Democrats support high taxes, both on incomes and in pretty much every other way as well. Some of us used to believe that the Republican Party stood for lower taxes, but their commitment seems to be at best lukewarm. There seems to be no question, however, with the Democrats. They live up to their rhetoric. They believe in high taxes, and when they have power, they generally act upon that belief.

Let's consider taxation for a moment. If we are to have a government at all, it must be paid for somehow. Originally, politicians figured out how to pay for government through tariffs and other indirect means. At some point, they decided that they needed more money, and someone proposed a direct tax on income. I suppose it makes some kind of sense. We all receive some benefit from having a government, in the sense that it is there to punish people who violate our rights and return whatever anyone unjustly steals from us. Today it does a whole lot more than that, but it seems that everyone can appreciate even a very limited form of government. Even if those were the only benefits it provided, it would seem that somehow it would need some resources to do them, and that seems to justify some kind of taxation.

Yet, I believe the income tax was originally 1% of one's income, and that was during a time of war. Furthermore, the income tax demanded by the Federal Government today goes towards all sorts of things besides the basic protection of our rights. Think about this. What if the government only demanded we pay taxes sufficient to allow it to prosecute federal crimes and continue its basic legislative and executive functions? How much tax would be demanded? A whole lot less, that's for sure. Perhaps we should add in a military, but I'm pretty sure some Americans would object to that as well.

My question is this: If you could keep that much more of your money, what would you do with it? Would you donate some of it? Spend some of it on yourself? Give some to charity? Buy items you've been putting off buying? Pay off some of the bills you have because you couldn't afford to live your lifestyle while the government did take more of your money? Would you use some to invest? I suspect you would do most of these things, and probably a whole lot more.

The point is that you would be deciding where and what to spend your money on. You would figure out what you value most, what your priorities and prior commitments are, and you would take care of them. Just like you do with the money your government allows you to keep now.

I hope you see what I'm getting at here. The money will be spent or used in some way. That's a given. Unless you are irresponsible and just hide it in your mattress, but even then, I think that should be your decision. You earned the money, you should say where it goes. Again, it will be used somehow, and the only real question is *who* makes the decision about *how* the money is used.

Should each individual be making decisions about how the money he earns is spent, or should the money be pooled together, and some authority figure get to decide how it is spent? I know what an organicist would say. There's no question that an organicist would support high taxes. That way, decisions as to how money is spent will be made by the whole and not by the individuals. The more the decisions are made by the organ analogous to the brain, the better.

Just how strongly at least some Democrats feel about this issue is revealed by a representative quote from Bill Clinton. In a speech he was giving in Buffalo on January 20th, 1999, the ex-president brought up the issue of the budget surplus. After pointing out that the surplus was over $70 billion dollars, and would likely continue far into the future (how mistaken that was!), he asks the question "what do we do with it?" He begins to answer his question this way: "We could give it all back to you and hope you spend it right. But I think – here's the problem. If you don't spend it right, here's what's going to happen. In 2013 – that's just 14 years away – taxes people pay on their payroll for Social Security will no longer cover the monthly checks." He goes on to paint a horrible picture about how the lack of available money will basically mean the collapse of Social Security and Medicare, and the only way to save them is if the government gets to keep the money. He then contrasts what will happen if he allows individuals to decide what to do with the money, which he imagines is spending the money on a new car, to what will happen if the government spends the money. He puts that rosy scenario this way: "If we keep driving the debt down, then you will keep interest rates down, you will keep home mortgage rates low, you will keep credit card interest rates low, you will keep the interest rates that you pay on your car payments low, you will keep more investment coming in to Buffalo and Erie County, you will have more jobs here."[59]

The obvious conclusion is that it is in all of our best interests to allow the government to take more of our money, because it knows better how to spend and allocate the money for the right things. You, as a part of the society, don't know what is best for you or how to best spend your money, but the government does. It seems to me that this is precisely the way an organicist looks at the world.

I haven't yet argued that this view is right or wrong, all I am saying is that Mr. Clinton's views, which I believe are representative of Democrats in general, match those of an organicist. I don't think anyone should be defensive at this point. If you are a Democrat, consider for yourself what you believe. I'm pretty sure a strong case could be made that, for many people, the government could spend their money in better ways than they could themselves. Don't reject something which you believe to be true because you're afraid that I might use it against a person or group for whom you have admiration.

The real question is whether that fact, that some people are very bad at spending their own money, justifies the state in taking it from them, and then spending it in ways which will benefit that person. Mr. Clinton apparently thinks it does, and all I'm saying now is that this fact about him means we should classify him as an organicist. If you agree, then you are also an organicist.

Mr. Clinton made another comment later that year which buttresses my argument, and which reveals the jealous nature of an organicist who has decision-making power for any other decision-making body within the society. When asked why he did not want to allow local school districts to make their own decisions as to how to spend federal money which was given to them, he responded "because it's not their money."[60]

Perhaps we could defend Mr. Clinton, and say that it really is money that was taken from people all across the country, and it doesn't belong to the local school districts. And of course, it would be irresponsible for the Federal Government to hand over that money to some other lesser authority without ensuring that the money was spent responsibly. This seems like a pretty good justification to me, but it still begs the question of why the government is taking the money from individuals in the first place, especially when it is just giving it to groups which it doesn't feel are intelligent enough to make competent decisions about how to spend that money. And it still indicates that Bill Clinton takes an organicist view of things.

The instinct for a strong central authority is a definitive feature of organicism, and it is a central feature of Democratic ideology. The

Democrats stand for Social Security, Medicare, and other government programs which are run by the Federal Government, and most Democrats today are pushing for the Federal Government to take over the entire Health care system within the United States. These programs are funded by money coercively taken by every working person. It seems to me that all of these programs really only make sense under an organicist mindset.

Let me make it clear now that I disagree with the organicist philosophy, as I hope will be made clear in the following dialogue between a young person just setting out on their career and an organicist government.

"Just How Much of My Money Do You Want"

YOUNG WORKER: Hey, I realize that you are responsible for protecting me from outside military and terrorist threats, and you punish criminals and protect me in other ways which I couldn't do for myself, so I am willing to turn over some of the money I earn to help ensure you do those things.

ORGANICIST GOVERNMENT: Of course, you are. You realize that we all are better off when we unite and give authority to one central power to make decisions for us.

YOUNG WORKER: Wait a minute, I'm not sure I agree with all that, but I do think it makes sense for me to give you some of my earnings to do those things which I can't do for myself, within some limits I guess. I suppose 5% of what I make would be about reasonable, although maybe that should be for all government and not just the Federal Government. I make about $30,000 a year, so that would be about $1,500 a year. Wow, that actually sounds a little high, but I suppose I could go for it.

ORGANICIST GOVERNMENT: Well, actually we in the government have decided that it's a little more than that. So, we are going to demand that you pay more like $7,500 a year.

YOUNG WORKER: You've got to be kidding! I'm pretty sure that whatever you provide me is not worth that much. Besides, one of the things you're supposed to be doing is making sure that people from another country don't come here and take my job, or cause my wages to be reduced due to wage competition at the lower end of the economic spectrum. And you are doing a miserable job at that. And I'm not so sure you're doing such a great job on keeping me safe from criminals, either.

ORGANICIST GOVERNMENT: Regardless of whether any of that is true, it's still our decision to make. You haven't done the studies, you haven't spoken to the experts. You just have to trust that we know what we're doing, and that we know the value of what we provide better than you do.

YOUNG WORKER: I suppose that's partly true, but there still seems to be something unseemly about you're arrogance. Perhaps I should just hold on to more of my money, and then I can decide what it's used for. That seems like it's the more responsible thing to do.

ORGANICIST GOVERNMENT: Look, it's not your job to be responsible, it's ours. We carry responsibility for everyone in the country, which means we have to make the decisions. You can of course do whatever you want, but there will be consequences. Imagine what would happen if we say that we provide people with a certain amount of services, and then we just allow everyone to make the decision whether to pay the fee or not. There will be a lot of people who just refuse to pay. And then, no one will respect any of our decisions. So, we have to insist that you do pay the amount we tell you that you owe.

YOUNG WORKER: And what happens if I don't?

ORGANICIST GOVERNMENT: Well, fortunately for you, we are smarter than you. We have already put a system in place so that it's unavoidable for you to pay. You see, we have directed your employer to take the money out of your paycheck and send it to us. You really don't have a choice.

YOUNG WORKER: But, what if I tell him not to take the money out?

ORGANICIST GOVERNMENT: Are you serious? Do you think he will risk his business for you? We simply couldn't allow employers to make those sorts of choices, and if they do, we take measures.

YOUNG WORKER: Like what?

ORGANICIST GOVERNMENT: Fines, fees, hassles, regulatory oversight. We have all sorts of means to ensure compliance. And for those who are especially recalcitrant, we throw them in prison.

YOUNG WORKER: Wow, you guys really do mean business. But what if I were to be self-employed? Couldn't I just refuse to pay you? Considering that you're basically extorting from me?

ORGANICIST GOVERNMENT: Hey, only private citizens can engage in extortion! And you better watch what you say about us. We can afford much better lawyers than you. As for your question, there's a reason people fear getting an audit more than seeing a proctologist. Try to avoid paying what we decide you owe, and eventually you'll see the inside of a prison cell.

YOUNG WORKER: All right, you haven't done anything to convince me that I owe more, but I understand an appeal to force when I see it. You've got the power, so I guess I just have to give you the $7,500 you demand.

ORGANICIST GOVERNMENT: That's better. You'll see that it gets easier. Once you realize that we're really looking out for your best interests, it will be much easier for you to accede to our demands, or perhaps I should say requests.

YOUNG WORKER: They're not really requests if you will throw me in jail for refusing, are they?

ORGANICIST GOVERNMENT: Okay then, demands. But don't you agree that you ought to do that which your government commands you to do?

YOUNG WORKER: I'm not really so sure anymore.

A couple weeks pass, and the worker gets his paycheck. It turns out that not only $7,500 (annualized) has been extracted, but an additional $5,000 (annualized), under several headings, including FED MED/EE and OASDI/EE, not to mention the state income tax. So, our worker heads back to talk to his government.

YOUNG WORKER: Hey, you told me you would be taking out $7,500 a year from my income, but now you're taking out an additional $5,000 a year.

ORGANICIST GOVERNMENT: And what of it? Remember, we get to decide how much of your income we take, not you.

YOUNG WORKER: Wow. I think I really had a different view of government before. I just don't think this is right.

ORGANICIST GOVERNMENT: What would you prefer? Every individual making decisions for his or her self? You know that there would be irresponsible people out there who wouldn't pay their fair share. That's why we in the government have to make the decisions.

YOUNG WORKER: But can't you make the wrong decision?

ORGANICIST GOVERNMENT: Ah, but who would be capable of deciding that, one individual? No, only we have the authority and the capability of deciding whether we've got things wrong, and then we can change them. You've got a representative, why don't you contact him.

YOUNG WORKER: I suppose that's right, but still, something seems wrong here. And anyways, what made you change your mind?

ORGANICIST GOVERNMENT: Oh, we never changed our mind. We just failed to mention that we would also be requiring you to pay into the Social Security system and Medicare. In our defense, we thought you knew. The money we talked about before was just for regular governmental spending, but Social Security and Medicare are there to help you. Oh, on your next paycheck, get ready to spend a little more. We're adding a benefit to our citizens, and we have decided to pay for their healthcare through the Worker's Health Organization. WHO will care for all your medical needs. WHO will pay for all your doctor's visits, including psychiatric visits and acupuncture, as well as all your medications. Isn't that great?

YOUNG WORKER: Wow, that does sound kind of great, although I'm not sure I really need all that. Still it would be nice to know that I never had to pay the doctor. They seem to me like they pad their bills quite a bit. How much will you be taking out?

ORGANICIST GOVERNMENT: Only a mere $6,000 a year, which is significantly less than the average American spends on healthcare a year.

YOUNG WORKER: Are you insane?! I can't afford that!

ORGANICIST GOVERNMENT: Of course you can. If you usually pay $7,000 for healthcare to the doctor, we've actually reduced your cost. We're actually saving you money. You should be thanking us.

YOUNG WORKER: But I don't pay that much right now! I'm a healthy person. And I don't think I'll be paying that much for a long time. Which reminds me, why am I paying into Social Security anyway?

ORGANICIST GOVERNMENT: Let's cover only one issue at a time. Even if you're not paying that much now, you should be. If you were responsible, you'd be paying for health insurance. Or your employer would be. You never know what will happen. We are just ensuring that you are taken care of if something bad happens.

YOUNG WORKER: Shouldn't that be my right to decide?

ORGANICIST GOVERNMENT: Look, if you would make the right decision, then of course we wouldn't have to make the decisions for you, and you could spend your own money in the right way. Since you won't, then we have to do it for you.

YOUNG WORKER: But that's just it, what is the right decision for me? If I look at the risk and determine that it's more rational for me to forego health insurance until later in my life, then wouldn't that be the right decision for me? How can you force me to do something that is irrational? I mean, apparently you can, but aren't you violating me in some way if you do?

ORGANICIST GOVERNMENT: That's just it. It may be rational for you from an individual point of view, but we have to look at things from a more holistic approach. We have to look out for the interest of the whole society in all facets, and from that perspective, it is better to make your decisions for you, and mandate that you act in the interest of the whole society.

YOUNG WORKER: It's not that I don't think your heart is in the right place, I guess, but it's just that I think I can do a better job at running my own life than some government official who has never met me and doesn't know anything about me.

ORGANICIST GOVERNMENT: But everyone needs healthcare, don't they. And as for your other comment earlier, everyone needs a retirement income.

YOUNG WORKER: So, you're saying that Social Security provides retirement income.

ORGANICIST GOVERNMENT: Exactly, so it would be irresponsible not to pay into Social Security. Isn't it a good thing for the government to require people to be responsible?

YOUNG WORKER: I guess I might have thought so, but are you really requiring people to be responsible, or just taking away all responsibility from them? Couldn't I take my Social Security money, the money which is mine, but which you take from me, and put it into the stock market, or buy some other investment which will provide retirement income. That would be responsible, wouldn't it?

ORGANICIST GOVERNMENT: Maybe it would, but you see, most people wouldn't do that.

YOUNG WORKER: Well then, why don't you just make those irresponsible people pay into Social Security, and let those of us who are responsible do what we want? I'm confident I could invest that money and get a better return on my money than Social Security would provide, plus I would actually still own that money.

ORGANICIST GOVERNMENT: Oh, but we can't treat people differently. We all have to unite together, and that means sometimes doing something you don't want to do for the sake of others.

YOUNG WORKER: But in essence, aren't you really just punishing people who are responsible because of those people who are being irresponsible? If that's the case, why would I want to be responsible for myself?

ORGANICIST GOVERNMENT: Now you are beginning to understand. You are not supposed to be responsible for yourself. That's what the government is for. We will make decisions for you for your own good. And we've decided that it is best for you to pay into these programs, and these programs will provide for your needs.

YOUNG WORKER: But that's just it. It's not really better for me. I'm planning on living responsibly and taking care of myself. I would do better on my own than if I gave it to you. But those people who are irresponsible will be much better off. So, I ask again; aren't you just punishing responsible people for the irresponsible behavior of others?

ORGANICIST GOVERNMENT: All we can tell you is that it is better for society as a whole if we all go along with the decisions of the government. Let's say that there are some people who wouldn't be responsible for themselves, would you really want them to make their own lives miserable? Would you want them to forego medical care and fail to provide for their own retirement, until all of a sudden we as a society would have to care for them anyway?

YOUNG WORKER: But doesn't that just encourage people to be irresponsible?

ORGANICIST GOVERNMENT: Oh you give us too much credit. We can't influence how people behave.

YOUNG WORKER: You can influence me to pay you half of my income by threatening me with financial ruin or worse.

ORGANICIST GOVERNMENT: Exactly, because you realize you have something to lose. But for those who are irresponsible, nothing we can do would change their behavior. So we should all be made to contribute to alleviate the problem.

YOUNG WORKER: Again, I don't see how this is alleviating the problem, but anyway, I think I should be able to make my own decisions.

ORGANICIST GOVER GOVERNMENT: Well, then, it's a good thing you don't have that right. It's a good thing that we can make your decisions, because it seems clear to us that you would make the wrong choice.

YOUNG WORKER: So, then there's nothing I can do.

ORGANICIST GOVERNMENT: Of course, you can use the political process to change the government, and put in place people who think more like you, and then they can make the decisions.

YOUNG WORKER: But that takes a great deal of money, and right now you seem to be taking most of it. I don't really have any more left for politicking.

ORGANICIST GOVERNMENT: We have a solution. We will take some more of your money, and we will ensure that each person will have equal political influence.

YOUNG WORKER: Oh great! I shouldn't have said anything. It seems like you have the same solution for everything. Take more of my money to put in place whatever you decide.

ORGANICIST GOVERNMENT: It seems like it's working so far.

YOUNG WORKER: It sure does. So, I'm wondering then. Are you going to make pre-marital sex illegal?

ORGANICIST GOVERNMENT: What on Earth are you talking about?

YOUNG WORKER: Isn't one of the main reasons a lot of people have financial difficulties, besides the taxes you take from them, because they have children too early, at a time when they can't really afford them? That seems like irresponsible behavior to me, and it seems like it's negatively affecting their own children. Wouldn't it be best if the government prevent that from occurring?

ORGANICIST GOVERNMENT: Are you some kind of puritanical tyrant? How dare you impose your views of responsibility on others. People should be free to make their own decisions regarding their own life choices, without being punished or hounded by others. Besides, we already agreed that we can't expect irresponsible people to act responsibly; that's the definition of irresponsible.

YOUNG WORKER: I don't think I'm gonna win this one. I should shut up before I say anything else that somehow makes you raise my taxes even more.

Perhaps I was a bit extreme in a few cases, but I think I pretty much captured the general worldview of the organicist, at least in regard to political justification. The central authority should be making decisions for all members of society, and the members of society are mandated morally, or at least coercively, to abide by those decisions. That seems to me to be the heart of the matter, though a few other issues seem to have crept into the dialogue.

It should have been obvious how I see coerced contributions into Social Security and Medicare, and a possible healthcare system or government-financed electioneering, are supported by an organicist philosophy. And these are all ideas being pushed by Democrats. High taxes and other governmental regulations on businesses, such as a federal minimum wage, tend to fall into the same category.

What gives the federal government the right to decide whether I can work for $1 an hour? If I decide to do it, why should the government prevent me? I will explore this issue again in the next chapter, but even here it seems to betray an organicist predisposition. Ultimately, it is the central authority which decides what should be allowed or disallowed. The choice is taken away from individuals, and made by authority figures in the government.

Another area, as we've already touched on is public schools. Criticizing public schools in any way is anathema to Democratic sensibilities, much less asking why they even exist in the first place. Think about public schools. Who decides what gets taught? Whoever puts in place the curriculum. Who puts in place the curriculum? The central authority of the state.

So every child across the state learns the same material at the same time as every other student. Well, we know that's not true, but that is how the curriculum is set up. Every child is expected to learn the same information, regardless of his or her interests, aptitudes, or prospects. It's as if the central authority has decided to design schools along the model of an automobile factory. Our states have largely abandoned education for McEducation. Nothing against McDonald's, which works great as a fast food company. I just don't think it's an appropriate model for teaching young people.

From where are innovative ideas in education coming? Certainly not the left or the Democrats. All they seem to want to do is consolidate power in the hands of the few. They fight intensely against any measure to increase diversity among schools, in terms of content taught, or method of teaching, or home-schooling. They fight against vouchers, and any effort to allow parents more control over their children's education.

They also require that anyone teaching in a public school go through education classes, which are largely centers of indoctrination. And then they discriminate against free-thinkers when they hire people. In fact, they require everyone teaching in a public school to join a union. You don't even have an option. Either you join the union, or you don't get hired.

Actually, I should make it clear that most of what I've said so far only applies to grade school and high school education. When it comes to college, leftists generally take the exact opposite attitude. In fact, they often fall off the horse on the other side, by refusing to adopt or adhere to any standards whatsoever. At least within the humanities and several of the social sciences.

Maybe some of these measures can be supported on rational grounds, but that's not the point. And perhaps the apparent inconsistency within leftist ideology can be explained reasonably, although I have trouble imagining how. I'm only pointing out how Democrats and leftists generally do adopt an extremely centralized decision-making authority when it comes to lower education. They adopt an attitude which is only appropriate for an organicist political worldview.

One Man/One Job

Here's one more piece of evidence. Listen to people who have worked in and among unions, and you'll eventually hear stories about how people are locked into one individual role, and they are not allowed to do the job of any other role. Many people can tell you about their experiences where there was some simple task to be done, which anyone could do, and which they couldn't continue doing their job until it was done, but they had to wait for someone else to do, because "it violated union rules."

I hope I don't need to explain that unions are largely supported by Democrats, and vice versa. No, it's more than that. Union activism and Democratic activism are largely synonymous. They fight for the same issues, they support the same causes, and they have the same enemy. They may not be identical, but they have the same view of the world. So, I think it is appropriate to discuss them together, even though I recognize that there are some strains within the Democratic party which would have some problems with some of the things unions do, or vice versa.

I've heard numerous stories like the ones I mentioned above over the years, and I apologize for not cataloging them. I'm confident that you won't have to talk to union members for long before you hear them yourself. Whenever I hear stories like them, I always hearken back to Plato's description of the organic society. In it, it is inappropriate for one class of people to try to do the role of another class. In fact, Plato identifies this with injustice.

That seems to me to be exactly the attitude of modern unions and many of their members, especially their leadership, and by extension, it seems to be the view of many Democrats. It seems clear to me because of this and everything else I've presented so far that at root, the Democrats have an organicist view of society, and support the kind of government which is appropriate to that model.

The reason that I am not a Democrat is that I reject the organicist analogy, whether construed metaphysically or figuratively. I hate it as a model which is supposed to be used to draw conclusions about society, but I can't even stand it as an illustration in any way. Society is not an organism, and the members of society are not merely parts of an organism. Nor are they fundamentally, or even primarily, only their relationships. They are people. Each of them is an individual, with his own mind, and the right to use his mind and make decisions for himself.

An Alternative View

I have a different view of what society is and who should be making most decisions within it. My view goes back to Hobbes and the political thinkers who followed in his wake. They rejected the organicism of their history, and introduced a new idea to the world. The idea was the primary importance of the individual.

In this view, no individual owes allegiance to his society by his very nature, such that society (or its representative) can lay any claim against him that it finds reasonable. Instead, each individual is primary, and each individual is sovereign over himself. He makes all decisions for himself, and does only that which he thinks is right.

In his groundbreaking work *Leviathan*, Hobbes begins with the clear insight that individual men are not just parts of the society, and that they each have sole discretion over what to do with their lives, even to the point of killing other men if it be conducive to their survival, and again, only each man can make that determination for himself. Even though he refers to society as a body, he also makes it clear that he considers it an artificial body, constructed by individual men for a reason. In this model, society is not primary, each individual person is. Society, and the government which runs it, is a construction of man, each of whom understands that he is better off by entering into it than by remaining outside of it in a perpetual state of war, where life is "solitary, poor, nasty, brutish, and short."[61]

Hobbes' model for society is not an organic body, but a contract between men, who are wholes themselves. Accordingly, this theory, and the numerous offshoots and varieties which have sprung from it, has been called social contract theory. Hobbes may have gotten a lot of things wrong, but I agree with his basic insight that men are whole as individuals and do not derive their value from their country, state, nation, society, family, or any other relationship, in some secondary way.

Hobbes actually thought that his theory led to a society which was just as authoritarian as any organicist philosophy. That was one of its benefits in his view. His fellow countrymen who were organicists could not then condemn it for being a revolutionary work, although some men did well see the seeds of a doctrine, which in its full implementation would rock the foundations of the world.

John Locke took Hobbes' Social Contract theory and gave it a decidedly more liberal bent, one which is more acceptable to an individualist. Hobbes began with a theory of individuals, but he seems to end with an almost absolute rejection of individual rights. Locke considers that contracts are only entered into for mutual benefit, and if one side refuses to adhere to its commitment, the contract is nullified. Locke also made it clear that any government can only be justified through the consent of the governed. One only enters a contract through one's own free will.[62]

Since a rational person would only agree to follow the power of government if it would benefit him, the government must guarantee something in return for obedience. It must guarantee that no individual's rights are violated. It must secure each person in his person and property. If it can't do it proactively, it must endeavor to find and recover property from any perpetrator, and punish him accordingly.

The government is instituted to protect individual rights, and is just only insofar as it achieves that end. If it fails to do so, then it reneges on its side of the contract, and it no longer deserves to be obeyed. As Thomas Jefferson put a similar point in the Declaration of Independence, "when a long train of abuses and usurpations, pursuing invariably the same object evinces a design to reduce them under absolute despotism, it is their right, it is their duty, to throw off such a government." The people can put up with quite a bit of injustice, but ultimately, an unjust government does not deserve to exist. After all, it is doing exactly the thing it was put in place to prevent.

So, do individuals have the right to decide how much of their income to spend on charity, and how much to spend on their retirement? Do they have the individual right to put that money where they want it to go? I think they do. I think they have the individual right to decide where their children go to school and what they are taught. I think they have the right to decide how much health insurance they would like, and to obtain it where ever they want, or not.

I believe people own their property, and it is a violation of their individual rights for the society as a whole to take it away from them and redistribute it amongst its members. If one holds that society has its own rights, and those rights override those of the individual, perhaps these policies could be justified, but I reject that it does. I reject organicism.

I think one point will show you my commitment to the value of individual human lives: I would rather see the United States gone than to see one innocent life destroyed, whether that person be American, Iraqi, Korean, or anything else. If that sounds incredible, keep in mind that I believe that lives can be destroyed in ways other than killing, as by enslaving or other forms of oppression, and that I believe the United States does as much or more to protect innocent human lives than arguably any other country, organization, or individual throughout history. I have such faith in the individuals who compose the United States that I believe that we would reconstitute ourselves into a new free union of peoples. No group as a group, not even the United States, is more valuable or important than a single individual. I have the highest honor for the United States mainly because I believe it was founded on and continues to support these principles of individualism.

Final Thoughts

The point of this chapter was not to convince you to be an individualist. That is a choice you will have to make. The point was to make it clear why I am not a Democrat. They adopt a political metaphor, or at least I find their views flow out of a political metaphor, which I find demeaning and insulting, and which I think leads to policies which deny individual rights.

You are welcome to try to get me to change my mind. But you should know you really only have three possible ways to convince me. First, show me that the Democrats don't adopt the organicist analogy, or at least that the policies they endorse can be firmly justified without it. Second, show me that I should reject individualism and adopt organicism (or relationalism, or communitarianism). Or Third, convince me that even though I find organicism demeaning, unjust, and pregnant with authoritarianism, I should join the Party which governs according to it anyway.

Good luck. Just so you know, attacking the Republicans, and saying they are the true organicists will do you no good. For one, it strongly seems to me that Republicans are much more in favor of individual rights. For another, how is that supposed to show either of the three logically possible ways to convince me? It won't show me that the Democrats don't support organicism; it won't show me that I should adopt organicism; and it won't show me that I should join a group which supports a view that I find so distasteful.

Finally, in case you were wondering. The two quotes I listed near the beginning of this chapter. The two quotes from Organicists who lived in the twentieth century. I should tell you that the first one was by Mussolini, and the second was by Hitler. I'm not trying to rely on a genetic fallacy in order to show that the philosophy is wrong. I'm just saying that if you adopt an organicist view of society, you've got some interesting company.

CHAPTER FIVE
Whatever Happened to the Separation of Church and State?

Experience should teach us to be most on our guard to protect liberty when the Government's purposes are beneficent. Men born to freedom are naturally alert to repel invasion of their liberty by evilminded rulers. The greatest dangers to liberty lurk in insidious encroachment by men of zeal, well meaning but without understanding.
–Justice Louis D. Brandeis dissenting,*Olmstead v. United States*

Many years ago a brilliant philosopher developed an innovative idea which would affect the world long after his death. The idea was that there can be a legitimate state authority separate and not subsequent to religious authority. We in America happily live in the world created by this distinction. The Philosopher: Jesus of Nazareth.

When confronted by interlocutors who asked Jesus whether Jews should pay taxes, Jesus responds "Give to Caesar what is Caesar's, and give to God what is God's." (Matthew 22:21) Jesus deftly avoided the trap; he didn't take the position that Jews did not owe the tax, which would have put him in the revolutionary zealot camp. But he also didn't say that Caesar can overrule God.

It is inconceivable that a Jew of the period would not give God ultimate authority in a sense, but while God saw fit to allow the Romans a secular authority, the idea was that it was their prerogative how to use it. One could not refuse to obey secular authority in any matter by a simple appeal to the fact that the secular authority did other things of which even God would not approve. If this is the right interpretation of Jesus's words, one might argue that it doesn't get us the full separation of church and state, but it was an important step along the way.

In any case, we in America are very proud of the fact that we live in a society which has some kind of separation of church and state, even though we sometimes bicker over where the line should be drawn. There may be a few fanatical Americans who would call for a complete theocratic society, where religious authority and secular authority are inseparable, but they are few and far between. Most of us support some kind of separation between the two.

There is, however, a great deal of debate about what the separation of church and state entails. Does it require us to remove the words "In

God We Trust" from our money? Apparently, many people do not think it does, while some people do.

Regardless of my view, I am confident that most people have a seriously distorted understanding of doctrine of the separation of church and state. Many people don't even have the slightest clue that the Establishment clause, as they understand it, would directly conflict with the Free Exercise clause of the First Amendment to the Constitution. If the Establishment clause dictates that we strip the public sphere (including, especially, the schools) of all mention of God, as many people seem to think it does, then there is no room for people to freely exercise their religion. The Free Exercise clause most definitely does not say that each person is free to exercise his religion as long as he does it in private.

Despite our disagreements in this area, there seems to be widespread agreement that the Republican Party is the group most responsible for incursions across the divide. I must admit that before I really thought about the issue, I agreed with this conventional wisdom. I have since come to believe that the conventional view is born of political biases and groupthink. I do not expect anyone to change a major part of their belief system just upon my saying they are wrong, so I will instead offer numerous examples to firmly establish my current view. We have little to fear from incursions into our religious liberty from Conservative Republicans, but much to fear from Democrats of many stripes.

Let me say before I begin that I am an atheist. I do not believe there is a God or gods. I have respect for many religious traditions, and believe that there is great wisdom in many religious people and religious texts. I also think that sometimes there is great foolishness in some religious traditions, just as there can be much foolishness in all groups of people.

Next, even when I agree with the morality found in Christian tradition, I do not believe that Christians should be able to force the rest of the society to abide by that Christian morality. It doesn't matter whether it is Christian morality, or Hindu, or Jewish, or Daoist, or Sikh, Muslim, Jain, or any other religious or pseudo-religious tradition. People should be free to follow their own moral and religious traditions, unless their individual actions are violating another person's freedom. I've already expressed in an earlier chapter how I believe it is wrong to force morality in general on people. In this chapter I will focus specifically on Christian morality.

Specifically, I will show that Democrats do impose their Christian moral views on the rest of society. They do it unashamedly and unabashedly. And yet, because no one points it out, the rest of us blithely ignore these incursions. Most of us don't even realize it happens at all, even though it happens right in front of our faces.

Defining Christian Morality

As in every philosophical enterprise, out first task is to understand our terms. Unless we know what is meant by Christian morality, there will be no reliable way to determine whether anyone is trying to impose it on others. I am relying on my own background experience in defining Christian morality. I can't say that every Christian will endorse every position I will outline below, but I do believe it captures the traditional Christian view on morality. As always, each reader is allowed to make his own judgments about how close I have gotten. I am confident that my ultimate conclusion will follow for any reader's definition of Christian morality.

Let's begin with sexual matters. Christianity seems to say a lot about sexual matters. First, it says that pre-marital sex is immoral. It also frowns on activities which might be seen to encourage pre-marital sex, such as pornography. Christians generally find homosexuality to be immoral. Some forms of Christianity even say that contraception is immoral, as well as divorce.

Let's face it, Christianity has a lot to say about the morality of sex. However, if one thought that was the extent of Christian morality, one would be gravely mistaken. Here are a few more: Christian morality forbids one to take advantage of others. It also mandates that one help others who are in need, as presented in the parable of the good Samaritan. Christianity requires those who have more to give to those who have less. Numerous Biblical passages support this moral stricture. One must also forgive those who have transgressed against oneself, as Christians are commanded to "turn the other cheek". Jesus also seemed to reject hierarchical authority, telling his apostles that the first among them would be last. This admonition is usually understood to command recognition of the equality between people. The Bible also condemns those who judge others, telling them that they will be judged by God as they judge others.

These examples may not be exhaustive, but I believe they are fairly representative of the views of Christians as I understand them. If I had to make a list of what are the basic positions of Christian morality, it would look something like this:

1. Pre-marital sex is immoral.
2. Pornography is immoral.

3. Homosexuality is immoral.
4. Contraception is immoral.
5. Divorce is immoral (specific to some branches of Christianity).
6. Adultery is immoral.
7. It is immoral to take advantage of others.
8. It is immoral to ignore those in need, in particular the poor.
9. It is immoral to be selfish.
10. It is immoral to be covetous.
11. One should not judge others.
12. Everyone is equal.
13. One should be tolerant of others (non-judgmental).

There may be some disagreement about some of the particulars, but I am confident that most Christians would find this list to be fairly close to what they take to be Christian morality, with perhaps some clarifications or qualitifications. So, in order to see which groups are forcing Christian moral values on other Americans, all we need to do is determine who wants to impose these values on the rest of society.

How Conservative Republicans Fare

Let's first look at conservative Christian Republicans. They certainly accept many if not all of the aspects of Christian morality I listed. Which of them do they want to make illegal? It seems to me that it would be... none of them. I'm not naïve. I know there are a few people who would want to make homosexuality itself illegal. Some people recently defended anti-sodomy laws in Texas (though perhaps on the basis of their view of the vertical separation of powers upon which our Constitution insists). I don't know, however, of any politician, Republican or otherwise, conservative or otherwise, who has publicly called to reinstate laws against homosexuality.

Many conservatives rail against the dangers of pornography, but they seem willing to allow people to deal with the issue as individuals. There is little likelihood of a crackdown of people engaged in the industry of pornography.

Conservative Catholics, whether politicians or not, who find contraception and divorce immoral, are nonetheless fine with allowing other people to engage in those acts, despite the fact that they believe they are immoral. No prominent Christian wants to make adultery illegal.

Of all these thirteen aspects of Christian morality, I don't see a single one that Conservative Christians want to impose on society. From where then, does the common perception come that Conservative Christians do want to force Christianity on others?

One might argue that I've left a few things off my list. I have not listed either abortion or same-sex marriage. Then there's that whole prayer in school thing. And let's not forget "In God we Trust", and "one nation under God."

Yes, it is true. Conservatives, in particular Christian conservatives, want to outlaw abortion and prevent gay marriage. They also want children to pray in school and keep God on our coins and in the Pledge of Allegiance. Some of them even want to put the Ten Commandments in our courthouses.

Yes, Christians believe that abortion is immoral, and most of them would like to make it generally illegal. My first impulse is to say that opposition to abortion is not really an aspect of Christian morality. Nowhere in the Bible or in Christian scriptures is there a clear proscription against abortion, as Christians who are in favor of allowing abortion like to point out. Next, I am not a Christian and I think that abortion should generally be illegal. I don't think that position depends on Christianity at all, nor on a belief in God or a soul. I probably should include a whole chapter on this issue, though, so I will leave it until then.

As for gay marriage, it is very clear to me that to have gay marriage is to impose one moral outlook on society. Let me put it this way: to allow individuals in society to engage in homosexual activity, or to allow them to live together in exclusive relationships, is not to endorse the practice, or for society to say that it is moral or immoral. There is no stamp of approval given from society. But society is also not declaring that it is immoral. That seems to me as it should be.

But for society to offer a certificate which recognizes such relationships IS for society to endorse the practice, and to declare that it is morally good and desired. Why should society make such a declaration? Perhaps you agree with me that homosexuality is morally permissible, but why would you want society to declare it to be morally good? Do you think that people who think homosexuality is immoral should feel welcome to use government to declare their view that homosexuality is immoral, say by making it illegal?

In fact, that was the standard view 50 years ago. Homosexuality was considered by the majority of people to be immoral, and they had no problem using the government to have society announce that viewpoint and act upon it. People could be thrown in jail simply for engaging in homosexual behavior.

Wasn't that a bad thing? And wasn't it the case that the only way to fix it was to adopt the view that society shouldn't be deciding such moral issues? It certainly wasn't by convincing the majority of people that homosexuality wasn't immoral! No, we convinced people (a majority of them at least) that even though they thought homosexuality was immoral, they shouldn't use government to force their view on others.

Aren't those who support gay marriage doing exactly the same thing today, only on the opposite side? Okay, the effects aren't exactly the same. On the one side, people were thrown in jail, and on this side people are only asked to endorse the practice of homosexual marriage, and to provide resources to protect such marriages and to pay more in taxes, though not much more. And not to revolt while their government endorses a practice they find to be absolutely immoral. But it seems to me the principle is the same. People who support gay marriage will not be happy until society declares that homosexual relationships are just as good as other relationships. That is just not something that the government should do.

I hope it has been clear that I do not think that opposition to gay marriage is to force a certain viewpoint on people, but instead an effort to prevent some people from forcing their view, the view that homosexuality is as good as any other relationship, on everyone else. Ultimately, I think this shows the Democratic propensity to respect only their own moral views, and to dismiss any other set of moral views, such that if they think something is morally good, who cares what the rest of the people think, they should be made to accept the correct view of the Democratic Party.

When it comes to "In God we Trust" and "Under God" let me say that if I had my preference, I would not have them. I'm not sure what slogans I would include on money, but I wouldn't have them refer to God, either pro or con. But, let me also say that I don't feel the slightest bit oppressed or put upon by the slogan "In God we trust" on our money. As far as I can tell, it spends the same regardless. Yes, I do think it is a little presumptuous of our leaders to put it on our money, but after all, something like 90% of Americans believe in God, of one sort or another. So, as far as presumptions go, I'd have to say that this is about as innocuous as it gets.

As for the Pledge of Allegiance, many people are unaware that it originally did not include the words "under God." That being said, I do not think it should be included now, but not only because of some desire to return to the original, true version. If we expect all children in school to be saying the Pledge, there will be atheists whom we are forcing to say something against their beliefs. It would seem to me analogous to atheists forcing God-fearing children to recite the pledge while saying "One nation, without God." It just should not be done, either way.

Having said that, I think that many teachers, such as I did when I substituted in junior high and high schools, do not require every student to recite every word in the pledge. In fact, I know that some of them don't even have students stand during the pledge, much less recite it. I don't see how anyone could require a student to use those words. I still think that there is a problem with the pledge as it stands, but a fairly straightforward compromise is that atheistic children just refrain from saying those words when they recite the pledge. It's not a perfect solution, and I still think it should be changed, but again, it doesn't seem overly problematic to me either.

As an atheist, even now, when I recite the pledge, I think I usually include the words "under God", but when I'm paying attention I leave them out. I don't feel forced upon when I do. It has never made me question my beliefs or doubt myself as a person. I know that I am a fairly-strong willed person and always have been, and I realize that not everyone is as strong as me, but I still would find it hard to sympathize with a student who really felt like the state was infringing on their life choices by having the *class* recite the pledge including the words "under God." Yes, we shouldn't do it, but I can't get all that exercised about it either.

I'm actually more concerned with forcing children to say a pledge at all. I don't think that should be done. Call me a leftie, or a sixties radical, but it smacks of authoritarianism to me. Still, I find that it is easy to avoid any compulsion by simply not reciting it. I don't know of any teacher who would punish a child for not saying the pledge, as long as he stood silently and respectfully while it was recited by other children.

I suppose my attitude is the same when it comes to prayer in school. I would oppose daily prayer in public schools, but I wouldn't oppose a moment of philosophical reflection, or a moment of silence. In fact, I would see a great deal of good in them. And it seems to me that with a moment of silent reflection, fewer people would really push for prayer in public schools, and most conservatives would be happy.

I would go even further. I would have no objection to a moment of philosophical reflection which was led by students who chose their own sources for philosophical reflection, and if some of them chose to do it using prayer, then I would still have no objection. As long as those students who chose to use purely secular reasonings would not be barred from doing so (and they were respectful and courteous). I have no desire to purge the public sphere of religion or prayer or any mention of God, and I think that anyone who does suffers from intolerance and authoritarianism.

Nor do I have any real problem with putting the Ten Commandments on the wall in a courtroom. Symbols don't worry me, reality does. As soon as conservatives start trying to enact laws based on the Ten Commandments, that's when I will be gravely concerned. It's probably not a good idea to have purely Christian religious symbols in our public buildings, but I wouldn't feel threatened by them, as long as the law remained liberal, in the classical sense.

I personally would think that a panorama of lots of different religious traditions would be a great idea. Heck, if I were decorating a church or synagogue, or some other building for a religious group, I might even suggest a panorama including lots of other religions. Why not have a Catholic rectory include religious motifs from Islam, Buddhism, and Jainism? To do so would not necessarily be an acceptance of the veracity of a religious tradition, but might only be intended as a display of respect. If a city council put one of those up in some city building, I wouldn't object in any way. In a courthouse, I wouldn't be bothered at all by representations of laws throughout history from different countries, cultures, or traditions. And even if they were all religious, I still wouldn't object. I would find an atheistic example, and then ask them to include it. If they then refused to include it for no other reason than that it were not religious, then I would have a problem.

I love Christmas and Easter. I think they are American traditions and should be protected and honored. I don't care that they have their roots in Christianity (as well as paganistic views, as anyone who has researched them knows). They are holidays precisely because we live in a country largely built by Christians, largely because they were Christian, and they should be respected, along with their history and the religion they practiced. To ignore that history and the actual development of the country is, frankly, ridiculous. It wasn't Republicans who turned "Christmas Break" into "Winter Recess", or "Easter Holiday" into "Spring Break". I wonder if college students would do nearly as much drinking and carousing if they were away from school because of "Easter Holiday".

I hope I have made it clear that all of these areas where leftists rail about the intolerance of Christians and how Christians are imposing Christianity on the country seem to me trivial and unimportant. Most of them don't bother me at all, and I don't see that any of them violate the Constitution or my rights as a citizen, or anyone else's. If there is an imposition, it is a trivial one, and is generally in an area where I think the majority should be able to do whatever it wants. In general, I find that conservatives do not want to push their religion or their religious values on others in any objectionable way, and I find most of them take very seriously the idea of having a secular government, as well as the freedom of religion.

How Democrats Fare

When it comes to Democrats, I believe the picture is much different. Few Democrats want to impose Christian practices in terms of worship, or indeed Christian morality in terms of sexual issues, on others. In fact, in these areas, they positively reject imposing Christian values. Nonetheless, I believe that they are generally willing to force Christian values on others in many of the policies they endorse.

If we look at our list of thirteen aspects of Christian morality, it is clear that they do not want to outlaw the first five. In case you've forgotten them, here they are again:

1. Pre-marital sex is immoral.
2. Pornography is immoral.
3. Homosexuality is immoral.
4. Contraception is immoral.
5. Divorce is immoral.
6. Adultery is immoral.
7. It is immoral to take advantage of others.
8. It is immoral to ignore those in need, in particular the poor.
9. It is immoral to be selfish.
10. It is immoral to be covetous.
11. One should not judge others.
12. Everyone is equal.
13. One should be tolerant of others.

After reexamining the list, I'm not sure most Democrats even believe the first five activities are immoral, even when they identify themselves as Christians. That would explain why they wouldn't want them to be illegal. Most Democrats would probably condemn adultery as immoral, but I think they will agree with Republicans that adultery shouldn't be considered an imprisonable or fineable offense. As we have already seen, most Democrats don't even consider adultery by itself, or even when it includes perjury, a high crime or misdemeanor egregious enough to impeach a President (although I think many of them might change their mind if the President were a Republican).

Also, generally speaking, Democrats seem to me to be very unlikely to support prayer in schools, and somewhat unlikely to support "In God we Trust" on our coins and "Under God" in the pledge, although I think we could find many Democrats who would. Democrats generally seem to agree that the form of worship associated with Christianity should not be forced on everyone, and they seem to be on the forefront of trying to stop that from occurring, sometimes, in my opinion, going way too far overboard.

I hope to show you, however, that when it comes to the other aspects of Christian morality, it is actually the Democrats who are trying to force everyone in the country to live according to Christian values. I understand that many of my readers will think I've lost my mind, but the argument seems utterly convincing to me. You tell me if you can find any flaws.

One policy which Democrats strongly support which betrays their impulse to impose Christian values is the minimum wage. The minimum wage is a law which prevents people from entering into certain contractual agreements. If I offer a job for one dollar an hour, and you accept it, then this contract is deemed illegal by minimum wage laws, such that I can be fined and forced to pay you more than I want to, and likely additional fines beyond even the minimum wage at the time, including back pay.

Why is it that in a free country some voluntary contracts are deemed not legally acceptable? The answer is that in a completely free country they would be, but those who support minimum wage laws have decided that they would rather take away freedom from people than to allow such voluntary contracts. Because they believe that it is immoral to offer such contracts, they have decided that they should not be legally permissible.

I know many people, especially those on the left, will bristle at my characterization including the term "immoral", but that's what their position is, even if they do not realize it. I subscribe to the principle that if an action is morally permissible, then it should be legally permissible. So, if it is morally permissible to pay someone a dollar an hour, then it should be legally permissible, as well. It would be an incredible kind of totalitarianism that held that actions which were morally permissible could still be made illegal by the government. Democrats in general seem to hold that even if the majority of people think an action is morally wrong, it is even worse for the government to punish people for their immoral actions.

People on the left often seem to think that only people on the right have moral views, and will reserve the adjective "moralistic" for those on the right, but I can't distinguish the attitudes that those on the left have for violators of minimum wage laws from the attitudes that those on the right have for people who engage in premarital sex, for example. They frown upon such people, and consider their actions to be morally wrong. Oh, the one distinction I do see is that people on the left want to punish violators of minimum wage laws, while those on the right do not want to punish promiscuous people.

If you are on the left, and you really don't want to say that paying someone too little for their work is immoral, then what would you call it? Whatever term you use has to be a negative one, and will necessarily be judgmental. It will also involve morality. Try it. Do you think it is inappropriate? Corrupt? Selfish? Wrong? Criminal? Unethical? Unjust? Rude? Impolite? Improper? Offensive? Harmful? Disrespectful? It doesn't matter which of these terms you use, because they are all aspects of morality.

To say that people should not offer other people below a certain amount to work is to say that it is immoral, no matter what language you use to avoid saying so, and to make laws punishing people for doing so is to impose one's moral outlook on the rest of society. To use a probably inappropriate colloquialism, "duh".

In fact, if the worst you could say about paying someone one dollar an hour was that it was impolite or inappropriate, and you still wanted to have a legally mandated minimum wage, then you clearly think it is the job of the government to enforce etiquette using the force of law. What kind of totalitarianism would that be?

Don't ask me how otherwise intelligent people can belittle Republicans for wanting to force their moral views on society while supporting minimum wage laws. It doesn't make any sense to me to deny it. To impose minimum wage laws on others is to impose one's moral viewpoint on them, that much is undeniable. But one could still deny that those who support minimum wage laws are trying to force *Christian* morality on others.

In fact, I suspect that at this point any supporter of minimum wage who has continued reading this far has already begun to engage in all sorts of mental gymnastics in order to protect their belief system. I think the most likely defense is that the principle to which Democrats are appealing in supporting minimum wage laws is not a Christian principle, but a basic moral principle that any rational person would recognize, or something along those lines.

I hate to be mean, but sometimes it's called for. It would be unbelievably hypocritical for many such people to try to use such a tactic, as many people on the left have serious doubts about whether any such morality can be so justified. I probably need a whole chapter for this, but those on the left generally put forward a rather crude sort of moral relativism or subjectivism. They often reject the idea that morality can be grounded in rational principles, such that there is a single morality which would apply to everyone on Earth. So, let me deal with that later.

For now I will only consider leftists who would argue that it is simply common decency not to pay someone too little, and that common decency requires us to make it illegal. Note that common decency is another dodge to avoid using the term immoral.

What I want to argue is that this sense of common decency rests on Christianity. If I successfully do so, then I will have established that minimum wage laws are supported directly through Christianity. This would show that those people who support minimum wage laws are in reality the ones who are forcing Christian views on the rest of society, and what would follow from this is that the common view of the American people, especially the media, is flipped squarely on its head. Let me get started.

What we need to identify is exactly what is wrong with paying someone a dollar an hour, or perhaps $4.50 an hour? If we consider the extreme case, what if someone offered a job for one cent an hour? I suspect that most of us would say that there is something wrong with that. The question, as it is usually, is whether it is wrong in such a way that we should make it illegal. Perhaps we aren't really sure what is wrong with it, it just feels wrong. We might make a direct appeal to our emotional reaction. Perhaps that is it.

Now, I could see an absolute dictatorial tyrant thinking that it was acceptable to require the rest of society to abide by his emotional whims, but how could anyone who wants even the pretense of a free society? An organicist might say something like this, but even they would usually have more sense. And certainly accepting this principle would allow Christians, who are the majority in America, to outlaw anything that made them uncomfortable. I certainly cannot accept that anyone with an ounce of sense would seriously argue that this was the basis for minimum wage laws, that the majority of us just find it icky. Unfortunately, I suspect that far too many Americans have no deeper basis than this.

No, I think if we really reflect on it, our emotions and our intuition must rest on something a bit more solid. Here is a suggestion: the person offering a job for one penny an hour must be taking advantage of his prospective workers. Really, who would work for one penny an hour? Someone with no skills who was absolutely desperate, obviously. Anyone who would take advantage of such a desperate person would be an absolute monster with no heart. Really. They would be making a killing off the hard work of someone else, and taking advantage of the person who has no skills and can't find employment anywhere else.

The same basic analysis goes for a dollar an hour, at least here in the entire United States. Anyone who would work for a dollar an hour must be extraordinarily unskilled, desperate for money, and unaware of any other opportunity for employment or money. And anyone who would take advantage of such a person would deserve condemnation. Most Americans would probably agree.

Exactly what amount people should pay others, and what minimum amount would be morally acceptable is no doubt debatable. Some people even argue for a legally mandated "living wage" of something more like fifteen dollars an hour, so obviously they think it would be immoral to pay someone less than that without, presumably, taking immoral advantage of someone. Perhaps you might even say unjustly taking advantage of someone, but if something is unjust, it is by definition immoral.

If you, reading this explanation, found yourself agreeing wholeheartedly, and thought that no one in his right mind could disagree, and thought that you had justified minimum wage laws, then welcome to the world of religious intolerance. I suspect that you never realized how intolerant of other moral perspectives you were. To condemn another person for taking advantage of another person is intolerant. Perhaps we shouldn't be tolerant of such people, just like perhaps we shouldn't be tolerant of homosexuals, and we shouldn't be tolerant of abortion, right?

I suspect that most Democrats reading this cannot even fathom a moral viewpoint which allows one to take advantage of others. Yet, it still follows that one who is intolerant of people who would take advantage of other people, is intolerant of their religious, philosophical, moral perspective.

I haven't yet connected Christianity to support for minimum wage laws, but it should be clear what I have in mind. Not taking advantage of others is a core component of Christian morality. Minimum wage laws rest upon this moral principle. So, those who support minimum wage laws for this reason are forcing a Christian morality on the rest of society.

Anyone who disagrees is likely unaware of history and of alternative moral visions that exist even today. Many Capitalists would adamantly disagree that anyone has a moral obligation not to take advantage of other people. In fact, they would invite you to try to take advantage of them. They would say that everyone has a duty to take care of themselves, and obviously some people will do better than others.

You may find their moral views immoral, repugnant, and disgusting, just like many other Christians find homosexuality immoral, repugnant, and disgusting, but the question we have to ask is whether that means you should require them to accept a Christian morality through the force of law.

Ayn Rand was a moral/political philosopher and author who adamantly rejected this moral principle. She had an alternative moral vision where every person was responsible for him or her self, and it probably wouldn't even make sense in her philosophy to acknowledge that anyone could "take advantage" of anyone else, unless perhaps they were lying or coercing someone in some way. Everyone finds themselves in different positions at different times, and no one owes anyone anything, so if anyone accepted an offer of employment it would be their choice, regardless of how much they accepted as payment. Ayn Rand's books, especially Atlas Shrugged, have sold multiple millions of copies in America over the decades, which shows that at least some Americans favor, or are sympathetic to, her moral vision.

Existentialist philosophy also takes a fairly strong stand that everyone makes his own choices and is responsible for his own life plan. On my understanding of existentialist philosophy, for the government to step in and prevent you from making a contractual agreement, even when everyone else thought it was a horrible deal for you, would be a nauseating disrespect of your individual autonomy. It would be to force you to live an inauthentic life. There may not be many existentialists out there, but they do exist.

Anyone who looks even superficially at history knows that this principle, the principle that it is wrong to take advantage of other people, was not accepted anywhere, in the Western world at least, until the advent of Judaism. Yet, it was not widespread in the Western world until Christianity took it there. Greeks and Romans would not have accepted it, from my understanding. I haven't studied the Huns or other Germanic tribes, or Vikings for that matter, but from what I have heard of their moral outlooks, it doesn't seem to me that they would adopt the principle that it is wrong to take advantage of others.

What follows is that minimum wage laws are based firmly on a moral tradition that is characteristically Christian, or Judeo-Christian, in origin and temperament. So, those who support minimum wage laws want to force a distinctively Christian doctrine on their fellow Americans. Is it too quick to say, "Case Closed"?

All right, I don't want to pretend that there are no logically available defenses. One escape is to argue that there is a different principle upon which we are relying as our support for minimum wage laws.

Unfortunately, if you identify any principle such as "it is wrong to be greedy", or "it is wrong to ignore those in need", or that we have any kind of obligation to help the needy, then you're going to be right back where we started. Those are principles which Christians widely accept, and many other people do not.

One could say that one is not a Christian, but one still supports minimum wage laws. So, wouldn't that show that support for minimum wage laws is not based on Christian morality? The answer is not necessarily, and even if it were, there would still be problems with the view.

First, anyone who grew up in America has been shaped and influenced by the Christian morality which pervades American society. So, even if one does not identify oneself as a Christian, one might still be pushing Christian values and morality on others in some sense. I think that it is undeniable that for nearly all Americans, their support for the principle that taking advantage of others is wrong is intimately tied to the fact that they grew up in an overwhelmingly Christian environment. Perhaps they would still hold the principle if they grew up in a non-Christian environment, but they didn't. And if they did, then there is no guarantee that they would still accept the principle.

Let's consider those who did not grow up in America, as well as those who have a different religious tradition which informs their values. One might point out, and indeed it is a fact, that many different religious traditions include some type of admonition against taking advantage of people. I mentioned Judaism already, but Muslims and Sikhs, among others, would accept the principle, at least generally speaking.

I fail to see how that fact shows that I am mistaken. I suppose it would mean that the principle against taking advantage of others used to support outlawing wages that are too low is not distinctively Christian. But it would still be strongly religious in nature. Historically, cultures which have not accepted modern religions have not accepted the principle, and it is often organized religions throughout the world that have tried to push it into the general mindset of their respective countries. So, perhaps for some people, they could argue that they are not trying to push Christianity on the rest of society; they are only trying to push their religion, or religion in general, on the rest of society.

I meant for everyone to realize that this shows that it would still be wrong, but it strikes me that some people have such disdain for Christianity in particular, and admiration for other religions, that they might instinctively feel that there would be nothing wrong with pushing Hindu religion, or some other more tolerant religion on the American public. But I can't imagine that anyone would try to defend that view with a straight face.

Still, perhaps one might think a doctrine which was exclusively Christian is different from a doctrine which is accepted in many, even the majority, of religions. Maybe one could hold that in that case it is permissible to force moral doctrines on others, specifically when many religions agree.

Maybe, but it still would go against the doctrine of the separation of church and state, wouldn't it? The state should not be shoving religion on its citizens, even in a non-sectarian way. At least that's what I thought liberalism was all about. Whether it is one particular religion, or the views common to many religions, it is still enforcing religious views on others.

Furthermore, most religions throughout the world also agree with Christianity that homosexuality, pre-marital sex, adultery, and pornography are immoral, and a great many would say that women's work is in the home (Does Christianity?). I'm not sure about abortion, but what if it turned out that many religions were opposed to abortion. Imagine the rhetorical door one is opening by saying Christian views can be forced on the American people, as long as those views are supported by other religions in the world.

No, it seems to me that if one backs up the principle that it is immoral to take advantage of other people using religious grounds, one is in the same boat one started in, only with a different flag. One is still forcing one's religious views on the rest of society. So, if there is any hope of defending minimum wage laws without imposing Christianity or other religious views, one must find some non-religious grounds to support it.

And how, I wonder, would anyone do that? One possibility, which I have heard people express, is that somehow the older principle, that one can do whatever one wants to others, as long as they consent, is, well, old. The new principle is new, it is civilized, it is progressive. The old principle is a relic of an older time, and it should be left there.

Unfortunately, this is simple question-begging. Yes, the newer principle seems newer, and nicer for that matter, but why does that make it better? One can simply assert that it is more moral, but that is no different from someone simply asserting that homosexuality is immoral. One can point out that "no one gets hurt" in homosexual relationships. I think this is an important part of people's justification (rationalization?). One might make the case that homosexuals do not hurt anyone, but taking advantage of people does.

First, not everyone will agree. Many groups, including Christians, will deny that homosexuality does not hurt anyone. Yes, the damage they discuss probably only arises from their worldview, but if it is their worldview, they would have to consider it. I don't think I would agree myself that homosexuality itself is hurtful, although it can be in many cases, just as heterosexuality can be. But, I don't want to bicker about the comparative risks.

The more important objection is that those groups I mentioned earlier will vociferously argue that one cannot hurt someone when they consent to something. They are agreeing to it. Again, if someone deceives them, or is using coercion against them, those can be considered hurtful, but in their absence, whatever people choose to do cannot be hurtful.

It does seem odd to me to call it hurtful to offer someone a job at a certain price, and having them accept it. All of us have accepted agreements which we didn't want because we were in an unfavorable bargaining position. Would we want the government to go back and nullify all of those agreements? Okay, many of us probably would react emotionally and say yes, but isn't that a childish, immature, unreflective impulse? Could we really think justice requires the government to do so? In fact, wouldn't it be unjust for the government to do so?

The only way I could agree that it would be hurtful is if someone could convince me that we each do have a moral obligation to refrain from taking advantage of others, or that when someone is in a bind, we each have a moral obligation to assist him. In essence, I would have to be convinced that those aspects of Christian morality are indeed objectively true. Then, I would probably agree that some aspect of hurt or harm is involved. But even then, in order to support minimum wage laws, one would have to argue that the hurt involved there is such that we can legally prevent it, and that the hurt involved is of a sufficient level that it would overwhelm the harms involved in having the government enforce the restrictions. The first hurdle seems high to me; the second and third hurdles, from my perspective now, seem insurmountable.

Think about it this way. Even if Christians could convince me that there was some harm involved in homosexuality, I would still be reluctant to make it illegal. Making something illegal involves all sorts of things, many of which are harmful in their own right. Taxes must be forcibly collected in order to enforce the law, and in enforcing the law, other people could be put in harm's way.

Also, added to the mix in my mind is that many people argue that minimum wage laws actually reduce the number of jobs at the very bottom rungs of the economic scale, and so make things better for some people at the bottom, but worse for others *at the bottom*. They also increase prices, hurting everyone, but disproportionately hurting those at the bottom, and also hurting everyone who owns a business. So, supporting minimum wage laws can be seen as supporting one method of redistributing goods, in the form of money, and harms, in the form of higher prices and less money. But one must also hold that every other method of distributing those goods and harms is morally wrong.

Either way, one is taking some moral viewpoint about what society should look like, and forcing everyone at the threat of fines or imprisonment, to adopt that moral viewpoint. Or, if not to adopt that moral viewpoint, at least to behave as if they accept it, which may be even worse.

I have argued that at root, the moral impulse involved traces back to Christianity, so that I believe that most Americans who support minimum wage laws are trying to impose Christian morality on the rest of society, whether they are Christians themselves, or if their moral view simply arose by being raised in a culture steeped in Christian morality. Even if one can argue that for some of them it does not, it would seem like their support is based on their own religious tradition, and so it would be just as wrong to impose it on the rest of society.

Many such supporters will still probably insist that their support does not depend on Christianity at all. My response is that I'm extremely skeptical about that, as it is very difficult to sort out the experiences and sources of the ideas and beliefs that make us who we are. Christian moral impulses could have entered one's consciousness even though one is fully unaware of its influence. In fact, one may argue that he got it more from some respected person who wasn't Christian. But even then, that person could have been influenced by the Christian perspective.

Nonetheless, let's say that there are some few people out there who support minimum wage laws because they are morally opposed to people being taken advantage of, and that their moral view is not derived from Christianity in any way, then I must agree that for them, they are not trying to force Christian morality on the rest of society.

So what? I do not believe that will apply to the vast majority of people who support minimum wage laws, nor to the vast majority of Democrats, or people on the left side of the political spectrum. So, I think my thesis in this chapter would still hold strong, that Democrats in general are trying to force Christian morality on the rest of us.

And even in those other cases, there are two possibilities. Either their support derives from some other religious tradition, or it arises from some deep place inside of them, perhaps their spirit or soul, or mind, or judgment. I have already argued in this chapter that if it arises from some other religious tradition, it falls into the same category as if it were Christian, such that it should not be imposed on other people.

If, on the other hand, it arises from some intuitive sense deep within them, it should be increasingly clear that I still think they have no business imposing that view on others. There seems to me to be this false distinction between religious views, on the one hand, and deeply held moral views, on the other. In fact, the more I think about it, it is a distinction between moral views which are informed by one's religious commitment, and moral views which are informed not by one's religion, but instead by one's intuition, perhaps even a very reflective intuition.

It seems to me that some people are very exercised when people try to impose their moral views which are informed by religion, but they yawn, or even support, those people who try to impose their own intuitive moral views on others. For myself, I cannot see any distinction. I am disturbed by both. I think both are unjust and must be resisted. Except for the basic moral requirement mandated by liberalism, the moral command that one not harm others, our moral viewpoints, whether religious or not, should not be imposed.

In case anyone thought that I am only referring to minimum wage laws, that is only the beginning. There are numerous other policies which are supported by Democrats which seem to me to be distinctively Christian in origin. Mandated charity, for example. Yes, it is true, you never hear it put that way, but that is exactly what the government welfare system is. Democrats do not believe that private charity will meet the needs of the poor, and so they have devised a system whereby that moral obligation can be met.

The government simply takes the money by force from those who wouldn't give it freely, and then hands it out to those who it thinks need it more. In other words, since some people are not Christian enough to give money to the poor in sufficient amounts on their own, the government will require them to meet their Christian obligation. I won't go through all the considerations again, but it should suffice to say that I believe it is generally Christian in origin, but even if it isn't, it is still unacceptably religious.

Christianity is also the basis for much of the egalitarian impulses of the left. It was Jesus who insisted that no apostle should be so as presumptuous as to place himself first ahead of others. Jesus also admonished us against judging others, and appealed to us to forgive others.

These policies inform Democrats' views in numerous areas, including the demand for equal treatment in all sorts of areas, legislation requiring tolerance of other viewpoints, as well as their lenient approach to retributive justice.

When one listens to Democrats attack people who make a lot of money, one gets the unmistakable impression that they believe that the highest immorality is to be selfish. This intolerance of selfishness is the hallmark of Christian morality. Selfishness is anathema to Christians, who constantly pontificate against it.

Now, ask yourself what is more immoral: selfishness or homosexuality? If you say that selfishness is, because there is nothing wrong with homosexuality, fine. But just consider that many other Americans will disagree. Is it okay with you to outlaw homosexuality? Or do you think that anyone who wanted to do so would be a totalitarian dictator? Then ask yourself whether you think it is okay to outlaw selfishness. Why wouldn't the same judgment apply?

Isn't that exactly what Democrats do? You might have balked at the idea that one could outlaw selfishness, but isn't that exactly the justification for minimum wage laws, progressive income taxation, inheritance taxes, universal health care, and a whole host of other issues? It is selfish for the haves to keep what they have and not to give some of it to the have-nots, and if they have to be forced to do so by law, then so be it.

I realize that conservatives will sometimes attack leftists for being selfish, which might weaken my hypothesis here, but not when everything is considered. Yes, conservatives give more money to charity, but they criticize leftists for being selfish in more than their financial leanings. For example, many conservatives will criticize leftists for their sexual lifestyles, especially premarital sex, and for the way they will quickly get divorced with seemingly little concern for the effects on their children. They criticize the "me" generation for being self-obsessed, and for caring only about themselves.

All that is true, and I'm not sure what to make of it. Many of these very same people are the ones who will most strongly support government welfare, and other laws which restrict freedom. It's as if leftists realize that they are selfish, and they realize that it is very, very bad, and they also realize that they do not have the strength to resist the temptation on their own, so they want the government to force them, and everyone else, to act in an unselfish way. But only when it comes to money. Don't dare let the government interfere in sexual selfishness.

The Seven Deadly Sins

Perhaps there is no absolute, universal Christian morality, but there are certainly some moral values which are shared by most if not all

Christians. Another way to get at Christian morality besides just listing some aspects of it as I did above, is to ask what items were traditionally considered the seven virtues and the seven cardinal vices by Christians. The seven deadly sins were lust, gluttony, greed, sloth, wrath, envy, and pride. These are supposed to be strongly immoral character traits, and they contrast with the seven holy virtues: chastity, abstinence, temperance, diligence, patience, kindness, and humility. These may not be official doctrines for any specific branch of Christianity, but even now they do give a good general picture of the things Christians find morally praiseworthy or morally wrong.

One way to ask how much Christians are forcing their morality on others is to ask which of the seven deadly sins do they want to make illegal. If we look at Conservative Christians, the answer is clear: none of them. Even though most conservative Christians will say that every one of the seven deadly sins is immoral, I do not see any prominent conservative Christians making any attempt to make any of them illegal, much less having any success.

As far as Conservative Christians are concerned, each individual can be as lustful, gluttonous, greedy, slothful, wrathful, envious, or proud as he or she wants to be. They believe such people may pay a price for their character traits and actions, but they are not the ones who will make anyone pay. They also seem to insist that no one else should have to pay for the poor vicious choices of their neighbors. Perhaps the one exception is homosexuality. Any conservative who wants to outlaw homosexuality does want to legally curb lustfulness in at least some way. I still think that it is a very rare conservative who would actually make homosexuality illegal.

Consider again the seven deadly sins: lust, gluttony, greed, sloth, wrath, envy, pride. For some of these dogmas of Christian ethics, it would be ridiculous to think that leftists want to legislate against them. Lust is the one which stands out in my mind. Leftists instead prefer to think that lust is a basic right everyone deserves, far from anything immoral. In fact, I think most leftists go so far as to promote lust in people, and think of it as liberating, or positive in some way. I'm not so sure about sloth either. I could see an argument that easy rules regarding welfare, unemployment, and worker's compensation or disability, which are easily taken advantage of, actually promote sloth in people. But I certainly do not see Democrats trying to outlaw laziness.

Envy, or covetousness, seems to be heavily promoted by Democrats as well, for partisan political purposes. John Edwards did it with aplomb in nearly every speech he gave. His "Two America" speech is a perfect example. The point is to instill jealousy and covetousness in the underclass. Those in the "other" America have all sorts of things, and everyone should want them, and feel entitled to have them. And if they don't have them, they need to do something to get them. No, not hard work and dedication over decades, all you need to do is give him political power, and he will take those things that you don't have away from people who have them, and give them to you. The entire purpose of that speech is to instill jealousy and envy in people who are poor.

So, Democrats are far from making most of the seven deadly sins illegal and even promote some of them as good. But greed, that's a different story. Greed is not good. People who have it are the enemy. They need to be stopped, and since individuals cannot make them give up their greed, the government has to do it. When they want to greedily hold on to the money they have earned, then the government has to go in and take it from them. We cannot tolerate that.

In one way, it seems to me that in America, conservatives focus on sexual immorality, as defined by Christian ethical doctrine, and leftists focus on economic or financial immorality, as defined by Christian ethical doctrine. Conservatives attack and criticize what they perceive as selfishness in the realm of sex, and leftists attack and criticize what they perceive as selfishness in the economic realm.

As I think I have shown, however, conservatives have been moving further and further from using the government to force people who disagree with living their lives in ways which would conform to Christian sexual ethics, while leftists move more and more to regulate all of our lives as if we accepted Christian ethics in the sphere of our economic interactions. Leftists have been successful in their project, while conservatives keep retreating from using government power to control our lives. Yes, there may be some trivial ways in which they are fighting back, but they don't concern me much. They seem more symbolic than substantive.

Conservatives will condemn homosexuality as abhorrent, yet the vast majority of them would now fight to ensure that it is not made illegal. They believe that premarital sex is highly immoral, and yet if someone proposed a law to make it a crime, how many, or should I say few, conservatives would support it? I suspect no prominent conservatives or Republicans would do so. Yes, some conservatives have made moves to regulate sexual content on the internet, but does anyone think they have had any success? And anyway, their efforts seem to be focused on protecting children, but still allowing an anything goes approach for adults. Laissez-Faire sexuality is accepted, while Laissez-Faire economics is not just morally wrong, it is against the law.

Where are the Democrats who take the analogous position? They could condemn scummy sweatshop owners all they want. They could even propose boycotts and refuse to buy their products. They could go on television and condemn them as immoral and selfish. But they would stand by their principles and insist that the government should refrain from any punitive action against them. Why, of all the deadly sins, is greed the only one which we can legislate against?

Oh, I did forget gluttony. I'm not sure about that, but it seems to me more and more that Democrats and leftists want to legislate against that as well. Bans against greasy foods, more specifically trans-fats, have occurred in leftist cities. I'm not sure about smoking. Leftists seem to be on a crusade against smokers today. Is smoking selfish? It seems like it to me. At least when one is breathing out smoke into an enclosed space.

In case anyone would accuse me of being greedy or selfish, I would say some people probably would think I am, and others would think I'm not. If I were hiring people, even for relatively unskilled jobs, I think I would give them as large of a salary as I could, probably to the detriment of my family. I would have a problem with myself if I only gave minimum wage. I'd probably try to provide all of my employees with retirement and health benefits. I'd probably also go out of business. That's why I teach.

But again, the point is not about what I think is moral or immoral, Christian or non-Christian. It is whether I am willing to use the government to force other people to follow the guidelines of my morality. Even though I may not be selfish, should I use the government to punish people who are?

I do not believe so. I do not believe that the government has the right to do so. It is unjust for the government to take any aspect of Christian morality, or any other religious or secular morality beyond the basic liberal demand that we allow others to live their lives as they want without unduly harming others, and impose it on society. As such, I cannot be a Democrat. It seems to me that they support numerous policies which do exactly this. The government they support and want to see in America is fundamentally unjust to me.

Whether they support those policies because they are mandated by Christian doctrine, or any other religious or ethical doctrine, or because they believe in an organicist philosophy, or because they just think that in any community, certain behaviors are just necessary, such as caring for what happens to strangers. Whatever their reason for doing so, their widespread support for such policies means that I cannot be one of them. I agree that in many cases, one should care what happens to strangers, but that is a part of my ethical code, and I realize that it is morally wrong for me, and for anyone else, to ask our government to punish people who disagree, or who act in selfish ways.

The Smoking Gun

Imagine that a prominent politician were to unabashedly quote Christian or Jewish scripture in support of their public policy positions. Wouldn't you expect the media to call them on it, and to ridicule them into submission? Wouldn't every media outlet ominously discuss the implications for the doctrine of the separation of Church and State? Get ready to be surprised.

Nancy Pelosi is the Speaker of the House. She is arguably the most powerful woman in American history. And as recently as April of 2008, she explicitly quoted the Old Testament in support of her public policy positions. In an official statement for Earth Day, Ms. Pelosi wrote "The Bible tells us in the Old Testament, 'To minister to the needs of God's creation is an act of worship. To ignore those needs is to dishonor the God who made us.' On this Earth Day, and every day, let us honor the earth and our future generations with a commitment to fight climate change."[63]

Perhaps the media only worries about the separation of church and state when politicians use the Bible to support policies the media doesn't support. There was some controversy of Pelosi's quote after Earth Day, as well as the numerous times she used the same quote the year before. Yet, it was not over the problem regarding separating religious scripture and one's support for legislation. No, it was about the fact that no one could find the quote or any close paraphrase anywhere in the Old or New Testaments.[64] Maybe the mainstream media gave Pelosi a pass because she wasn't really quoting scripture, even though she was trying to.

Barack Obama also seems to be fond of pseudo-quoting scripture. Here is one of his favorite themes to which he refers again and again:

> In the end, then, what is called for is nothing more, and nothing less, than what all the world's great religions demand - that we do unto others as we would have them do unto us. Let us be our brother's keeper, Scripture tells us. Let us be our sister's keeper. Let us find that common stake we all have in one another, and let our politics reflect that spirit as well.[65]

This quote is taken from Mr. Obama's widely hailed speech on religion. I'm not sure what the Golden Rule has to do with being my brother's keeper, but only the former is scriptural in origin. The Bible never tells us to "be our brother's keeper", but perhaps there is some such sentiment in the Bible. I won't quibble with Obama's scriptural interpretation.

My beef is with the fact that he is interpreting scripture, and using it to justify his public policies. And my beef is with people who feign outrage when conservatives make references to their scriptural beliefs, while ignoring when Democrats do the same thing. I say "feign" because it seems to me that if they truly found it outrageous when conservative Republicans do it, they should be equally outraged when Barack Obama does it.

To see how strong is Barack Obama's commitment to imposing his Christian religious values on the rest of the country, all we need do is listen to his advisors. According to his campaign's director of religious affairs, Joshua DuBois, many of Obama's political views are "an outgrowth of his reading of some of the seminal parts of the Bible about doing unto the 'least of these' just as we would have done unto Christ. He takes very seriously the numerous passages in the Bible that talk not only about poverty, but of people of faith taking God's words and extending them beyond the four walls of the church."[66]

If you truly support the separation of Church and State, you will join me in condemning this attitude and this approach to justifying one's public policies. Democrats may not be the only ones who have this approach, but they seem to be the only ones who are currently using this approach in such a monumental way. And they seem to be the only ones who get a pass for doing so by most of the media.

Final Thoughts

I am not a Democrat because in my experience Democrats abuse the separation of church and state in numerous ways. They impose their Christian values on others blithely without the slightest bit of introspection. Some prominent Democrats are even comfortable justifying their votes on legislation using naked Biblical references, without any pretence that doing so might go against one of their most deeply held principles.

Unless the principle they use rhetorically to attack their opponents was never meant to apply to them. I don't care how legislators justify their votes, as long as they vote in line with the principle of liberalism which I follow. The line to be drawn is not how a legislator justifies his political and moral philosophy, but is he voting using principles which violate individuals' rights to live their own lives and make decisions for themselves. That is the line I care about.

Until a great deal of these things change, I will not become a Democrat. Until Democrats come to a proper and consistent understanding of the separation of church and state, and until they refrain from hypocritically attacking Republicans for relying on their religious views, while enthusiastically relying on their religion to dictate to other people how to live their lives, I cannot be one of them.

CHAPTER SIX

Eat, Drink, and Be Merry, and Let Future Taxpayers Pay

There is a difference between happiness and wisdom: he that thinks himself the happiest man is really so; but he that thinks himself the wisest is generally the greatest fool.

—Francis Bacon

I think I have launched quite a few major criticisms of the Democratic Party so far, and yet I feel there is so much more to say. The problem is organizing my complaints in a coherent manner. My next criticism is about the shortsighted and capricious nature of much of the reasoning I see Democrats employ. They seem to prefer going along with the crowd instead of logically analyzing whatever problem we seem to be having.

People used to think that the political spectrum of left and right was just a way to portray a person's attitude to change. Liberals wanted change, and Conservatives wanted things to stay the same. Radicals wanted immediate, violent change, and Reactionaries wanted to return to some previous position. I always thought that this way of characterizing political viewpoints was idiotic. "Change" in itself, I thought, could not be a "value." No one, I thought, could possibly just want things "to change", without any concern for what change is being made, or the

current state of things. I thought a proper way to characterize political viewpoints was to articulate actual values, and that progress toward those values could be used to judge society. People with different actual values would have different political philosophies, and whether and how anyone would want society to change would depend on their judgment of how close society reflected their values.

After observing how well Barack Obama has done with his very non-descript slogan for "Change we can believe in", I've started to reconsider my view. I've come to the conclusion that there are some people who really do value "change" without any concern for what direction the change is. And I've come to the conclusion that they tend to be Democrats. I think the problem is related the very wise philosopher Thomas Sowell's criticism that some people tend to think in only a short-term fashion. He calls it "stage-one thinking", which is the failure to think "beyond the immediate consequences of decisions to their long-term effects."[67] My criticism is more specific, though, in that I believe the reason many leftists tend to think in a more short-sighted way is that they have come to value change in itself, and not because change might make things better in some other sense.

Perhaps we can call this valuing of change for change's sake "trendomania" or "fadophilia". Though I now recognize that such people do exist, that fact by itself by no means implies that I think this approach is reasonable or rational. In fact, I think it is diametrically the opposite of reasoning. It is anti-rational in the sense that rationality requires the use of reasons for action and an analysis of those reasons, whereas for fadophiliacs action is always justified. It makes sense then, that this sort of person will be more likely to jump on whatever trend is happening or fresh, and he will be much more likely to adopt fleeting fads for little or no reason. The fact that something is new and dynamic is justification enough to endorse it, at least for a fadophiliac.

One might point out that jumping on the bandwagon won't always have negative results, and that is certainly true. The fact is that sometimes the bandwagon is headed in the right direction, but the problem is that it is silly to think that it will always be headed in the right direction, or even that it will be more of the time than not. And far too often, it will be headed in the wrong direction. Sometimes, it will even lead to harm and damage to the very people it aims to help.

I've made quite a few claims here without any support. I think this approach is appropriate, since I want to first tell you why I am not a Democrat, and second convince you that my position is based on careful reasoning and not any personal bias or rash generalizing. Let me now begin to address the second concern.

After thinking about this for some time, I think the clearest example of how Democrats tend to be fadophiliacs, and thus think capriciously and in a short-sighted way, is the case of the War in Iraq. I don't think I need to argue that most Democrats wanted to pull troops out of Iraq before the surge. But I do need to argue that pulling troops out of Iraq at that time would have been shortsighted and capricious.

The War in Iraq

I have serious problems with killing other human beings even in war, and so I am sympathetic to people who are pacifistic, although I think my views have been maturing in this regard. I can see how someone could take a principled stand against authorizing the use of force. I could also see how someone could argue that it is better for us in the long run to mind our own business and let the world progress on its own without any forceful intervention. Ron Paul seems to make this argument. Of course, one could disagree with isolationism and still not think that we should have invaded Iraq.

Yet most Democrats do not take these principled stands, especially Democratic politicians. President Bush did not have to drag along the Democrats, against their internal opposition, into the war in Iraq. In my recollection, most of them were competing against each other to show how strongly they were behind the legislation. There were some who argued very early on that our invasion of Afghanistan was good, but thought we should not invade Iraq, but they seemed to be in a very small minority.

Immediately after the murderous attack on September 11th, nearly everyone supported whatever course the President suggested. It seemed to me, however, that the tone began to change as the campaign for the next election rolled around. As anyone who has any experience with politics knows, if you say your opponent is doing a good job and you support his policies, you've got about a zero percent chance of being elected. It seemed to me that this was motivating a lot of the impetus behind criticism of the President's policies in Iraq.

I am not saying that the President made every decision correctly, nor will I say that everything went well in Iraq. I'm not even sure that going into Iraq was the right choice. But the question at the end of Bush's term was whether we should pull our troops out, and it is important to realize that the reality that men and women in our armed forces were being killed in Iraq does not necessarily imply that we should have.

In any case, after Bush's first term in office, most Democrats changed their viewpoint and believed that we should pull our troops out of Iraq, which was one of Barack Obama's main platform positions, which probably got him elected (although even Barack Obama quickly and completely abandoned his commitment to an immediate withdrawal). My question is this: what changed to justify such a strong reversal in the Democratic position? I realize that one must sometimes change one's views when presented with new evidence, but only when that evidence justifies changing one's position. One cannot justify a change in position by observing that things change. Of course things change, but which change in particular justifies the new position?

Democrats wanted to send our troops into Iraq early on, presumably with the dual goals of overthrowing Iraq and putting in place a less hostile democratic regime. We have accomplished the first goal, but arguably we have not even yet completely accomplished the second (as of 2010, though hopefully we soon will). What could possibly justify pulling our troops out before we accomplished the second goal? As I've hinted at, it seems a bit like the real change that motivated this position was the then upcoming election, but that would only explain it and couldn't justify the change. Of course, perhaps that's exactly the problem. Perhaps there is no justification. No, that couldn't be right. Everyone just knows that the changes in Iraq justified our pulling troops out; why should we even think about it?

I refuse to sheepishly go along with anyone. I can't just believe something because that's what the majority believes. When I would ask my students about the Iraq war, in particular, and why they hated George Bush, they didn't really seem to have reasons, but just the feeling that any smart person held those positions. I can't tell you how infuriating that attitude is to me. It's why I teach philosophy; to get people to stop jumping on the bandwagon. Why do I feel like the Democrats are fighting me every step of the way?

Sorry for that brief indulgence. The point is that I can't just accept that we should have pulled troops out of Iraq because people thought we should have. I can't accept that the Democrats so radically changed their viewpoint for a justified reason, unless and until they can provide me with the new information which justified them changing their position. Or I can continue my present belief that Democrats will shortsightedly accept pretty much anything, as long as it is considered new (especially if they judge that it will brighten their political prospects).

The idea that people who radically change their views should have some kind of justification for that change is a basic principle I think most of us accept, but sometimes we ignore it for emotional reasons, or because the person changing their view is someone we like. Consider Mitt Romney. He apparently changed his position on whether abortion should be legal, and now believes that it should not be. Everyone jumped on him, trying to see whether such a radical change could be justified by some intellectual reflection, or whether it was done in an insincere way just for political gain. Of course, the Democrats, and the leftist media, were the ones who most criticized him, and they were the most likely to be skeptical of his attempted justification that it came about as he was considering stem-cell research and his observation that our society was beginning to value human life less and less.

I even recall a news story which looked back at the timing of the debate over stem-cell research in Massachusetts, I believe, and the timing of Mitt Romney's epiphany on abortion, arguing that they were too remote in time to have been a causative factor. The story seemed more like an attempted "Gotcha Journalism" piece, as it ignored the fact that people don't see an event and then immediately change their deeply-held beliefs. It often takes months of ruminating before one changes one's views.

Let me be clear that I think that the principle used to criticize Romney was proper, even if many media organizations applied it inconsistently and sloppily. He had a major change in policy which he could use for political benefit, and it is reasonable to believe his radical change was made for purely political gain unless he can provide a justifiable reason for the change in position. I don't dispute the principle, I just want to apply the same standard to Democrats.

So, what exactly happened in Iraq or the world which would have justified the change in view for Democrats? It might appear so obvious to you that you can't imagine how I don't see it, but in my experience that is exactly when it is most often that precision and careful analysis is most revealing. I will try my best to identify the changes which might have justified it, and then consider each one.

So, here are the possible reasons I have heard for changing one's position from support for keeping troops in Iraq to withdrawal from Iraq:

1. There were no weapons of mass destruction.
2. The members of our military were being killed.
3. Our presence in Iraq drove the international community to disapprove of, if not hate, us.
4. It cost too much financially.

It seems to me that these are the main reasons cited by those who criticized President Bush about his policy to remain in Iraq until Iraq could take care of herself. Let's honestly consider each of them, and see whether they can really do the work required of them. Could they really take a person who supported the war in Iraq, and justify that person changing to a position that we should withdraw all of our troops as quickly as possible?

No WMD's

One of the reasons cited for the invasion of Iraq was the possibility, no, probability, that Saddam Hussein had weapons of mass destruction, most likely chemical agents, but also possibly bio-toxins. He had apparently not been able to acquire nuclear material, but was purportedly considering it. Those who mistakenly think it is a certainty that he did not have them apparently have no more sense than those who thought it was a certainty that he did have them.

Now, if this probability were the only reason we had for invading Iraq, then the invasion would not have been justified. After all, India and Pakistan both created nuclear missiles, and it doesn't seem like we should just go invade them. Anyone who argues as if the possible presence of weapons with the potential to quickly kill large numbers of people was the sole reason for us invading Iraq is using a straw man, a particularly un-artful one at that, which makes it all the more galling that so many people fall prey to it.

The reason for going to war with Iraq was much more complicated than that, although the probability of WMD's was a central part of it. In order to evaluate whether the lack of WMD's could justify the change in view of Democrats, we need to have some understanding of the reasons we invaded Iraq in the first place.

In my recollection, the argument for war went something like this: Saddam Hussein had invaded another country without any provocation when he took control of Kuwait. He had already invaded Iran, but we tended to ignore that because, well, the Iranians took over our consulate way back, and we were still really pissed about it. We also mostly ignored it when he used chemical weapons in that war, and we ignored it when he used those weapons on Iraqi Kurds. Maybe ignored is not the right word, but overlooked, or allowed. It is true that when a leader kills his own people, we tend to allow the U.N. to get involved. But we couldn't ignore it when he invaded the peaceful nation of Kuwait, so George H. W. Bush got the nations of the world together, and sent in troops to remove Saddam from Kuwait.

Many people at the time argued that we should have gone all the way to Baghdad and ended his regime then, but cooler heads prevailed. Notice I didn't say wiser. It was argued that the coalition had only been formed to liberate Kuwait, and not to remove Saddam from power. If we tried to do that, then the coalition would fall apart, and that wasn't something Bush was willing to risk. It was thought that Saddam would be contained, and that sanctions would rein him in. He could be controlled if the world stood firm against him.

As we all know in hindsight, that didn't happen. He toyed with the U.N. weapons inspectors, he bought off ministers in the U.N. through the oil for blood money, I mean food, program, and he did everything he could do to show he was defiant, and that he was still housing stockpiles of chemical and biological weapons. He had his political enemies killed. He also had his soldiers fire missiles at our planes which were enforcing the no-fly zone. We told him not to, but well, what were we going to do to him, invade?

He also sent money to the widows and children of terrorists who blew themselves up in the middle of crowded cafes. Sure, one could argue that he was a great humanitarian, but if a Muslim is considering making such a sacrifice (such an indecent, abhorrent one), and he knows that his family will be taken care of financially, he will be much more likely to do it. In fact, if the Muslim world convinced these potential terrorists that their families would be shunned, how many of them would still be motivated to kill others?

So, Saddam Hussein was a real bad guy, with ambitions to expand his power. All of this would arguably be enough to invade Iraq and remove him from power, but considerations of the loss of life prevented our leaders from making that decision. We already had an enormous number of personnel, resources, and effort merely to contain Saddam Hussein, and these resources could have been used to combat global terrorism throughout the world. Perhaps it would have been better to just leave, and allow Saddam Hussein to do whatever he would have done.

Or perhaps that would have been irresponsible. The basic arrogance and defiance of Saddam Hussein hadn't changed. Nor had his willingness to kill his political enemies or his desire for hegemony in the gulf. George W. Bush, however, recognized that something had changed. To allow a dictatorial tyrant to possess WMD's when he had used them in the past, and when he had been willing to invade other countries was one thing, but the knowledge that there were groups of people who were intent on using such weapons against the people of the United States made for a whole different ball game.

Would Saddam Hussein use the chemical weapons everyone suspected he had? Would he sell them to a terrorist group, perhaps Al Qaeda? Should we wait to find out?

Whatever you and I would decide now in hindsight, George W. Bush decided that we could not, as did nearly every other politician who looked at the data, including the Democrats in Congress. In my recollection, George Bush never guaranteed that Saddam Hussein had stockpiles of WMD's, and insisted that even if he didn't, it still made sense to remove him from power, simply because of the risk that he did, and the near certainty that he would try to rebuild his stores once the pressure was taken off of him.

We can disagree now, seeing that he did not have stockpiles of active WMD's, but without that knowledge, nearly everyone who had access to privileged information and considered the situation said that Saddam should be removed. I do not see how the revelation that we were mistaken about whether he actually had stockpiles of WMD's changes anything about the decision when it was made.

Let me put it this way: it may have shown that we didn't need to go in with the urgency that we thought, but it could never show that we made the wrong decision given the available evidence. I know it's a subtle distinction which many people will have a difficult time grasping, but it is very important. Every decision has to be made with the information available at the time. It is always the case that new information can be obtained, which would have the effect of changing one's decision. But sometimes not making any decision and waiting around just in case any other information turns up is a worse choice than making a decision based on incomplete information.

It depends on how certain the information one has is, or at least how strong one takes it to be. And apparently we were strongly convinced about the claim that Saddam had stockpiles of WMD's hidden somewhere. So sure, in fact, that only a handful of Democrats disagreed with the need to use force against Saddam in order to remove him from power.

George Bush strongly made the case that even if Saddam Hussein was not an imminent threat, we could not risk him becoming one. Implicit in that case, it seems to me, is the idea that Saddam might not have stockpiles of WMD's. If he did have them, he would be an imminent threat. So, Bush's argument was subtle and did not depend on the fact that Saddam Hussein actually had stockpiles of WMD's, despite the fact that nearly everyone today portrays the argument as if it did.

Even if one thinks the Democrats were not smart enough to see that subtlety, and that they voted to use force because they were convinced that Saddam Hussein had stockpiles of usable WMD's, their change in policy would still not be justified. I don't see how the failure to find such stockpiles argues that we should pull our troops out. In fact, it seems to me that it would actually make it even more clear that we could not pull our troops out of Iraq. The fact that there were no large stockpiles of usable WMD's would not justify the change in position so many Democrats have made, but reveals it as politically motivated at best, and downright foolish at worst.

Let me use an analogy to make my point. Say we have a police officer who has his gun trained on a known felon. He suspects the felon is carrying a gun. In fact, multiple witnesses say they saw him carrying a gun earlier. The felon has a trenchcoat on, and refuses to open or drop it. There are 50 people within range of being shot if he does have a gun, and he has murdered 17 people before. The police officer continues to tell the felon to drop the coat and then put his hands up.

Now, without even acknowledging the police officer, the felon reaches deep into his coat, and begins to pull something out. So, the police officer shoots him. Let's think carefully about this case.

I think the police officer did exactly the right thing. He made a decision based on the available information that he had. What if we found later that the felon did not have a gun? Would that invalidate the police officer's decision? In the police officer's judgment, if he had waited to confirm a gun, there was a high likelihood of other people being injured or killed. Perhaps one can judge that the risk was warranted, and that we should allow felons a chance to kill others before we shoot them, but can anyone really condemn people who disagree?

If the police officer knew that the felon did not have a gun, would the shooting have been justified? No. But that is not the right question. It is a hypothetical with an easy answer, but it is a counterfactual conditional nonetheless. It is like asking if the police officer would be justified in the shooting *if* he knew the felon was not a felon, but instead was Mother Teresa. The question to ask is whether the fact that it turned out that the felon did not have a gun, but was reaching for his cell phone, would show that the policeman acted rashly.

I know the analogy is not perfect, but it is similar enough to ground all the conclusions I draw from it. The decision to invade was made on incomplete information, yes. But it was made on the basis of very strong information, and there was a risk of injury and loss of life if we waited to make the decision. You can disagree now, but at the time nearly everyone, *including the Democrats*, agreed.

It should be clear by now that the failure to find stockpiles of WMD's could have no bearing on the decision to invade Iraq. The decision was either right or it was wrong, but if it was made sincerely and carefully, then it was the right decision regardless of what we found out later. And if it was the wrong decision, it would have to be wrong because of some piece of information about the decision-making process, and not some after the fact discovery that some of the information we had was wrong, even if the decision was based solely on the information that turned out to be wrong. It might be a tragedy, but we couldn't criticize the people who made the decision. We might be able to criticize the people who gave us the information, which would include the CIA and apparently the analogous organization in nearly every country in the world, but I have neither the expertise nor the knowledge to attempt any such criticism. I wonder if any of my readers do.

So, it is clear that the failure to find stockpiles of WMD's could not have invalidated the decision to invade in the first place. Yet, this doesn't address the question of whether the lack of these weapons could have justified the decision to pull troops out of Iraq. To answer that, let me return to the analogy.

Say the police officer shot the felon, and the felon died. It turned out that the felon was a single father who had 10 children who depended on him. Let's presume that the felon did have a gun, and it was loaded, and he intended to use it to kill as many innocent people as he could. The question I am asking is whether the police officer owes anything to the children. I would say not. One could argue that we as a society perhaps still have an obligation to raise those children, although I realize some people will disagree, but no one could dispute the fact that the police officer did nothing wrong, and doesn't owe the children anything personally.

Now, let's say instead that the felon was actually reaching for a cigarette. He didn't even have a gun. Could any of my readers possibly think that this would *lessen* the police officer's responsibility? I could see how someone would insist that it didn't increase his culpability, as long as he made the decision in a careful way. But consider what happens in the real world when police officers do exactly this sort of thing. Republicans generally say, tough, the police officer was doing his job, the kids now should go into foster care, and it was the fault of their father if it was anyone's fault. Democrats in general seem to wail that an injustice was done, and often want the police officer to lose his job, pay restitution to the children, and have the city pay restitution to the children as well.

So, let me make my analogy clear. We invade Iraq, in simplistic terms simply because Saddam Hussein had stockpiles of WMD's, and it turns out that he didn't have any. And Democrats turned around and argued that this lack means we had no further obligation to the people of Iraq, and could withdraw our troops at any time and allow the people of Iraq to fend for themselves. Really?

Wouldn't that only strengthen the claim that we had a moral responsibility for invading the country and throwing it into turmoil? How arrogant and narcissistic is it to think that we can go into a country and screw it all up because we thought something that turned out to be false, and then we can just bail out of that country, leaving it to be assaulted and its people attacked while they are defenseless? Really?

Did Democrats take even one second to really think about the implications of what they were saying? They were saying that we screwed up, but it wasn't our responsibility to put things right. Many of them were saying that we can invade a country on trumped up charges, but we have no obligation to undo the damage that we did. Honestly, I can't imagine anything so callous and indifferent to the suffering of others. For Democrats, who seem to think that we were morally responsible for a great deal of that suffering, their position seems all that much worse.

Seriously, it is hard for me to convey the depth of my revulsion for this view, as well as the willful blindness it seems to require. A few seconds of careful thought makes it obvious to me, but it seems that most Democrats couldn't even be bothered to do that. Even if we found WMD's, wouldn't we still be responsible for bearing the brunt of the hard work required to rebuild the country. We could hardly expect an oppressed, tyrannized population to do it for themselves, could we? The lack of stockpiles of WMD's could in no way lessen our responsibility, but could only strengthen it. That responsibility involves using our military to help the Iraqi people rebuild their country, and to help protect them against the murderous thugs who are attempting to kill them in order to gain political power.

Perhaps, however, the lack of stockpiles of usable WMD's was not the main reason most Democrats supported a pullout of our troops, but that one of the other reasons I mentioned was the real reason. So, let's turn to those.

Americans were being killed

Perhaps the fact that we had lost thousands of men and women justified the change in view of the Democrats. I don't mean to be overly cynical and I know they don't mean to, but at times it sounded like some Democrats reveled in every death in Iraq, and they made hay when the tally of the dead reached a numerically striking total, like 2,000. Let's agree that we should mourn the death of the 1,999th soldier killed just as much as the 2000th one.

In any case, when I would ask Democrats why we should pull the troops out of Iraq, the fact that we were losing soldiers and marines figured prominently in their reasoning.

But is the reasoning sensible? A big part of deciding whether the loss of life we were suffering dictated that we should change our view toward pulling troops out is the original estimate of how many lives we were risking by invading in the first place. If we had planned on losing a hundred troops in the invasion and the aftermath of our victory, then it might make sense to reevaluate whether we should keep troops there. But if the estimates were in the hundreds of thousands, then it would seem odd.

Let's face it, there is no such thing as war where no one dies. That is why we want to avoid it at nearly all costs. That is why we shouldn't go to war unless we believe the consequences of failing to go to war are worse than the deaths of thousands upon tens of thousands of brave men and women dying. Sometimes, often, I get the sense that Democrats voted to support the use of force without really thinking through the consequences. It seemed like they suddenly decided that the loss of life was not justified, and so we needed to pull the troops out, as if they never envisioned that people would die in the first place.

I do not recall the estimates for our casualties in the lead up to the invasion of Iraq, but it seems to me that it must have been in the tens of thousands. Plus, if Saddam Hussein had WMD's, the casualties would likely have been much, much higher. He could even have used them against Israel, Iran, or Kuwait, and killed hundreds of thousands of people. When I consider this, all I can say is thank God he didn't have stockpiles of WMD's.

It was Congressman Stark, Democratic Congressman from California, who said that President Bush basically enjoyed seeing our soldiers killed. Really. He criticized the Republicans in Congress for blocking a vote on SCHIP, a bill to fund children's healthcare costs, by wondering whether enough children would "grow old enough for you to send to Iraq to get their heads blown off for the President's amusement".[68] He later apologized, but what an incredible statement. In Stark's mind, the only way he could comprehend the President's decision to keep troops in Iraq was that he enjoyed it, because in Stark's view, there was no other possible reason to keep them there. It is another case where a Democrat thinks that his point of view is the only rational point of view, so that anyone who disagrees with him must be irrational, if not downright immoral or worse.

No one wants to see our soldiers die, except for members of Al Qaida and other terrorist groups. Did President Bush want to see our soldiers die? No. Could he have stopped it? Yes. He could have prevented the deaths of thousands of our troops by pulling all of them out of Iraq. This was apparently all the reasoning that needed to occur in most Democrat's eyes. Why think any deeper about consequences, or results, when we know that we can reduce the number of our troops being killed? Why think about what will happen to innocent Iraqi women and children? Why worry about the possible repercussions on American civilians if we were to let Al Qaida gain a stronghold in the Middle East?

Because that is the honorable and responsible thing to do. Think for more than two seconds, and we know exactly what would have happened.

Imagine if Barack Obama would have fulfilled his campaign promises by immediately pulling all troops from Iraq. The killing would have undoubtedly continued, but now, without our troops there, the killers, emboldened by what they would have perceived as a victory, would escalate their murderous attacks. Every day numerous Iraqi men, women, and children would have had their arms and legs blown off. The slaughter would have continued unabated. We would see six months of hell in Iraq, and then the United Nations would decide that something must be done about all the bloodshed. How would Obama have responded? Probably by sending the troops back into Iraq, this time under the banner of the United Nations.

Fortunately, Barack Obama, as well as every other Democrat who aspired to the Presidency knew the likelihood of this scenario, and so would never have pulled the troops out completely. That didn't seem to stop them, however, from using irresponsible rhetoric against anyone who freely admitted that we must keep troops in Iraq.

Another way to think about it is this: Democrats said they wanted to end the war in Iraq, and people, especially the press, thought them noble and principled, and caring. But a moment's reflection reveals that they did not want to engage in the hard work, and yes, death of our soldiers, that it would take to end the war. Instead, they just wanted to end *our involvement in the war.* If we would have pulled out our troops before Iraqi troops were competent to take over, the war would have continued. No one thought that the killing would somehow miraculously cease. So, our withdrawal would have meant that our soldiers would be safer, but it would mean that the war would continue, with thousands of men, women, and children being killed over a few months time. Who knows how many would have been dead by the time the killing was finally over?

This is the legacy the Democrats wanted to leave to the country we invaded for our protection? I could understand it if the Democrats just said that the lives of our soldiers are worth more than the lives of Iraqi citizens, but no Democrat would assert that this is true, would they? Shouldn't we simply have asked this question: Will fewer innocent men, women, and children be killed if we remain in Iraq? Everyone agreed that this was true. Didn't that fact alone justify our being there?

And wouldn't that make anyone who wanted to remove our troops precipitously either callous, indifferent to suffering, or imperialistic?

Yes, yes, I am well aware that many people condemn our invasion as imperialistic, but if that was imperialistic, we sure go about it in an odd way. We practically immediately turned over sovereignty to the local people. I don't ever recall a truly imperialistic country doing this.

Isn't it imperialistic to think that we can just go invade a country (as the Democrats believed), and then abandon it because our soldier's lives are more important than the people who live there? That would qualify as imperialism in my mind.

I keep coming back to this, but how does any of that justify pulling troops out? I especially cannot see how anyone who cares about people throughout the world, and who cares about living up to his responsibilities, could even consider pulling troops out of Iraq.

Perhaps one is thinking that I am being hyperbolic here. After all, there are a lot of people around the world who are being unjustly killed. Wouldn't my reasoning justify sending our troops all around the world? I don't recall any specific examples, but I have heard exactly this charge leveled against people who argued that we should keep our troops in Iraq.

I find the criticism frankly rather childish. It seems to be a perfectionist fallacy which follows this general line: because we can't save every person in the world from being blown up, we shouldn't save anyone from being blown up. Wrong. We should sometimes do things to protect people around the planet, even at some risk to ourselves, and even if we can't save everyone.

Even so, I think this approach is missing the point. It fails to realize that our actions were directly responsible for the situation in Iraq, where terrorists were killing people nearly every day. How could anyone have just ignored this fact?

Would I take the position that it doesn't matter how many of our troops were killed? No, although I'm not sure that is saying much. By the time Barack Obama took over, there wasn't much chance of getting to the numbers of deaths required to reach that point. As I have already stated, the Democrats must have been willing to accept tens upon tens of thousands of deaths when they accepted the use of force. Whatever casualties we had taken, we would still have to ask the question: can a change in tactics change the casualty count? At what stage would we give up entirely, and say that nothing we can do will end in Iraq being a stable, self-supporting government?

There is something unseemly about Democrats who rushed to that judgment so quickly. Democrats seemed to be so willing to pull troops out that they jumped to the conclusion that there was no hope in Iraq, and publicly announced it, even with so little evidence. In fact, George Bush insisted that if he had more troops and changed the rules of engagement, then the situation in Iraq would turn around. Today, there is wide agreement that he was correct.

If we had listened to the Democrats, we would have pulled our troops out, and we would have never known that there were ways to reduce the casualties, and which we can expect will continue reducing them. Not only casualties of American troops, but of Iraqi citizens. Could anyone really think that they support the troops when they don't believe they can succeed with their mission? If so, then it is support that our troops do not need, nor do they want.

Would I want every single member of the coalition forces to continue living? I wouldn't even respond to such an idiotic question if someone posed it, which they should. After all, the rhetoric of some Democrats seems to suppose that anyone who supports keeping the troops in Iraq wants soldiers to die. Just think about Stark. Of course he apologized, but his words still revealed his thought processes and basic inclination in belief.

Just for the record, I do not want any of our soldiers to die. I want them all to live long healthy, happy lives. But I also want every man, women, and child to live long healthy, happy lives. And I also wish that everyone on the planet wanted the same thing.

But there are some people who do not, and they are willing to end the lives of innocent civilians in order to get their way politically. They have also shown that they are more than willing to kill our soldiers.

I imagine some readers are saying right now that our soldiers are more than willing to kill them. I believe that this is true. But to equate the two would be the worst form of fallacious reasoning imaginable. Our soldiers are willing to kill people who have pledged to slaughter innocent men, women, and children. How is that supposed to be morally equivalent to them wanting to kill our soldiers, because, what, we are willing to protect men, women, and children?

If terrorists decided tomorrow to stop killing innocent civilians, how long would it be before we would pull our troops out? A month. Two months. We are not there to die. We are there to prevent people from dying. Our military does whatever, in the opinions of its civilian authorities, will reduce the loss of life overall, and if that involves killing people who seem to have no qualms about destroying the lives of innocent people, then they think that it is more than justified, and I think the vast majority of Americans would agree.

The World was Against Us

Many Democrats seem to argue that we should have pulled out of Iraq in order to restore our image in the eyes of the world. I hope that for most people this isn't just some kind of blatant *Ad Populum* fallacy, but I have my doubts. Should we care about what the world thinks of us? I can't imagine anyone saying that we shouldn't, not even a Republican. Everyone thinks that we should try to uphold a positive image in the world.

The only question is whether we should sacrifice our other values in order to keep a positive image. For instance, our image throughout the world would probably be greatly enhanced if we killed homosexuals. Maybe the countries in Western Europe would go apoplectic, but most of the countries in the Middle East and around the world would think we took a step in the right direction.

My point is that when someone is doing the right thing, it would be asinine to stop doing it because someone might frown upon what you are doing. We should care about what they think of us, but that shouldn't get us to stop what we are doing. It should only get us to try to convince them that we are acting honorably and from noble reasons.

Another way to say it would be that the fact that the entire world would frown on certain behavior could never establish that the behavior is wrong. We would need some independent reason. Without that, I think we should act in accord with our own values. In order to justify changing course, we would need a reason that what we are doing is wrong in the first place. Then we should stop doing it.

Anyway, all of this presupposes that it really would have enhanced our image around the world if we pulled troops out of Iraq. My previous discussion should make it clear that I have strong doubts about that. In fact, I think it would severely undermine any support around the world that we have. Imagine that we up and left while men, women, and children were being blown up. We just pulled out without a thought to the people who would die in our wake. And the killing continued, or as is more likely, increases. Just how the hell is that supposed to make the German people say, "Oh, now the Americans are doing the right thing." Such thinking seems so counterintuitive to me that I have a hard time understanding how supposedly mature adults could hold such a view.

Did our withdrawal of troops from Vietnam enhance our standing in the world? And even if it did, was it worth it? Yes, we lost a lot of good men and women during the war. But our withdrawal resulted in the deaths of millions of people. Are American lives more valuable in the long run than Cambodian or Vietnamese lives? Even if you thought they were, our withdrawal sent the message that we were a paper tiger. Al Qaida has cited it as a reason to believe that if they keep hitting us and killing civilians, then we will soon turn tail and run. If you ask me, that put many more American lives at risk in the long run.

Yet, those are not the questions Democrats seem to be interested in. What will take care of the immediate problem? That long term thinking may be beneficial in the, well, long run, but it doesn't get you elected.

Besides, the claim that our reputation throughout the world was harmed because of our invasion and keeping troops in Iraq is highly suspicious. The Germans and French recently elected leaders who were explicitly pro-American. From these results and others, it doesn't seem like we are suffering a deficit of respect from most of the globe. As Dennis Prager, a nationally syndicated radio talk show host, put it, "The world doesn't hate America; leftists from around the world hate America." It does seem like leftists and other fascists from around the world use the same rhetoric as leftists in America do. I remember hearing a speech from a leader in Al Qaida where I heard quotes which could have come right out of a Democratic fund-raising letter.

Please don't hyper-react and think I just said that Democrats and Al Qaida were in cahoots. All I am saying is that America, as it is, is well-respected by many people around the world, and it is considered as deeply flawed by many people around the world, both within America and without. Much of that disrespect comes from differing values. We shouldn't forget about those people who still look up to America, because, certainly, those people who hate America are not going to change their opinion because we pull troops out of Iraq.

In fact, I am fairly sure that if we did pull our troops out of Iraq, we would be hated even more by those around the globe who hate us now. This is what I mean by Democrats being shortsighted and capricious. They would pull troops out of Iraq, partly because they say it has contributed to our global image being tarnished, even though doing so would make the problem even worse. Convince me that this move isn't shortsighted. Let me know how this move could possibly be anything other than capricious. Perhaps before I ask for counterarguments, I should consider one last reason.

It just cost too much

Some Democrats argued that the war in Iraq was costing us too much financially, and that for this reason we should have pulled our troops out. I must admit that the war was and is expensive. I would definitely support the idea of the Federal Government spending less money.

Yet, I can't help pointing out that anyone who voted to support the invasion of Iraq had to know it would be a terribly expensive proposition. And one would think that they would have calculated into their analysis of the decision how much the war and its aftermath would cost. And even if there were never any terrorist attacks in Iraq at all, we would still have maintained a high troop presence for a while, and kept some troops in place for a very long time. We still have troops in South Korea and Germany, for example.

Undoubtedly, the cost is higher than one likely would have anticipated. But, as before, does this increased cost justify the decision to haphazardly remove our troops? I have a little more sympathy here for someone who would say that it does, but ultimately, I think they would be wrong.

We need to look at all the reasons we had for keeping our troops in Iraq, and then ask how much those things are worth. It actually matters less what we anticipated spending than what we are gaining by being there, or losing by pulling out. As I have argued, pulling out would have had enormous repercussions. Many more innocent lives would have been taken, and innocent lives which I think we as a nation owe some obligation toward protecting.

Our pulling out would also have severely affected our image around the world, and not in a good way. It would also likely have emboldened our enemies now and for a long time in the future. Al Qaida still draws inspiration from the Vietnam example. If we hadn't pulled out of Vietnam with our tail between our legs, Al Qaida probably would never have attacked us. We will never know for sure, but I think it is still an enormously important consideration.

The most important question to ask is whether we are safer as a nation with troops in Iraq, or are we safer with the troops brought home or redeployed elsewhere? It may be less important to us overall than to the Iraqis themselves, but it still seems to me that our pulling troops out before Iraq was completely stabilized would have made us less safe. If the government of Iraq is too weak at any time to fight the insurgents, which everyone seems to agree is true at the time I am writing this (although there are now finally signs that in the near future they will soon have that ability), then our pulling out will only serve to destabilize Iraq, and perhaps the entire Middle East. And I'm pretty sure that people around the globe will blame that on us.

Ultimately, I cannot see any good reason that would have justified pulling our troops out of Iraq. I can only surmise that there is no good reason, even though the majority of Democrats, and perhaps even Americans, changed their position in the aftermath of the war. Whether it was a predilection for fadophiliac thinking, or just capriciousness or indifference to long-term consequences I cannot be sure. But I can be sure that I would not want to be a member of a party which encouraged its members to think this way.

Other examples: Crack Cocaine

If the war in Iraq were the only area where I thought the Democrats were thinking poorly, I think it would be a pretty serious flaw, but not insurmountable when it comes to convincing me to give them my vote. No one person or group can think perfectly all the time. It seems to me, however, that this is just the latest in a long series of the same thing. Here are a few more examples.

When I was in high school or shortly thereafter, I remember a new scourge which had to be combated: crack cocaine. My recollection is that people were very concerned about drug use in the inner cities and among minorities, and crack cocaine was much cheaper than powdered cocaine, so poorer people would be more affected than any other group. Rich people would still buy powdered cocaine, but the relative cheapness of crack cocaine meant that many more people on the lower end of the economic scale would be affected by the new drug.

I wasn't all that concerned at the time. I remember a girl in high school that I had a crush on said that she had taken cocaine, and I thought she must have had a lot of money to burn. I never intended to use any hard drugs, but knew people who had. I wasn't sure what should be done about the issue of drug use, but I did think that the people who were fighting against the new scourge were leftists concerned about the disproportionate effect of crack cocaine on the people that they cared about.

That was exactly why they increased the penalties for the selling and possession of crack cocaine. They were concerned about people, and from an economic perspective, if a criminal activity costs less to engage in, then the penalties must be higher in order to gain an equal deterrent effect. It seemed eminently reasonable, assuming the government has the right to criminalize the use of drugs in the first place.

It must have been five or ten years later when what I now realize was inevitable happened. Just think about it. If the penalty for powdered cocaine, which is generally used by rich white people, is less than the penalty for crack cocaine, which was generally used by poorer minorities, how long will it be before someone screams racism, and not just someone: Leftists.

Perhaps not the same leftists who thought it was a good idea in the first place, but leftists nonetheless. The stories which came out then were about the racist government, out to attack and bring down minorities. I was utterly astounded. I was especially astounded that I didn't see anywhere a discussion of the original intent of the law, or the discussion surrounding it, or who had supported it, or the fact that it may have been brought about by an emotional appeal in the media on behalf of poor people and the dangers they were facing.

It was especially astounding that it seemed like an equally emotional appeal on behalf of poor minorities which was guiding the new stories. I started to understand that leftists, largely Democrats, do seem to get immediately absorbed in the emotion surrounding a debate, and seem to ignore the long-term implications. They seem to sway back and forth with whichever emotional appeal the media is making at the time, and don't step back a minute to engage their intellectual capability.

Nowhere did anyone make the case that lowering the penalty for crack cocaine, say equalizing it to powdered cocaine, would unquestionably mean that drug use would increase among poor minority population, like they had been a relatively short time before. I shouldn't say nowhere. At the time I only read newspapers and watched network news. I have no idea about what any alternative media was saying.

The Fairness Doctrine

The so-called "fairness doctrine" is another example. It was the law of the land before Reagan eliminated it. It held that media outlets needed to include "fair speech". In essence, the idea was that if a broadcaster had on a leftist viewpoint, it had to give equal time to someone with a rightist view. I don't know enough history to know who supported the law originally, but it seems to me like a clear violation of the first amendment. It puts "fair speech" above "free speech." It values a certain balance, or equality, by taking away freedom. It sounds perfectly leftist, which values equality over freedom. It seems to me it had to be leftists.

In any case, one problem with such a law is the perennial issue: who decides what is fair? In fact, it seems to me that it would be easy to hide behind the law in order to be even more manipulative of people than otherwise. Let's say a radio station has on an articulate leftist to present his view. People will listen, and may be persuaded, but any educated person should realize that there are other perspectives out there.

Now, follow up the articulate leftist with a bumbling rightist, and it will be harder for people to sort it out. They will hear one side with a strong argument, and will only hear a horrible argument on the other side. Nominally, it meets the demands of the Fairness Doctrine. But it certainly isn't fair, and it doesn't even support the goals stated by those who support the Doctrine, namely allowing people to hear both sides so they can make a careful, informed decision. Again, how are we supposed to decide whether two speakers are of equal rhetorical ability?

A few Democrats, including California senior Senator Dianne Feinstein, have recently talked about reexamining the "Fairness Doctrine." I can't help but wonder if she has really thought it through. I suspect that she has fallen into the trap of thinking that mainstream media are fairly neutral, while talk radio is unabashedly conservative. Perhaps she will let me know if I am wrong.

The facts tell a very different story.

A recent study concluded that television news programs, especially morning shows, had a clearly statistically significant bias in favor of Democrats, as did a handful of major newspapers that were studied. Cable programming was a little more mixed, but still slightly tilted toward Democrats.

Common sense among most Democrats would tell them that the story would be vastly different for talk radio, but their common sense would be wrong. While the study found that Republicans received slightly more positive coverage than Democrats on talk radio, *they also received slightly more negative coverage*. It would seem that talk radio as a whole might be more balanced than some people think.

Of course, that doesn't consider individual programs, and only media in segments, but I think the point is clear. If Dianne Feinstein got her way, the positive coverage of Republicans throughout most every media segment would increase, and on talk radio, it would likely stay the same. I wonder what would happen if we applied the fairness doctrine to classrooms across the educational spectrum.

Oh, as I have heard many leftists say when they ridicule people who see bias in the media, anyone can put forward a study. I could understand leftists rejecting a study that showed that the media is biased toward the left if it were conducted by some right-wing think tank (although many of them have impeccable credentials), but this study was done by The Project for Excellence in Journalism and the Joan Shorenstein Center on the Press, Politics, and Public Policy which is associated with Harvard University and the John F Kennedy School of Government[69]. The study focused on coverage of the Presidential primary races, but I think it would be fair to generalize to political coverage generally.

Also to be fair, I should note that the Senator didn't call for the "Fairness Doctrine" to be reinstated, only studied, but even that much tells me that she can't have thought about the issue very deeply. I would say a lot more against the fairness doctrine here, and I am opposed to it, but my main point is only that prominent Democrats, and Democrats generally, don't think too deeply about the major policy decisions they make and what implications and effects they might have. I am fairly certain that anyone who carefully listens to what prominent Democrats say, and remembers it, will not have to listen too long before they come to the same conclusion.

Immigration

One area where I think this propensity is especially problematic is immigration. It seems to me that not a week goes by that I don't hear some disparaging comment about Republicans along the lines that they are racists who hate immigrants, or some variant on that theme. Republicans have no doubt made some political blunders in the debate over immigration, and Democrats have certainly taken advantage of that fact and bludgeoned them about the head and shoulders. It has helped the Democrats that the mass media at large is biased in a leftist direction. Still, this is all political. I personally don't care about political gamesmanship and who can score points by using manipulative, rhetorical tricks. I want to know the truth about what is right, just, and best for our country.

It seems to me perfectly sensible to have some sorts of restrictions on who is entering our country, either for travel, or to live. I see at least three basic categories of reasons to enact such restrictions. First, is racism or xenophobia. Second, is security and safety. Third, is everything else, including a whole host of domestic concerns.

In my formative years, in fact, all throughout my education including grad school, the main reason pushed for why we have immigration restrictions has always seemed to be racism. It was xenophobic hysteria that drove the legislature to crack down after several massive waves of unchecked immigration. The pure white Protestant Americans couldn't handle so many of the unwashed masses, especially of a darker pigment. The swarthy Southern Mediterranean Italians and darker were the worst.

Of course, the fairly skinned Irish didn't fare much better. Maybe Americans just have an inherent distrust of people who speak differently or have different values. Maybe like most every other group of people on the planet.

Of course, some of us have high ideals. We don't think it is proper to denigrate or harass a group of people for such trivial reasons as their speaking a different language or worshiping differently. We ungrudgingly welcome them into our society, and offer them the same opportunities as everyone else.

Perhaps more people think like this in the Democratic Party than the Republican Party. Perhaps. But I have my doubts. I have talked to quite a few Democrats and Republicans, and it seems to me that they both basically share the same view here, with some exceptions, and it seems to me that Republicans are just really bad at expressing their side. To put it as succinctly as possible: Republicans insist that all immigration be done legally. Democrats seem not to mind whether it is illegal or not.

Add to this that the Democrats and many in the mainstream media make every effort to portray Republicans in a bad light, and, well, you get the picture. I find it hard to believe that the laws restricting immigration were done primarily, or even in large measure, for racist reasons.

So, that leaves the other two types of reasons. I have no doubt that at the beginning of the twentieth century there were security concerns, but these have primarily arisen in arguments opposing open immigration after the 2001 terrorist attacks on the World Trade Center. Perhaps I missed some, but I don't recall anyone using the danger of terrorists as a reason to try to end illegal immigration before that. I'm sure that when immigration laws were originally being debated their supporters would have pointed to any immigrant who committed a crime as part of their justification. In similar vein, news commentator Bill O'Reilly has recently used the crimes of illegal immigrants to justify his position that illegal aliens should be deported, but only those who are arrested for serious crimes.

Still, it seems to me that security concerns are secondary to other domestic concerns, even today. Let's say Al Qaeda attempts to send twenty men over the Southern border, what are the chances that they can be caught, even with a wall and advanced technology? Besides, isn't it more likely that they will just buy a plane ticket direct? They've got money, and they won't be sending any of their higher-ups of whom we might be aware, but instead anonymous men who wouldn't even be on our radar screens.

Let me put it this way. If the only reason we were worried about people crossing our borders illegally were terrorists, I'm not sure it would be cost-effective or worthwhile to build a fence. Moreover, it couldn't even come close to explaining why we are only building a fence along our southern border.

So, it seems to me that the real reason that our legislature decided to put in place quotas on the number of immigrants we will accept each year had to be domestic concerns, and it seems to me domestic concerns must be the reason why we continue to have such laws today.

To what kinds of domestic concerns am I referring? Just about everything, but one of the most important involves wage competition. The more people competing over certain jobs, the more downward pressure on wages there will be. One primary reason to restrict the number of people who can immigrate into our country is to alleviate some of this pressure.

Imagine if we allowed as many people to immigrate into our country as wanted every year. What is to ensure that each of them will have a job? It is simple economics that says that if more people are competing for scarce jobs, the wages they will be able to demand will be lowered. So, one way to ensure that immigrants have employment at reasonable wages, as well as to ensure that current workers (both immigrants and native-born citizens) aren't pressured into accepting lower and lower wages, is to limit the number of people who can move here, temporarily or permanently.

Of course, the minimum wage attempts to do a similar thing, but it does so by restricting the rights and freedoms of American citizens. Unless one thinks that everyone in the world has the God-given right to live in America, it doesn't seem to me that restricting immigration violates anyone's rights. It also seems like the minimum wage laws can be easily subverted when there are large numbers of illegal immigrants who can't risk complaining about sub-minimum wage labor.

The way I think about it is this: as a college professor, I don't have anything to worry about from a large volume of immigration. My job won't be at risk, nor will my wages likely be suppressed because of it. But every person in non-skilled or lower-skilled (or if you're P.C., those jobs which require skills which are available to nearly every adult human being) will be affected negatively. They *have* been affected negatively: stagnated wages, lack of availability of jobs, and in numerous other ways.

Again, let me be absolutely clear on my position. Having no limits on immigration will harm the people who are the most poor, especially recent legal immigrants. It seems to me that this is why leftists originally supported having limits on the level of immigration in the first place. But by no means was it the only reason involving domestic concerns.

Another range of concerns is the question of integration into the American culture. Will immigrants pick up English well enough so that they are not exploited? Will they abandon those aspects of their culture which we frown upon? Will they accept the values that we cherish in America? I know modern Democrats seem to belittle these concerns, and act as if Republicans are merely xenophobic for bringing them up, but in many ways leftist Democrats should be most concerned.

Many of the people who move here from Latin America have an almost disdain for education, especially for young girls. Is this a part of their culture that we would wish them to leave in Latin America, or are we okay with it spreading throughout America? Many of our recent immigrants think it is proper for women to remain in the home, bearing children, and being obedient to their husbands. They discourage young women from going to school, even high school, but certainly when it comes to college. I have learned about this attitude directly from many of the girls who have still somehow absorbed the American ideal of getting an education, and made it into my community college classes.

The point is that the more immigrants who come to America, the harder it is to get them to acculturate to a level with which American leftists would be comfortable. I know they speak as if they are comfortable with any culture, but the culture of machismo which is predominant in many Latin American countries is the first thing they try to stamp out when they come across it, using the law, social pressure, and just about anything else they can.

On another front, think about many of the problems with our society against which leftists rail. Let's see, there's inequality between the rich and poor, there is overcrowding of prisons, there is the environmental impact, including global warming, there is lack of access to hospitals. Everyone complains about traffic, overcrowded schools, drought conditions and lack of availability of basic utilities, including water and electricity. Think about the price of gas. I'm sure I'm leaving a few out, but you can fill in some of them.

It seems to be an inescapable fact about every one of these problems that they are exacerbated by high levels of immigration. I can't imagine how anyone can overlook such a basic fact about society. A city can handle a large number of citizens. What is much harder to handle is when the number of citizens who must be organized and planned for increases rapidly and unpredictably. Large numbers of immigrants can't cause a drought (unless one believes that their acculturating to American consumerism will mean more carbon dioxide in the air, which will cause global warming, which will cause droughts), but they can make a drought much more difficult with which to deal.

I would hope that it is becoming clear why I think the Democrats have a lack of ability to think carefully here. It seems clear to me that they were behind efforts to institute immigration controls in the first place, though I haven't researched the issue, and it is possible I am mistaken. What I cannot be mistaken about is that the simplest way to make progress in a very broad range of issues which Democrats say they care about, would be to crack down on immigration into our country. Instead, we have enacted some of the most liberal immigration policies in the world, and have presumably set the number of immigrants at a level which would not have too dramatic of a negative impact on our environmental and urban planning. And yet, it seems impossible to find a high-ranking Democrat who wants to actually enforce the laws we have *now*. Instead, they seem to condone immigrants who migrate here illegally, and most of them support some form of amnesty, which would legalize millions of immigrants who violated the law to come here or are violating it to remain here. Furthermore, Democrats seem to ignore history and common sense and support amnesty, which is clear will encourage millions more people to immigrate here, which will exacerbate these very problems even more.

Democrats seem to have a preternatural aversion to saying anything negative about illegal immigrants. They even complain anytime anyone points out that a crime was committed by an illegal immigrant. Yet, it seems undeniable to me that illegal immigration has made so many of our problems worse, and more difficult to address. Of course it would be wrong to blame any individual immigrant, since no individual immigrant could intend to cause such widespread difficulty, nor could he. But that can't excuse anyone for ignoring the multitude of problems that arise from immigration as a whole.

It seems like a basic fallacy to me, called the fallacy of composition. It is as if Democrats are saying that one immigrant can't cause any problems, so immigration as a whole can't cause any problems. If this is not the fallacy being committed, then I really don't know how to explain the lack of reasoning exhibited by so many Democrats.

As I see it, Democrats refuse to tighten up enforcement of current immigration laws because it would hurt people, namely the individuals who have come here illegally, and even want to loosen up enforcement, if not completely eliminate such laws. All the while, they criticize anyone who points out that enforcing those laws would make life better for all other citizens, by way of reduced traffic burdens, reducing the demand for water and electricity which has become so precious in many areas, reducing pressure on emergency rooms to close up shop, reducing the need to build more jails and prisons, and reducing the need to build more schools and hire more teachers, including teachers skilled in teaching English as a second language, which takes away the money available to teach the rest of our children. There are many reasons why the quality of education in California has been decimated, but the rampant immigration is certainly a causal factor.

When it comes to immigration, especially in understanding the broad, complex implications that immigration has for other public policy areas, Democrats are clearly shortsighted. They seem less capricious in their policies here, though, at least for a few decades. They are very consistent in opposing the enforcement of existing laws, as well as any expansion of laws to make it even more difficult to immigrate illegally. I would still say that their views are inappropriately tied to their emotions in this regard, but it just so happens that their emotions in this area have remained constant, at least in current years.

Gun Control, Nuclear Power, and More

Washington, D.C. was sued not too long ago over its ban on handguns. The U.S. Supreme Court has recently decided that the ban was unconstitutional.

The background of the ban makes it clear how Democrats are completely shortsighted. All handguns were banned within the District. I believe they could only be owned if they were inoperable. As anyone with an ounce of common sense could tell you would happen, violent crime increased rapidly. When one makes a law against owning guns, all one does is hand an advantage to those who are willing to break the law. We have the civil, even human right to protect ourselves using guns, and anyone who fails to recognize it is not only myopic when it comes to reading the Constitution, but also when it comes to predicting the outcome.

As I heard recently, the oldest civil rights organization is the N.R.A. Democrats seem actively determined to undermine the civil right recognized in the second amendment. Imagine a law which says that we could say whatever we wanted, as long as what we say couldn't have any effect. Then imagine someone saying that this law was perfectly consistent with our right to freedom of speech. Now you know how I feel about Democrats who argued in favor of the gun ban.

I also recently heard a discussion about the use of nuclear power. Nuclear power is arguably a lot safer than burning coal, and it doesn't release any "greenhouse gases" into the atmosphere. You would think leftists would be all for it, especially leftists who are alarmists when it comes to global warming. Yet, it was leftists who fought against using nuclear power, going way back to the seventies. Maybe that was because back then the *cause celebre* was the dawning of a new ice age.

If we had switched over substantially to nuclear power, like the French did, we could have cut our emission of "greenhouse gases" drastically, as well as likely reducing our dependence on foreign oil. Oh yeah, that reminds me of drilling in the Arctic National Wildlife Reserve (ANWR), and off our coasts. It seems to me more globally and environmentally responsible to do our own drilling, where we can legislate responsible and safe drilling, instead of farming it out to other countries around the world, which will not be as environmentally safe. But maybe that's just me.

I'm sure I could find numerous other examples, but I should probably end this chapter now. It seems like every day I listen to political news I see another instance of Democratic shortsightedness, but I think I have presented enough examples to establish my case, if only partially.

Final Thoughts

One of the worst things I think a government can be is shortsighted. It is one thing to force people to turn over their hard earned money in order to accomplish something good, although even that can still be completely unjust. But to take money from people and use it in capricious ways, which later turn out to have been counterproductive, that is unforgiveable.

To use the power of government to impose certain views on the people of a society, only to rescind those policies when their ineffectiveness becomes obvious to everyone, when careful reasoning would have revealed the ineffectiveness from the beginning is not just foolishness. It is to impose foolishness on others at the barrel of a gun. It is to make the wise man suffer the fate of the fool, and make those who are responsible pay the burdens which rightly belong to the irresponsible.

Every government policy which takes from those who are responsible and gives to those who are not can only exacerbate the problem. It means there is less incentive for any of us to be responsible. And in my view Democrats do exactly this on issue after issue, which is why I cannot join them.

CHAPTER SEVEN

Tolerance is a Virtue, Unless You Disagree

Tolerance is the virtue of the man without convictions.
—G.K. Chesterton

Tolerance implies a gratuitous assumption of the inferiority of other faiths to one's own.
—Mahatma Gandhi

I am well aware of the conventional view that Democrats and leftists are extremely tolerant of others, and that it is their opponents who are intolerant. I hope to show that the conventional view is completely backwards, and that Republicans and others are far more tolerant than Democrats, although perhaps there is another word that might describe Democrats better. If I am right, then I think we have to begin looking at how Democrats and leftists are so powerful that they can shift and pervert the conventional wisdom of society in such an extreme way. That much power is truly dangerous, no matter in whose hands it lies.

Any moderately complete discussion of tolerance will necessarily include an aspect of morality, and that will lead our discussion into the question of cultural relativism. We, in America at least, are living in a society that has adopted relativism, at least for our simplistic musings in general. Relativism is with good reason associated with Democrats and leftists. The rhetoric of leftists teems with relativistic ideas, but I will argue that deep down, their policies and ideology depends on morality not being relativistic. So, not only are they not relativistic, but they push relativism on everyone else in their language. This deep inconsistency really damages young people, who are learning to navigate the world, while their teachers, who, let's face it, tend to be leftists, feed them a blatant contradiction. How can we expect students to think logically when this kind of thing is presented as the highest ideal in our society?

We can't. And I hope to help remedy this.

Defining Tolerance

The first order of business is to figure out what we mean by tolerance, or intolerance. We might possibly mean that we are intolerant any time we think that someone engages in immoral behavior. If that's right, then we are all intolerant. The only way one could avoid being intolerant would be to think that nothing is immoral. If this is the right definition, then I want to be intolerant, and the word should not have such a negative connotation. In fact, anyone who argues that we should be tolerant is by that very claim making a moral statement. They are saying that it is immoral to be intolerant. If all we mean by intolerant is that you think something is immoral, claiming that we should be tolerant is itself intolerant. I think we need a better definition.

Perhaps I'm being overly simplistic here, but the verb form of "tolerant" is "tolerate." Wouldn't it follow that someone who tolerates others, presumably other people, is a tolerant person, or has a tolerant attitude. So, what does it mean to tolerate someone? In general, I would say that to tolerate someone is to not kick them out or leave an area oneself, even when one finds them intolerable. If you like someone, it is not possible to "tolerate" them. You want to be around them. But if I have a friend whom I like, and they have a friend whom I dislike, I might still go out with the two of them. I would say that I will tolerate the other person. If it's in my house, I might kick out a person whom I find intolerable for whatever reason, but if someone I care about wants them to stay, I might tolerate them in my house.

It seems, though, that tolerance necessarily involves a judgment of distaste. I can tolerate someone whom I believe to be annoying, or bothersome, or smelly, or ugly, or crass, or... Pretty much any negative attribute can be tolerated. But you can't tolerate something which you like, or you think is good. The word just doesn't work like that.

When it comes to the question of political tolerance, it seems the word has a more specific connotation. It doesn't have to do with personal annoyingness, but with moral disapproval. In discussions of politics, when someone is called intolerant, it seems to involve their attitudes about right and wrong more than whether they are just annoyed. If you are in a restaurant and someone is talking loudly, and you ask them to be quiet, you aren't being intolerant. Or are you? And anyway, isn't that a moral issue? Is having respect for the other diners a moral issue?

Hmm. Maybe this issue is even more complicated than I thought. I don't think I would say that the person who asks a loud diner to be quiet is intolerant, but in a sense they are. They are not tolerating obnoxious behavior. But then again, why should we tolerate obnoxious behavior? And is being obnoxious also being immoral? When I really think about it, if one group of large men were so loud that other diners couldn't even converse, and no one said anything, I think that would be wrong. Certainly the owner of the restaurant should say something, and he would have the responsibility to do just that. The owner of the restaurant may be acting purely for his own financial benefit, but wouldn't it be the responsibility of anyone in the room as well. Or are we just supposed to ignore brutish behavior? Are we supposed to tolerate it?

I'm pretty sure that if no one said anything, it would be because of cowardice, not out of any sense that we are supposed to tolerate anything. If I were stronger, in any sense, than the disrespectful talkers, I would actually think I had a moral responsibility to the other people in the room to get the loud talkers to speak more quietly, even if I was dining alone and listening to my own mp3 player. Does that make me intolerant? If so, I think I should be intolerant. And so should you.

Perhaps intolerance is more about one's approach. To assume that the loud talkers are boors and irresponsible might be hasty. Perhaps they are unaware of the fact that their conversation precludes anyone else in the room from communicating. To just snarl at them, and shout that they "better keep it down, or else!" Maybe that would be intolerant. But tolerance would allow us to approach calmly and inform them of how loud they are, and kindly ask them to refrain from talking so loudly.

Only, I don't think that's tolerance. That's just good manners, and respect, and perhaps a few other things, including prudence. I don't see how it is tolerance. To allow someone to continue doing something of which I disapprove—that's tolerance. Or to stay in the same room with them, or, not to use whatever power I can muster to stop them or get them to leave—isn't that tolerance?

If that's the case, I can't help asking why on Earth anyone would want to be tolerant? If I asked a loud group to be more quiet in respect of other patrons, and they just refused, what should I do? Just tolerate it? Or should I get someone with more power to do something about it. I would ask the manager or owner of the restaurant, who presumably has the power to throw them out. If they refused the manager's request, and refused to leave, he would call either security, or the police, and they would use their power to get the group to either be quiet, or, as it would probably be too late at that point, would arrest them. Notice how we always look to someone stronger to help us enforce our ideas of what is right and good. Thankfully, people who are strong and have power often use it to help people who are weaker.

I'm glad that in our society we don't tolerate a whole bunch of things, even though sometimes Democrats make me feel guilty that I do. But maybe I shouldn't be feeling guilty after all.

What I think I'm figuring out is that intolerance is not necessarily a bad thing. Thus, a charge of intolerance is at best incomplete, and at worst a compliment (isn't it weird to phrase it that way?). But is there any case where it can be said to be good to be tolerant? There has to be, right?

Of course, there is. It is not always appropriate to use power, either one's own, or someone one knows, or governmental power, for that matter, to eliminate behavior which one finds immoral, or of which one disapproves in some other way. The importance of tolerance really arises when we realize that some of the things we do are disapproved of by others. In those situations, we certainly don't want them to use power against us to make us cease our behavior, whatever it is (or do we?). When we live in a pluralistic society, it is inevitable that there will be disagreements about what is morally right and wrong, or appropriate over a whole range of ethical concerns, even loosely ethical concerns.

If I am a woman, and I decide to have my hair cut short, would anyone call it unethical? Probably not, although many people would think it to be inappropriate for some reason. Perhaps because it blurs the line between male and female, which they think is important to maintain. Perhaps they just think it is not attractive, and they hate to see people making themselves less attractive, especially women.

Now, what would a tolerant person who disapproved of a woman's short haircut do? It seems to me they would still be friends with that person. They probably wouldn't make fun of that person. I don't think they would run that person out of town, and they wouldn't have the government, or other people in power, punish her, or take her freedom away in any sense.

Would they tell her that they didn't like her hair and thought it was inappropriate? I'm not sure about that one, but I tend to think that they should still tell her that they think her haircut is inappropriate. They could be as nice as possible about it, but I think it would be worse if they just remained silent and didn't express their disapproval. Maybe I think they don't need to express it, necessarily, but for us to put pressure on them to keep their disapproval to themselves, that I think would be very wrong. In fact, that would be intolerant on our parts, as far as I can tell.

Keep in mind that if I thought that her short hair looked good and was perfectly appropriate, then there would be no question of tolerance. I like it. I can't "tolerate" it, by definition.

As I think back to when I discussed ethical issues, it seems to me that there are a lot of things which conservatives believe are immoral, but which they have not tried to make illegal. In fact, they have gone along with allowing things in our society which they believe are horribly wrong. Homosexuality, for instance. There's also premarital sex, pornography, contraceptives (for some), violence on TV. Even when they oppose violence on TV, it's only on broadcast television. They are still committed to allowing grown adults to watch whatever they want on their own, at least generally speaking.

It is true that conservatives tend to think that many activities are immoral which leftists do not think are immoral, such as most of the things I just mentioned. So, leftists cannot "tolerate" these things the way conservatives can, and do. Overall, it's pretty clear to me that conservatives are overwhelmingly tolerant.

What about leftists? Are they tolerant? They are certainly more welcoming of people who have traditionally been marginalized, but I don't see how that makes them more tolerant. They have a different viewpoint about what is moral, and in some ways, their morality is more open or more accepting. This may be true, but I just don't think that "tolerance" is the right word for that. Yet, it is a neat rhetorical trick to pretend that it does.

In fact, in order to determine how tolerant leftists and Democrats are, don't we have to ask what activities *they* find to be immoral, and consider how comfortable they are in using power to exterminate those activities? When we consider it this way, Democrats fail miserably. Think about minimum wage, sexual harassment legislation, Indian-named mascots, political correctness, and a whole host of other issues. It seems to me that whatever it is that leftists find immoral, they try to use government to get rid of it. They punish it and look down on it, they ridicule and excoriate those who engage in it.

If you can find one thing that leftists find immoral or even disapprove of, yet they are not trying to stamp out using force, in particular the force of government, please let me know. Seriously. Perhaps I just haven't thought of it.

Even if you can think of something I haven't, it is still clear that my conclusion is true. Democrats are more intolerant than Republicans, in any real sense of "intolerant". Democrats don't tolerate homosexuality, they value it. They don't tolerate premarital sex, they absolutely revel in it. Perhaps one can argue that Democrats don't have to tolerate as much, because they have a less strict moral code, but that is exactly my point. They think that many things, things which conservatives think are immoral, are morally permissible, and so their moral code itself, perhaps, is more tolerant, but even here the word is not quite right.

Democrats don't despise the actions of homosexuals, so they can't tolerate them. But a person who finds homosexuality immoral, that person can tolerate homosexuals. I'm not making a judgment here about who is right or wrong morally, I'm just pointing out that only conservatives, more precisely only those who believe homosexuality is immoral, can be "tolerant" of homosexuality or homosexuals. Furthermore, voicing one's disapproval of homosexuality would not, if my earlier analogy is apt, make a person intolerant, depending on the way that disapproval is expressed.

Examples of Actual Intolerance

Attentive readers may realize that I haven't argued that Democrats are intolerant, but only that they fail to be tolerant, technically speaking. Now, I want to close that inferential gap.

I have always found myself at deep odds with the community in which I find myself. I'm not sure if it's some masochistic tendency in me, or it's just that my particular worldview combines concepts which are unlikely to be combined by most people. When I was growing up, everyone around me believed in God. I didn't. When I was a little older and was at a place where I was willing to discuss my lack of faith with others, I never felt attacked, or belittled. All I felt was concern for my well-being.

Today, I am a professor of philosophy. When it comes to atheism, I've got that around me in spades. I know of only one colleague in sociology who openly expresses her belief in God. But now I have a different problem.

I consider myself a liberal. To me, that means I think people should be generally free to do whatever they deem appropriate, unless they are directly interfering in someone else's life, or violating someone else's right to not be coerced. You've already seen a lot of my views, but they are not "liberal" in the way the word is generally used in America today. Yet, most of my colleagues are "liberal" in that sense.

Most of my colleagues do not know my views, and I believe that I would not be welcomed among them if they did. Perhaps the fault is mine, and I don't have enough faith in them, but in the few instances where I have let my guard down, the results have not encouraged me to be more open.

There was one case in particular. At one of the colleges where I sometimes teach, there is a wall near a faculty copy machine which is dedicated to "free speech". The faculty and administration haven't always gotten along, so they used the wall mostly to vent against the administration, sometimes in ways I considered rather childish. In any case, the closer I looked at the wall, the more I saw that it was really only left-wing views which were expressed. I should say left-wing to radical left-wing. I started to get a funny feeling. Either no one around me shared any of my political views, or else none of them had the courage to post anything on the wall of free speech. It didn't really seem like free speech after all.

Or maybe I was truly the only one who had any doubts at all about left-wing political ideology. I wouldn't call myself a conservative, but maybe there were absolutely no conservatives at the college. I started to think that was an even bigger problem.

So, partly out of a desire to spark debate, and partly to encourage any conservatives on campus, I made a move: I posted a comment. It was something about my fear that if I posted anything which didn't march in lockstep with "liberal" political ideology, I would be ostracized by the community.

I did get a few comments back, as I attached my name to the comment. They were mostly about how anyone should feel free to post anything they wanted. I even saw a colleague in the copy room later, and he assured me that there *were* comments by every ideology already on display.

So, I challenged him to find one. We were standing right in front of it, after all. He pointed to a flyer, and said "See, there's one right there which is about religion." I don't remember his exact words, but my challenge was to find something which represented a view which couldn't be labeled "liberal". I took a closer look. The flyer in question was a series of images. The first one, an egg, had the label "This is your brain." The second one said "This is religion." It was a frying pan. The last one was the egg frying in the pan. It, predictably, said "This is your brain on religion." It was a creative spoof on the commercials decrying drug use, and in a long genre of anti-religious argument comparing religion to drugs.

I'm not saying that there was no point to the flyer, I'm just saying it was not in any way, shape, or form conservative. And I couldn't imagine how anyone could even perceive it as being that way. I smiled, said nothing, and left. I didn't want to get in a loud argument, especially with students around. After all, as a part-timer, I am dependent on the whims of my colleagues whether I will have continued employment.

There was nothing on the wall which even hinted at anything like a diverse political ideology. Isn't that odd? On a college campus, where the diversity of ideas is constantly triumphed? Let me add that I posted a few other things over the next few months. Without exception, everything I posted was pulled off the wall within a week. One had some nasty comments written on it before it was taken down, although I should mention that students could easily have access there, so I can't say it was a faculty member. I should also say that I tried to ensure that my comments were respectful and I bent over backwards to only question leftist viewpoints, and not just assert my own beliefs, and I still got that kind of reaction.

At another college, I was in the mail room running scantrons, and two other colleagues were discussing healthcare. They were bemoaning the fact that we didn't have universal healthcare in our country. I tried to stay out of it. Eventually, one professor got around to saying something like "Everyone believes that people have a right to healthcare." I couldn't remain silent anymore.

"I don't."

The look on her face was hard to describe. It was as if she just saw a chicken give birth to a live snake. There was certainly surprise and shock, but also a tinge of disgust or horror. Her mouth opened, and she searched for words which wouldn't come.

I think she might have eventually muttered, "Really?", and I tried to explain the difference between a right construed negatively and a right construed positively, but I didn't really have the time.

At another college, during a department meeting, another colleague was energetically explaining about how she does everything she can so as to not make her students uncomfortable. Oh, except for Conservative Christian Republicans. But they deserved it.

Now, I have seen colleagues step up to defend the slightest insult aimed at homosexuals, minorities, or women, but no one said the tiniest thing. In fact, there was a bit of a giggle in the room. I just wondered how they would react if I said that I tried to make homosexuals feel bad. Even if I said it in jest.

I've heard similar comments directed at Christians from faculty members at some of my other colleges. If intolerance is using one's power over someone else to suppress that of which one disapproves, then these instances would be perfect examples of intolerance. And they displayed the sort of intolerance such as I had never witnessed by anyone on the right side of the political spectrum, at least in person.

Perhaps people on the right don't feel so comfortable around me, such that they let their guard down enough to let their true selves shine through. But I tend to doubt it. I have known some rather conservative people well. I would say that some of them knew me well enough to know that I have a pretty thick skin, and would be tolerant of them if they did say anything racist, and yet they still haven't said anything. The one person I know who may have said anything truly racist was my late grandmother, and she was a lifelong Democrat.

One might think I am generalizing a little too hastily, but professors are supposed to be the paradigm of tolerance. I think it is clear that intolerance exists in academia, at least on the left wing. I have also seen numerous examples of intolerance in left-wing magazines and in other sources. As I have already argued, leftists are much more likely than conservatives to force their moral perspective on others, which is textbook intolerance. Democrats and those on the left wing are not only intolerant, but in my experience, they are even more intolerant than hardcore conservative Republicans.

Tolerance and Objective Moral Norms

It seems to me that one reason leftists portray conservatives as intolerant (incorrectly, I have argued), is that many conservatives, especially Christian ones, are unabashedly objective in their moral view. They believe that right is right, and wrong is wrong. I think Democrats tend to use the rhetoric of relativism to condemn conservatives as intolerant and wrong, which not only makes morality less important and respected, but utterly hypocritical, as Democrats are the first to appeal to objective values when it suits them. Before I make my case, let me define what objective morality is.

Consider this statement: "The Earth is spherical in shape". We call this an objective statement. It means that it is about a factual matter, and since it is true we call it a fact. The opposite statement, "The Earth is flat", is also an objective statement, since it is about a factual matter. Since it is false, though, we don't call it a fact.

The thing about objective statements is that we think they are true in a way that precludes conflicting statements from being true. So, if "The Earth is round" is true, and "The Earth is flat" conflicts with it, then the statement "The Earth is flat" must be false. What follows from this is that when two people disagree about an objective matter, one of them must be wrong.

Now, consider the statement "Broccoli is delicious." Many people, including me, would say that this statement is true. But we would also recognize that many people would say that it is false. Yet, would anyone say that one group of people must be right and the other must be wrong? I would hope not. The statement "Broccoli is delicious" is not an objective statement. Its truth or falsity depends on one's state of mind or one's point of view. It is possible for the statement to be true from one individual's perspective, but false for another. We call this type of statement "subjective".

Just for you to get a sense of whether you understand the distinction, try to say what this statement is: "The Loch Ness Monster exists." Would you classify it as objective, or subjective?

Many people approach it this way: "Lots of people disagree about whether the Loch Ness monster exists. If I agree with one side, then the other side will get really upset, so I better just play it safe. I'll split the difference, and just say that the question is subjective. That way, everyone can be right, and no one will be mad at me."

Wrong. I'll be mad at you. I hate it when people say things that are clearly wrong just for the sake of political correctness. If you thought the statement was subjective, maybe you didn't go through such an extensive thought process, but that would just make it worse. In that case you have absorbed political correctness so extensively into your belief structure that you instinctively give obviously wrong answers, without even thinking. That is not only a problem, it's scary.

Maybe it's not political correctness, but then tell me what it is. The statement "The Loch Ness Monster exists" is clearly an objective statement. I know that something like half of my students think that the statement is subjective even after I explain the distinction. Something has to explain this.

If you still need convincing, think again about an objective statement. It is not objective because everyone agrees upon its truth. In fact, there may be subjective statements upon which everyone agrees. "Water is usually refreshing." Would anyone disagree? It's still a subjective statement.

A statement is objective because its truth does not depend on what someone thinks. My thoughts alone cannot make the Loch Ness Monster exist, or not exist. It exists or fails to exist independently of what I or anyone else believes. We can, of course, get into epistemological questions about how to figure out the truth about any objective statement, but whatever we decide on there, I think we must all agree that the statement itself is objective.

Every time I explain these things to one of my classes, I am always astounded that so many students have a hard time understanding it. Students have been pushed so far over to the subjectivist side, that it's hard to understand why they are in college at all. The basic underlying principle which organizes all universities is that there are numerous objective truths about the world, even in regard to controversial issues. Especially in regard to contentious issues. Unfortunately, students rarely see the contentious phases of research. The Heliocentric system did not slip in one day, with everyone waking up recognizing that it was self-evident. It took many decades of contentious debate before scholars began to reach anything approaching a universal consensus.

Think about it. Every opinion about a subjective matter is as good as any other. If colleges only dealt in subjective matters, then any one sitting on the street with no education would have just as good an opinion as a professor who had studied an issue for thirty years of his life. Does anyone want to defend that position?

Again, my only question is why students are so tilted to understanding the world as a subjective one. Someone must be pushing it on them. It could be their parents, but counterintuitively, I think it is their teachers. Their teachers should be the first ones pushing an objective picture on them. If one truly thought the world was purely subjective, they would have to think that any exam I made would be purely an exercise in me trying to force my students to accept my version of a subjective world. It would be like me trying to force them to tell me on a test that broccoli is delicious, whether they thought so or not.

So, of course, there is objectivity in the world, at least when it comes to certain areas. The next issue is the one which causes more dispute, and it is the one which I really want to discuss.

My next question is this: Is the statement "Murder is wrong" an objective or a subjective statement? Answer now in your head.

If my readers are anything like my students, then I suspect 90 to 99% of you answered that morality and statements making moral judgments are subjective. I would be very happy if it weren't that high, but if so, I would still have to ask why so many young people are indoctrinated with the idea that morality is subjective. You cannot get that kind of agreement without either indoctrination, or very careful analysis on an issue that is at least partly objective, and it's clear that my students haven't done much careful analysis.

The confusion in this area in our society is rampant, and it is somewhat discouraging. The position that morality is not objective leads to all sorts of confusions and contradictions that it is much easier to cover up. So, it leads to even more and more confusion.

For example, people in our culture think that legality and morality are two completely separate concepts. This misconception is completely bizarre to me. Is killing someone wrong? Yes, it is. And that is why it is illegal, and should be illegal. Some philosophers like to think that political obligation can be founded on pure rationality using some kind of contract theory, but as David Hume the philosopher argued long ago, even the demand to follow through on a contract is a moral demand.

The idea that something is wrong *because* it is illegal turns things exactly on their head, but I think it is the way many, if not most, Americans think. And I blame this on the fact that so many of them have been raised in a culture where moral objectivism is rejected.

If one is truly a subjectivist, then I don't see how any laws would be justified. In a morally subjectivist world, everything that we think is criminally wrong, including murder, torture, stealing, assault, rape, and more, are really just statements of taste. They would be exactly analogous to the claim that broccoli tastes great. Imagine someone trying to pass a law that said that every American had to eat broccoli once a week and like it. If morality is subjective, then what right would we have to force anyone to abide by any moral viewpoint. Sure, we as the majority might be able to use force to coerce people to do whatever we want them to do or refrain from doing, but that is a far cry from justifying that coercion.

Furthermore, if all moral restrictions are in this same boat, then accepting that any law is justified also implies that no laws are unjust. After all, if the majority can force its moral preferences on the minority, and its moral preferences are purely subjective, then there is no way to draw a line demarcating when government crosses into injustice. Basically, a subjectivist would have no way to condemn his government in such a way that the government should refrain from what it is doing. If the government says it likes to put black people to death for murder, but not white people, then me arguing that they shouldn't is like me saying that they shouldn't like vanilla ice cream.

Cultural Relativism is no Better than Subjectivism

I don't see how anyone could consistently accept pure subjectivism, at least not without accepting pure totalitarianism. Only a tyrannical dictator or group would assert that it had the right to force its emotional whims on everyone else in society. Fortunately, almost nobody does. Not even Democrats. But many people still seem to reject moral objectivism. One possible middle ground is called relativism, or cultural relativism. It holds that we do fall under moral obligations, but those moral obligations are culture bound, meaning that they can only apply to people inside one culture. According to this view, all cross-cultural evaluations are meaningless. It is not possible for a person in one culture to judge anyone in a different culture. It follows from this that there is no objective way to rank societies, such that one society is morally better in any objective sort of way.

Keep in mind that if morality is objective, it is possible to judge societies, by holding them up to that objective moral code. On this point of view, it is possible to say that one society is bad, or worse than another one. It is possible to condemn other societies in a meaningful, coherent way.

This aspect of objectivism seems to be the sticking point for many leftists. They really have a hard time with it, thinking that it is intolerant, and that it justifies all sorts of neo-imperialism and colonialism. They have, through indoctrination in early school years, imposed this view on millions of young people. Yet, the consequences of relativism are so contrary to some pretty basic ideas, as well as inconsistent with much of leftist political propaganda that it disturbs me that the conflict goes so unnoticed.

What I really think has happened is that in areas where leftists think actions are morally acceptable while others have a different view, they have pushed a relativist line, but for those actions which they think are immoral, they will in their rhetoric, if not explicitly, accept objectivism. Conservatives, on the other hand, generally insist on objectivity even in areas where their morality conflicts with the view of the majority.

I should first outline some of the basic problems with relativism, and then focus on problems specific to the American left. One of the simplest problems is that relativism ties morality to whatever the people in power in society say it is (although, maybe this is specifically a problem for leftists, who often rail about unequal power relations in society). If morality is equated to whatever each culture says it is, then the people who have power in each culture, those who have authority or political, social, economic power, they are the ones who will set the rules. After all, no one thinks that people who have no power are able to affect the moral code within any society. I don't know about anyone else, but I can't accept a theory of morality which grants to powerful people the ability to judge every aspect of morality.

There is also the problem of how we find out what actually is right or wrong. How do we decide whether a particular action is morally prohibited? I think that we should reason through our beliefs in some way, which presupposes that there can be reasons to justify actions, which reasons, I believe, are objectively available.

Consider what a relativist should do to decide whether something is morally wrong; he should consult the keepers of the code. He should find those people entrusted with deciding what the culture says about morality, and simply ask them. Their answer will be unquestionable. There is no way to question it, at least not under relativism. Of course, one might have to figure out who they are first. And frankly, in a society like ours, perhaps even that is impossible. Who sets our moral code as a society? There are lots of possibilities, although none of them good. Perhaps we should turn to Hollywood. Movies and television probably affect the moral views of people more than anything else. Does anyone think we should simply consult Hollywood in order to figure out what's right? That's a shame. Even if one did, there is no unanimity among people in Hollywood about what's right.

Who is it that actually shapes our morality? Our parents. Our teachers? Should we simply consult them, and let them tell us what is right and wrong. I know some parents would appreciate if their children just accepted their word on moral issues, but I'm not one of them. Besides, even if this approach worked for each individual, it wouldn't work for us as a group. In our culture, our parents have wildly different views about what counts as right or wrong. Our teachers wouldn't be much better.

Perhaps we can just say that our government tells us what's right. More specifically, we could say that law tells us what is right or wrong. I suspect that many leftists will turn to this view in some measure. It seems like it might be the only one they would have available that made any kind of sense. After all, isn't that why each person gets one vote? That way, everyone has some say in what counts as legal and thus moral, taking away the power differential that exists in non-Democratic societies.

This consideration will bring out another real problem for any theory of relativism. Are we really going to take it that whatever the law says *is* by definition morally right (or wrong)? If so, then it would be by definition wrong to criticize any law. If what the law says is by definition morally good, then how on Earth could anyone criticize, or even question it? It would be like a fundamentalist Christian criticizing what the Bible says.

It seems to me that leftists are often the first ones, perhaps often too hastily, to condemn laws. Think of the Patriot Act. Think of capital punishment. Think of anti-sodomy laws. Leftists criticize laws all the time. Thirty years ago, leftists fought against laws against abortion. If everything that was illegal was in fact immoral, then before Roe vs. Wade, abortion was immoral. So, how could anyone disagree? The answer is that you couldn't, if you were truly a relativist who thought that law defined morality. You could, however, if you had an objective view of morality.

If you believe that a law can be unjust, then you must believe that there is some standard for judging the rightness of laws which is higher than the law itself. Morality and justice cannot then be settled by appealing directly to the law.

I could see two approaches here. One is to say that we can declare a law to be unjust when it conflicts with the Constitution. It is certain that this is a reason which people will in fact use. Many people, both on the left and right, when they believe a law to be unjust, will say it is unjust because the law violates our Constitution. I can't see how this answer will work for a cultural relativist. It seems to suppose that a document written over two hundred years ago captures our moral principles better than the current legislature does. Or else it imbues our Constitution with some magical power to command us like the Bible does. Or both.

Furthermore, it just pushes back the issue. Can we ever consider any aspect of the Constitution unjust? It seems like we might want to, especially if we decide to amend it. I don't hear criticism of the Electoral College coming from the right. But if the left is condemning the Electoral College, then they think they must have a higher standard for right and wrong than the Constitution itself.

You see, I respect and revere the Constitution, but that is only because I believe it captures objective truths. I measure it against what I take to be objectively right or just, and I think it meets my standards pretty well. Not that we currently adhere to it all that well, but that's another story.

So, if leftists are adopting relativism, as many explicitly claim, and others will implicitly adopt it rhetorically, and they are still willing to call a law unjust, the only other source for a higher authority I can think of is the opinion of the majority. On this view, we can reject a law as unjust or immoral, when it goes against what the majority wants. On this view, the culture's morality is simply expressed by what the majority wants, and there is no higher authority.

Unfortunately, I don't see how this view will square with the actual practice of most leftists. Leftists routinely ignore what the majority wants when it comes to deciding the justness of laws. A majority of Americans want the pledge to include "under God", for example. For a relativist, then, anyone who wanted to remove those words would, by definition, be adopting an immoral view. So would anyone who put forward a view that was not shared by the majority of people. On this view, it seems to me that anyone who actively opposes capital punishment, since they are in the minority, is trying to move the country toward an immoral position.

If the ultimate standard for deciding what is right and wrong is the majority, then no other argument or justification would really matter. Why make any argument at all? The only way to settle an issue of morals would be to take a poll. And anyone who tries to convince another person because of some reason would have fundamentally misunderstood what ethics was. The only reason, on this view, that an act could be morally wrong is that the majority of people think it is wrong. So, if everyone adopted relativism, with the majority of people defining the morals of the culture, then there would be no basis to convince anyone that something was moral or immoral other than arguing that the majority of people think that it is. On this view, every legitimate reason for an act being immoral is simply a fallacious *ad populum* argument.

How could any leftist oppose torture? An appeal to the Geneva Convention? How could some document created by a transnational committee define the morality of *our* culture? I can't see that being accepted by a relativist. In fact, the only argument available to a majoritarian relativist would be to say that the majority of people oppose it. Number one, this is not the argument most leftists make, and number two, it is not clear that the majority of American are opposed to torture, at least not in all circumstances.

How about the Bible? Maybe we should just consult the Bible to settle our moral issues. If one considers that a strong majority of Americans revere that book, and consider it the word of God, I'd say it has a better chance of defining the moral code in our culture than even the Constitution. I'd like to see a leftist relativist arguing for the Bible as the ultimate determiner of American moral culture. Really. That would be interesting.

One other idea is just that a minority of Americans are the arbiters of what should be right and wrong in our society. We should just defer judgment to some small group of very intelligent people, and they can then tell us when a law is just or unjust. In essence, we can say that some small group of no doubt academic scholars just knows the morality of America in virtue of their pure and advanced intellectual prowess, and they know it better than the majority of Americans do.

Only, ceding that our American morality is simply known by some minority group of intellectuals, is the worst form of totalitarianism. It is precisely this view that has led to nearly all of the horrible tragedies of the twentieth century, including the Holocaust. Even if we got lucky and our oligarchy ended up being more enlightened than all those of the past, I would still argue that to cede our capacity for making judgments to any group of people is to abdicate our individual responsibility. Each of us has the right and the duty to use our moral intellect as diligently as we can in order to figure out what we think is right and wrong.

Any form of cultural relativism, when paired with the coercive authority of the state is going to run into the same problem. The idea of forcing relativistic morality on others is akin to totalitarianism. If morality is just whatever some group says that it is, and then they get to, by virtue of the power the group maintains, punish me for violating their wishes, then governmental power becomes nothing more than the strongest bully bullying everyone else. What justifies us forcing every individual in the country to follow our moral code, if our moral code is just what some group of us want it to be.

It makes sense to me to force people to follow a moral code and punish them for violating it, precisely and only because morality is objective in some regard.

Relativists Cannot Believe in Human Rights

If you haven't followed my argument so far, or perhaps you still have doubts about how cogent it is, let me say one further thing. Leftists constantly talk about human rights. They fight for human rights around the globe. For instance, they assert that the human rights of ten year old children around the world means they should not have to work in sweatshops. Now, if these leftists truly were relativistic, then they wouldn't go imposing their views on people in different countries. After all, in those countries, child labor may be considered culturally acceptable.

If you don't see it yet, let me make it clear.

If one is a relativist, one cannot believe in human rights. A human right is a right a human being has simply in virtue of being a human, but if all morality depends on one's individual culture, then one couldn't consistently believe in human rights.

If you believe in human rights, then you must believe in objective morality. As I think I have made clear, I don't object to Democrats because they accept the objectivity of morality, although I might disagree about exactly what that objective morality is. I reject Democrats because they pretend to be relativistic, and in fact ridicule anyone who presents an objectivist standpoint. I reject the Democratic picture of the world because it is a deeply inconsistent one riddled with double standards. They will condemn objective morality whenever it is put forward by a Right-winger as if it is the most backward, primitive view, and yet many of their policies depend upon objectivism. Democrats tend to be blissfully unaware of their own blatant hypocrisy.

That's one reason I'm not a Democrat.

Final Thoughts

I am proudly a moral objectivist. I believe that there is a right and wrong, and that it holds in some regard for every human being, and indeed for every self-conscious rational being with free will throughout the universe. I will not give up my belief in human rights for some trendy philosophy which is only held by people who inconsistently say they support human rights, when their very theory would make human rights impossible.

My views on what is moral or immoral may differ with yours, which is partly why I advocate a political philosophy which allows people to be immoral in many respects, from my point of view. This is why I will tolerate in my society many forms of behavior which I believe are immoral.

In my experience, Democrats rarely tolerate behavior which they believe is immoral. As I said, they may think that fewer kinds of behavior are immoral, but that just gives them fewer opportunities to be tolerant.

As soon as Democrats generally recognize that 1) They do accept an objective morality, 2) They should be tolerant of divergent moralities and viewpoints, and 3) Cultural Relativism is only consistent with a totalitarian political philosophy, then there will be three fewer impediments standing in my way to becoming one of them.

CHAPTER EIGHT

"The Cup is Half Empty, and Rich, White Men Drink It All Anyway"

Men of integrity, by their very existence, rekindle the belief that as a people we can live above the level of moral squalor. We need that belief; a cynical community is a corrupt community.

—John W. Gardner

I interact with students between the ages of eighteen and twenty-five on nearly a daily basis. I think most of them are somewhat hopeful about their own future, and believe that their personal lives will be decent, if not successful. But when I talk to them about anyone in a position of authority (except for teachers), they seem to take a routinely negative and cynical view.

Mention the word "corporation", and many of them will grimace. Perhaps I exaggerate, but I have seen an unhealthy cynicism in far too many students for me to be nonchalant about it. Students are practically eager to think the worst about any person in any of the following categories: Corporate executive, politician, conservative, rich person, most everyone else in authority. The only people who have power which don't elicit immediately cynical reactions from students are teachers. Teachers seem to be universally respected. At least about as universal as one can get with any generalization over human beings. And I shouldn't forget one other group: Democratic Presidents and Presidential nominees.

Students will readily, without any prompting by me, assign the worst motives to anyone in any of the categories mentioned above. The picture students have of these people is a monstrous caricature. They are more than willing to look at criminals and others with compassionate, understanding eyes, and will offer excuses and attempted reasons for why poor people commit crimes. But it is a rare student who will offer any kind of compassion for a rich person who commits a crime. They will never see rich people or politicians as being complex people with conflicting values and difficult decisions to make.

I suppose you can disagree with my experience, but I have to base my decisions on my experiences, and generalize carefully and appropriately. Even if I am right about my conclusions, however, we can still ask why students are so cynical. I think I have a pretty good idea of the cause.

How is it that teachers escape the scorn of students? I submit that it is because teachers are setting the bounds of the student's responses. It is teachers themselves that elicit the cynical responses of students toward authority figures, but teachers are careful not to allow that skepticism to reflect back on them. When you are the one dictating the tenor of the conversation, it is pretty easy to bring about exactly this double standard in students.

Just praise teachers over and over, and talk about how difficult their job is, and how they battle through conflicting values, on the one hand, and scorn every other authority figure on the other. Never ask in a balanced way what the motivations are for a company to move its production overseas. Just say that the selfish bastards who run the company don't give a crap about the Americans who lose their jobs, and just want to get as much money as they can. Even if it were true, which I do not believe it generally is, there is still a way to discuss it that makes them sound responsible. For example, they might be presented as interested in the long-term financial stability of the company, and that's just off the top of my head. Even if a company owner or CEO is just trying to maximize his own personal profit, is it the job of schools to push the view that they are acting immorally?

I am aware that not all teachers are Democrats. But the majority of them are, especially in the liberal arts and social sciences, and they seem to be more likely to express their political views to students. Add to this the fact that many grade and high school teachers majored in liberal arts. I may be generalizing here, but given that most Democrats are leftists, it's reasonable to conclude that most teachers are leftists. This generalization also matches my experience.

So, given that many teachers are leftists, and that leftists tend to lean toward socialism, which makes them antagonistic to capitalism, given that many teachers came out of the sixties and the aftermath of Nixon's resignation or the mentality that authority is always to be dismissed or attacked, given that many teachers have a negative attitude toward authority and big business, and given that many young people have a similar attitude, given all that, it seems to me that the only reasonable explanation is that teachers are imbuing students with this cynical, negative attitude toward certain kinds of authority.

I can't stress enough that I am giving you my impression, and perhaps I have overgeneralized a bit, but the reaction people have to my words will in part confirm or deny my impressions. Regardless, I would also hope that you take a step back and honestly reflect a little. Observe Democrats speaking while engaging that critical aspect of your mind, and perhaps you will find that I am right, even if your first impression is that I am speaking nonsense.

Without discussing actual incidents, which would be criticized as anecdotal in any case, and without cataloging hundreds of incidents, let me at least be as specific as I can about the areas where I see Democrats as being overly pessimistic and cynical.

Big Businesses and Business Leaders

The first area on the list has to be big business. Democrats hate big businesses. If you don't believe me, I honestly can't believe that you have ever listened to most Democrats talk about businesses. No objective observer of the last Democratic presidential debate before the 2008 Iowa caucuses could disagree. John Edwards, as he often does, started criticizing big businesses. Every time he said something negative about big businesses, the Democrats who self-identify with the term "Liberal" ratcheted up their approval rating. It was shown right on the screen with a graph.

The same thing would happen when any of the Democrats criticized George Bush, and it's pretty clear that they hated him. In contrast, it seemed to me that when a Democrat criticized another Democrat, the rating dropped. The average Democrat apparently isn't cynical and hating of everything; only certain things get them going.

John Edwards, although he is the paradigmatic example of the left's hatred of corporations, is by no means the only Democratic candidate who criticized them. Nor is it only political candidates who heap scorn on large corporations (that is, except when those large corporations have the word "Union" in their title). Listen to leftists in mainstream media and on talk radio, and it seems that there is a pretty universal hatred of corporations. I'd say that there is universal distrust of them, but among many, if not most, the feeling runs much deeper than distrust.

That Democrats are cynical of big businesses is just a fact, but one can react to this fact in very different ways. One could say that this cynicism is appropriate, and that this is one reason to support the Democratic Party, because it has an appropriate level of cynicism. This would be perfectly rational. One should find the political party which most closely holds the beliefs and attitudes which we think are most appropriate, and join it (or refuse to join one if none of them are close enough). We also prefer that a political party espouses our same values, or supports the same issues we believe in, but these can generally be captured by knowing the beliefs and attitudes of that party.

When I hear someone waxing eloquent (in their mind) advocating this view, namely that big corporations are horrible and the Democratic Party recognizes it, I'm not sure what to think. Here are a few of my jumbled thoughts on the subject.

Corporations do not exist. They are a legal figment of the imagination. There may be good reasons for us to act like corporations are persons in terms of the tax code or for other reasons, and the concept certainly helps to shield people from liability, but they are not a real metaphysical entity. So, there is at least one ambiguity here. Do Democrats hate the legal concept of corporations, or do they hate the people who make up the corporations? There is a kind of reification going on, which I am hoping to clarify. The same thing happens when people talk about government. People speak rhetorically as if it is a person with a mind, but obviously no such thing can be true. Such talk is at best metaphorical. If no real individual person who is a part of the government does anything, then the government doesn't do anything.

The same thing applies to corporations. It is true that psychologically, it might make sense to treat corporations as persons with minds and capable of making decisions, if only to explain people's attitudes toward them, but I find such talk to be dehumanizing. I think it is important, essential, to consider the decisions of a corporation to be made by real people. Yes, it is often in a complex way, not necessarily analogous to the way a single human being makes a decision, but made by groups of human beings nonetheless.

Perhaps most democrats have not even thought about the distinction, which might be so subtle that only philosophers can appreciate it, but this is part of the problem. I don't scorn people who engage in shallow thinking, and that alone would hardly be enough to keep me away from being a Democrat myself. But if that shallow thinking was gravely off or inconsistent, or led to negative consequences, and the person engaging in shallow thinking had power and control over me, that's another issue.

Questioning the existence of corporations as a legal entity is one thing. I am not sure myself why we should allow corporations in our legal system, though I have some ideas. I would be interested in this debate, and am not sure where I would end up. But I have no idea how this issue could inspire the hatred and cynicism I find in so many Democrats. This debate would be a staid affair, involving obscure issues about the arcane structure of the tax code. This is not the sort of thing that would lead people to hate corporations, or to despise their actions.

No, the only explanation is that people actually object to the decisions which are made by most corporations. If there were a corporation which only made decisions of which Democrats approved, I just don't see Democrats condemning it. For example, most unions. So, it seems to me that the objection is over the actual decisions most corporations make, and not the nature of corporations themselves.

Most Democrats think that the people who administrate corporations are bad people. They make decisions to protect their own financial interests, and don't care about the people that get hurt. By listening to their complaints over the years, I have learned that this is the way Democrats in general tend to think. If leaders and candidates in the Democratic party disagree, they certainly don't express it, and many of them, such as John Edwards, stoke the fires of hatred as often as they can.

They picture CEO's and business leaders as heartless, evil-minded bastards who care only about money, and don't deserve what they take. They think they exploit their workers, and would sell them out at the earliest opportunity if they could make a quick buck. Democrats criticize businesses for "outsourcing", which means employing people in other countries to do work for less money than that for which Americans are willing to do the work. Their view is that CEO's do this because they are evil, unpatriotic, soulless, monsters who are willing to take food out of the mouths of children if it means they can continue to sail on their yachts.

I'm pretty sure that if I were in a Democratic Presidential debate, my approval rating would be jumping off the scale right now. Prudent democratic leaders may not state the issue as bluntly as I have, but their rhetoric certainly foments these sorts of opinions in average Democrats.

This is not to say that sometimes CEO's deserve this sort of derision. Sometimes business leaders do criminal things, and sometimes they do stupid or negligent things. But so does every group of people. The question is whether it is right to generalize over all business leaders.

The thing that really disappoints me is how Democrats seem so ready, even eager, to think the worst about any business leader, but then how they bend over backwards to condemn anyone who generalizes over any other group. How often have Democrats insisted that there is no connection between Muslims and terrorists? In some ways, they're right. It is important to consider each individual as an individual, and not to stereotype in careless, inappropriate ways. But that is exactly what they do when it comes to businessmen.

Now, I know the cynical Democrats out there will say I am naïve, but if so, then I'm happy to be. I generally will think positively about people unless I have evidence to the contrary. After all, it is America.

Innocent until proven guilty and all that. I believe that most businessmen are honest. There. I said it.

True, that doesn't mean that they care about people in the way that Democrats think they should, but that seems to me much different than what I'm getting at. Most businessmen think that they are worth the amount of money they are getting, and believe that they are paying people fair wages. They do believe very much that people should be paid different amounts depending on their contribution, as judged by the owners of a business or the administrators they choose, in line with market forces. And they are generally unapologetic about it. And I think that's what drives Democrats crazy.

Democrats don't get worked up like that against any other group of people whom they consider to be criminals. In fact, they generally try to excuse, understand, and justify the admittedly criminal behavior of others. Mumia Abu-Jamal comes to mind.

I am not here debating the merits of any specific cases, and no doubt there are some cases where a forgiving stance is warranted. I'm just pointing out that if there is a case where one political party is pushing for a more clement attitude toward a criminal, it will generally be the Democrats. There will always be exceptions, which are often political cases, such as the Scooter Libby case, and the Compean and Ramos case. But in most cases, when anyone is pushing for leniency and forgiveness, it is Democrats. They are often advising us to take a more sympathetic and understanding view toward criminals.

But there is no sympathy whatsoever granted for CEO's and businessmen. Who is advising people to consider the situation from their point of view? Who tries to calm people's paranoid fears about the wicked businessman who is out to get them? No one. Even Republicans seem reluctant to stand up for him, cowed by the forces of conformity.

So, I think democrats tend to have a simplistic, stereotypical view of business leaders, which is allowed and even encouraged by their leaders. But even if the stereotype is generally true, I still wonder whether the hatred would be justified. Does an unrepentant capitalist deserve to be hated?

Even democrats seem to accept a repentant capitalist. Ted Turner and Warren Buffett readily spring to mind. If you are willing to work hard to get to the top, but then bemoan others who are in the process, telling them how wrong they are, then Democrats will like you. And, oddly, they won't even ask you to give any of your ill-gotten gains away. Is that direct hypocrisy, or hypocrisy by proxy?

But those capitalists who are proud and confident in their philosophical viewpoint, those are the ones who are truly despised.

They are the ones who are truly bringing misery and pain into the world, or so it would seem by the attitudes and words of many Democrats. Isn't the real difference an ideological one? Democrats believe in an equal society without haves and have-nots. They look forward to a radically egalitarian world, where everyone can get what they need, and so there is no excessive suffering. They will say it is unfair for some people to be able to afford, or obtain, health care, while others cannot.

Capitalists have a more individualist outlook. Any individual deserves to get whatever he can convince others to give him, or what he can obtain on his own. American businessmen tend to be unrepentant capitalists. The world they live in is a just world *because* it allows inequality in it. Would the world be nicer, or less harsh, with more economic equality? Perhaps. Probably. But capitalists will say that has nothing to do with justice. Social justice, as it is called, is at best an oxymoron, and probably just gibberish.

I have to say I tend to agree. Whatever my moral impulses are in this regard, I still recognize them as moral impulses. I can't delude myself into thinking that somehow economic matters transcend morality. But that is exactly why I don't think I should be able to force my moral viewpoints on business leaders. If they want to make all the money they can and keep it and hoard it while working their employees tirelessly, then it seems to me that is their choice. I may disagree with it, and I might try to convince them otherwise, but I don't think I have the right to use government to force my view upon them. The second a businessman tries to use the government to make it harder for his competitors to compete against him, that is when I can condemn him.

More to the point here, inasmuch as I might disagree with them about their moral view, I am not going to hate them. I reserve hate for people who truly destroy and hurt people. Those who cause the pain themselves, not those who fail to prevent it. Maybe that is because I do take seriously the distinction between acting and failing to act, but I believe there are good reasons for doing so.

I can find room for hating thieves, murderers, rapists, and those who defraud others. But I can't find room to hate those who deal honestly and competently with others, even if that means they end up extremely rich. It seems to me that many Democrats get that exactly backwards.

It would be one thing if it were just that I disagreed philosophically with Democrats in this area. I could probably overlook that and become a Democrat (if there were enough other reasons to do so), but it seems to me that this attitude can be extremely harmful, especially to young people, as well as people who are on the lower end of the economic spectrum.

Imagine a young person who thinks of the world in these terms: rich people own everything, and they are out to exploit you and use you for their own gain. They don't care about you at all, and they control everything. The only way for you to have a successful life is to bow down to them, and suck up any crumbs they deem to throw in your direction.

Just imagine the life prospects of a young person who absorbs and accepts this kind of rhetoric. Are they going to work hard to try and succeed, or are they more likely to give up, and forget about success? Certainly, there will be people who are pushed on even more by facing such a challenge, but in my experience they will be in the minority.

Wouldn't it be better to present to young people a more balanced, neutral view? One which isn't informed by socialistic, communist values, or disgust for capitalism.

Shouldn't we tell young people that those people who are rich got there for the most part by working hard and saving money. Not always, by any means, but for the most part. They do have power in our society, because people have given it to them, in exchange for giving them something in return. People become rich by figuring out a way to give people what they want for a price they are willing to pay, and doing it over and over and over again. Do they care about you? Who cares? They produce a product for which people are willing to pay them money. That is where they get their money, as well as their power.

Will they share some of their money with you? Absolutely, but not for nothing. They will expect you to do something for them. They will expect that you do a job for them that allows them to make more money. They will pay you as little as they can to keep you working for them. But if you are productive and work hard, you can make a decent amount of money, and if you don't spend it extravagantly, you can live better than 99.99% of all people throughout the history of the planet. If you live frugally, and invest your money, then one day you will be in their position, and can hire people on whatever terms you decide.

This version has dual benefits. One, that it is true. It doesn't sugarcoat anything. I wouldn't want to fall over the horse on the opposite side by presenting an untruthful, but glowingly positive portrayal of businesses. Second, it won't drive many people away from the corporate world. It won't turn many young people so cynical and negative about businesses that they sabotage their own futures.

Patriotism

If leftists and Democrats were cynical only about big businesses, that would be one thing, but they seem hopelessly negative about a whole range of things. They even seem to scoff at people who aren't cynical, thinking them naïve and simple. Here's an exercise. Find a group of leftists and in the middle of a conversation say, "I think American corporations are doing a great job, and they really make me proud." If they don't immediately start cracking up laughing, that's because their heads exploded.

I'm not a big flag-waver myself. I appreciate the American flag mostly because of the values it represents, which is why I am against any attempt to ban burning it. But I don't hang it up in my house or put it on my car. I don't have anything against anyone who does. Yet, some of my leftist colleagues have made fun of people who put flags on their cars. As if they were hicks, who didn't know any better that they were supposed to hate the flag. As if they were too simple and plain to understand that being patriotic was one of the worst things one could be.

That's another thing leftists are cynical about: America and American values. Ask people whether America is the best country on Earth, and see their reaction. If they scoff, you can be almost sure they are on the left. In my experience, if a leftist says that they love America, it's always an America just over the horizon: the America they hope and expect that they can make it. But never America as it is in the present.

Whatever foreign policy America employs, leftists will look at it cynically. If we intervene in the Middle East, America is just a money-grubbing, selfish nation. If we don't intervene, it's because we don't give a crap about the suffering of others. America is called imperialistic by those on the left all the time. It's as if they don't understand what real empire looks like.

Yes America and Americans want to see other countries adopt American ideals and values, absolutely. That's because they are the best values. Freedom and autonomy are essential social values, and it doesn't matter where one lives. To those on the left, attempting to bring about democracy and move a country towards more freedom is seen as imposing American values. If so, then I declare it a good thing to impose American values. After "imposing" American values on Japan, Germany, and South Korea, it seems like those countries are doing pretty well.

But I guess that's a naïve, simplistic view.

Again, the main motivation seems to be an emotional reaction against capitalism. Yes, America wants other countries to be capitalistic, but that is because capitalism is based on freedom. When it comes to economic matters, leftists definitely don't care about freedom. They despise it, because it inexorably leads to inequality.

Money

For similar reasons, leftists are very cynical toward money. The love of money is supposedly the root of all evil. Leftists seem to take that saying literally, much as fundamentalist Christians take the Bible literally (ironic, isn't it).

I would agree that greed is a problem, and can be excessive, but I contend that excessive greed has little to do with money. Somehow, through numerous nuanced and subtle forms of emotional appeals, our children are taught to think that money is a bad thing. Rich people are automatically condemned in this worldview. Again, I think that this is a pessimistic and cynical view that perpetrates harm against the young people who absorb it.

If we gave young people a more neutral or balanced view, then they would be happier and more optimistic about the future. And I think that's a good thing by itself.

I think of money as a place-holder for another person's time. If I want a man to do something for me, something that he doesn't want to do on his own, then I need to give him something to convince him to do it. Whether it is growing my food, producing some product I might want, finding and stocking shampoo that I can use, healing my leg, entertaining me. Whatever it is. I would be happy for him to do it for free, but the I.R.S. might have a problem with that, especially if I do something for him in return.

Now, I could always exchange some of my time for another man's time. As a teacher, I could teach the doctor's children for one hour for every hour that he diagnoses and heals me, but that system seems horribly inefficient. It also would be very difficult to keep track of and considering all the products I want, and the diverse number of people from whom I want them, I'm not sure how it could be done.

Instead, we can use money to keep track of all of this. Instead of giving you my time in exchange for yours, I give you money. Think of it like a simple database, keeping track of every individual exchange of time between men. If we throw in the purchasing of goods and resources, the story may get a little more complicated, but it is basically the same.

It just so happens that some people will give me an hour of their time for a lot less than other people will, for a variety of reasons, all of which are studied by the science of economics. The natural result will be economic inequality, obviously, and this is problematic enough for most leftists. When one recognizes the obvious connection between money and power, leftists become apoplectic.

One definition of power is the ability to get other people to do things for you. On this definition, and probably most others, the more money one has the more power one has. Leftists will argue that this fact leads to an anti-democratic distribution of power. After all, if Democracy is supposed to be one man, one vote, then as long as money affects power in society and we have an unequal distribution of money then there will be an unequal distribution of power. To those on the left, this is an anti-democratic distribution of power.

As a philosopher, I take it as my job to point out alternative ways of thinking about things, ways which most people overlook because of their closed minds, being locked into a certain way of thinking. It seems to me that money is actually the most democratic distribution of power. Every person is given money in proportion to how well they satisfy the desires of other people. Every person gives money to someone else in order to satisfy their desires. So, in one sense people vote with their pocketbook. They give money, and thus power, to people who satisfy their desires, and every individual can distribute his share of power, which he obtains from others according to their wishes or their "vote", to whomever he wants. The only exception to this is government. Taxes must be paid regardless of one's desire satisfaction.

From this perspective, it is legislatures who raise taxes which pervert the democratic distribution of power, for the sole reason that they do not like the way people do in fact distribute power. So, one small minority of people appropriate to themselves the right to alter this perfectly democratically decided allocation of power, and shape it in accordance with their moral vision.

I know there is a lot more to be said here, but I should emphasize again the idea that leftists have a very negative view of money and the role money plays in society, but there is a much healthier and more beneficial view of money that is available and that we should be teaching to our children. Money is power, and it is naturally distributed to those who satisfy desires most efficiently. If they desire to do so, they can factor that consideration in when they decide to give someone money. But they shouldn't hate money, or think it is inherently evil, or that it inevitably leads to corruption or evil.

Money can be used for malicious purpose, just like anything else, in particular other forms of power. Yet we don't condemn natural persuasive power or other natural talents as wrong simply because someone might misuse them. If someone is using money for ill purposes, the best thing we can do is to inform the people who are giving them money. If those people don't agree that they are using the money for ill purposes, then maybe we need to rethink our viewpoint. If we have, and we are confident we are in the right, then we need to do some very careful thinking about what that ill purpose is, and whether we are entitled to use force to stop it.

Governmental and Other Forms of Authority

I can be very cynical toward legislatures, but I think I have good reason for being so. A legislature which arrogates to itself more power that it rightfully deserves is a grave problem. Not only are they doing something inherently wrong, and which goes against my values, but I believe it puts us all at risk. As history shows, when legislatures get out of control, conflict and eventually warfare can be the end result.

A cynical attitude toward coercive power is a healthy one. I have always had problems with authority myself, and buckled under any kind of authority in my youth. I have thought long and hard about all kinds of authority since then, and I have concluded that there are appropriate forms of authority, even coercive authority. I don't know completely yet the contours of that authority, but I have come to realize that some kinds of authority are legitimate, and that as long as groups of people exercising that authority stay within the bounds of that authority, they are doing nothing wrong.

There are some people, however, who are dismissive, or even contemptuous, of all kind of authority. I trace a lot of it back to the sixties, and from what I hear about those days, all authority was mistrusted. Generally speaking one sees it in Democratic circles. For example, instead of political authorities in their commercials, Democrats love to put children. At the last Democratic convention, I believe they put up a twelve year old girl to wax eloquent about the problems in the healthcare system.

The current Democratic zeitgeist has emerged out of a belief system where all authority is corrupt and not to be trusted. Like I said, I can have a healthy skepticism toward government as well as other non-coercive forms of authority myself, and I do support individuals making decisions for themselves. So, I do not place absolute trust in any authority, whether the authority of tradition, the authority of social or cultural leaders, or the authority of government.

But I also do not reject everything traditional simply because it is asserted with the authority of tradition. With the rhetoric I hear from Democrats, I get the sense that they sometimes listen to what the authority of tradition says, and then immediately assert the opposite. It goes along with their tendency toward fadophilia.

Maybe I can put it this way. I think it is absolutely essential to question authority in all shapes and forms. But that doesn't mean we have to be skeptical of that authority. It seems to me that many Democrats, in particular the leaders of the Democratic Party, advocate a more skeptical and not a questioning attitude.

That is until they get power. Democrats seem to switch very quickly to a kowtowing attitude when they think of Democrats in power, and the imposition of Democratic policies. Don't believe me? Just ask a group of Democrats what they think about someone who wants to privatize social security. Social Security is a coercive social policy of which Democrats approve, and in many groups of Democrats, one can get mauled, psychologically at least, for even questioning the Constitutionality of the government forcing each citizen to contribute money without any guarantee that they will get it back.

Another example is welfare. Question the judiciousness of giving out money without any strings attached to anyone who is financially in trouble regardless of how they got there or what decisions they made to get themselves there, and we all know what will happen. Express doubt about whether we should give citizenship to any child born in America regardless of the immigration status of his parents, and one will be immediately tarred and attacked by those on the left.

As long as questioning the government leads one in a leftist direction, Democrats are more than willing to encourage it, but the second someone questions government in a way which would motivate someone toward the political right, they are pounced upon in all sorts of various ways. Democrats seem to have an asymmetric partisan cynicism for government. They are cynical and promote cynicism toward any policy or administration which promotes values with which they disagree, but show no cynicism when the shoe is on the other foot.

Consider Presidents Bush and Clinton. I suspect they are closer in policy than almost anyone today recognizes. There are no doubt some issues upon which they would support different policies, but they seem to agree in large measure on policies as diverse as the war (at least initially), immigration, and free trade. They may have different emphases and support them using slightly different values, but the policies they have enacted and supported are remarkably similar.

Yet, leftists view George Bush with heaps of scorn and cynicism, while they consider Bill Clinton the epitome of prudent government.

Even their cynicism seems to be employed for partisan advantage, instead of being real.

Consider the aftermath of Hurricane Katrina. FEMA was savaged over its failure to save lives in New Orleans. Could it have been that the Federal government did exactly what it has done in every other disaster, but that in those other cases State emergency workers did their jobs? FEMA has no first responders in my understanding, so its main mission is to come in after the fact and help to clean up the mess. From what I understand, they had no experience in dealing with a week long emergency crisis, like the one in New Orleans. Yet, that didn't stop Democrats from trying to take advantage of the entire mess politically. Somehow if the situation had happened under Clinton, which it very well could have, I don't see those deaths being used in a cynical way to undermine the competence of the White House. At least not by Democrats.

Not only was it used to undermine respect for the competence of George Bush's administration, but it was used to stoke racial cynicism as well. When it comes to race relations (I hate that term), Democrats seem to be more cynical today than they were fifty years ago. Democrats push people into believing that everyone is racist, and that most white people would abuse all other minorities, unless, that is, government steps in and prevents them from doing so (and only Democratically run government at that).

Again, it seems to be cynicism employed for the sake of political gain, but maybe that's just me.

Various Other Asymmetric Cynicisms

Democrats also seem very cynical and negative about men, in terms of the differences between men and women. Men are all to be distrusted and the masculine is inevitably portrayed in a negative light. There seems to be no attempt at balance, or at a sophisticated, not to mention sympathetic, understanding or portrayal of masculinity.

Democrats seem also to have an asymmetric cynicism for the media. They are cynical of right leaning media, and are prone to dismissing their arguments as self-motivated and thus illegitimate, whereas they envision leftist sources like the New York Times as being completely noble and objective. This view comports with other aspects of the leftist worldview: people with power and authority, at least if they use it to maintain the status quo, always act from nefarious motives, while the poor and downtrodden (even the phrase begs the question), anyone who stands up to those in authority in any way, they must always be acting for pure, noble reasons, and can never be criticized.

John Edwards, who fought against doctors and hospitals, is to be praised and honored. The fact that he became unbelievably rich by doing so is irrelevant, because he earned his money (supposedly) by fighting the good fight. Nevermind that his actions may have driven doctors out of business and hurt people in the long run. He fought to bring down big business, and that makes him good regardless of the consequences of his actions. (Of course, having an affair on his cancer-stricken wife brought him down in the eyes of most people)

I'd point out the cynicism Democrats have toward Christianity, but I think it's a little obvious. An area where one might not have recognized it is the area of global warming. It is my thesis that the fear of global warming coming out of the left is the direct result of the cynical, negative attitude that leftists have toward humanity in general.

No one knows what will happen in the future, unless it is the simple claim that at some point in the future the average global temperature will be higher than it is now, and that at some point in the future it will be colder than it is now. It is also clear that at the end of the last century and the beginning of this one, there seemed to be an upswing in the average temperature of the Earth.

Those facts are hard to dispute, but if that's what global warming is, it tells us very little about the future. Why is it that Democrats in particular are so apt to think the worst in regard to global warming? Why are they so quick to jump on the bandwagon that human activity is causing the warming, and that it will inevitably be so catastrophic?

Perhaps it is the same thing that made the same leftists jump on the bandwagon in the seventies about an upcoming ice age. Their basic pessimism and negativity. They always seem to think the worst, about practically everything except themselves. In the seventies there was only nature to be pessimistic about. The current scare about the environment adds a new twist: they can blame it on those bad, horrible, uncaring human beings.

It's hard to be cynical about nature (especially when one regards it as the result of uncaring, impersonal forces), and it's even harder to convince others to support the cause and send you money to fight it. But if the cause is human, and it is the result of human apathy and short-sightedness, somehow that cynicism can be parleyed into contributions to your political party.

I wouldn't be so cynical as to say that Democrats lie about global warming just to gain political support. That circumstantial ad hominem is committed far too often by those on the left. All I'm saying is that Democrats are far more likely to overlook possible financial motivations when it is on their side, and to hype financial motivations when it is Republicans advocating policies (Even when Republicans agree with global warming, they are portrayed as being in the pockets of the oil companies and other energy companies). I don't believe that Democratic politicians are reasonable and engage in careful analysis on the issue of global warming, only to realize that there is little evidence supporting it, and then are just lying to people to get them to donate money to the Democratic Party.

I think most supporters of global warming theories do so because they are not thinking carefully and instead roam with the flock, and the flock currently is afraid of what human beings are doing to the planet. Most Democratic politicians truly believe that global warming is a coming catastrophe, on the basis of horrible reasoning, partly because of their predilection toward a negative and cynical attitude about people in general, and that they use their faulty conclusions to scare people to contribute money to the Democratic party. Perhaps it is a subtle distinction.

Ultimately, all of this is one other reason why I'm not a Democrat: I'm not in favor of unbridled, unquestioning optimism, but I'm totally against a universal pessimism.

Divisiveness

Democrats routinely portray Republicans as divisive, and too often uncritical thinkers take that to mean that Democrats are generally in favor of unity. Just as a test, I want to run a few quotes by you, and see if you can pick up on something that really bothers me. Here goes.

Here is a quote of Hillary Clinton from an interview with John Stewart of *The Daily Show* on March 3, 2008. Jon Stewart comments on how he could see any of Hillary Clinton, Barack Obama, or John McCain serving in one another's cabinets, and then expresses his approval of that situation. Afterwards, Hillary Clinton responds:

> "A lot of our problems have nothing to do with Republican or Democrat. We've got to start acting like Americans again and roll up our sleeves and solve our problems, and there are good ideas across the political spectrum. Obviously, I think that the Democrats should have the opportunity to lead again because after George Bush, we

gotta lotta repair work to do. But then there'll be an opportunity to bring the country together."[70]

On May 20th, 2008 in Iowa, after claiming the majority of pledged delegates for the Democratic Party, Barack Obama stated the following:

> "The other side knows they have embraced yesterday's policies, so they will also embrace yesterday's tactics, to try and change the subject. They'll play on our fears and our doubts. They'll try to sow discord and division, to distract us from what matters to you and your future. They can take the low road if they want, but it will not lead this country to a better place."[71]

I suspect some sharp readers caught the complete hypocrisy in Senator Clinton's comments, but I wonder how many saw it in Senator Obama's words. Just to be clear, Senator Clinton seems to be calling for unity, for a leader who will bring the country together to solve our problems. And then she proceeds to bash then-President George Bush. Maybe it's hard to see reality in her circles, but at the time she spoke there were still around 30% of the country who approved of the job President Bush was doing. How the hell is poking a stick in his eye supposed to bring us together? It is obvious that she has no desire to actually bring people together, but to appear to desire to do so in order to cynically manipulate those who do wish for politicians to work together. Yes, she wants to unify Democrats together to defeat Republicans, but I can't help noticing the difference.

If you didn't notice it, Barack Obama did the exact same thing, if only a little more subtly. He never identified anyone's name, but left it as an amorphous "they" for which each listener is able to fill in his favorite bogeyman. While criticizing "the other side" for sowing discord and division, what does Barack Obama think he is doing? What road does Mr. Obama think he is taking when he says such divisive and belittling things about his political opponents? And where are the people who criticized President Bush for polarizing people with his "with us or against us" comment?

Could it be that they support Barack Obama, and that their ideological blinders don't allow them to see clearly?

The truth is that Democrats constantly seem to call for unity and putting aside our differences, while in the same breath beating up on Republicans for their divisiveness. If only we could work together in order to solve our problems, they lament, but those mean Republicans won't let us. What they seem to ignore is that our differences are precisely about what counts as a problem, and what solutions will work, or are acceptable morally. Again, leftist closed-mindedness raises its ugly head. Leftists seem to have a hard time understanding that anyone could see the world in a different way from them. Anyone who sees the world differently, who thinks that government intervention is a more egregious violation of rights than economic inequality, for example, is not just an American with a different view. It is someone with a vile perspective who is dividing us and preventing us from achieving what we all know is best for our country.

Am I dividing us by pointing out the hypocrisy of Hillary Clinton and Barack Obama, among other Democrats? Perhaps. But I think it would be worse if I ignored it altogether. If pointing out what I believe is true in as careful a way as I can divides us, then so be it. I suppose I value truth over harmony. Sue me. At least I am not engaging in the folly of launching careless, distorted assaults against my ideological rivals while at the same time pretending to be very concerned about uniting us all together.

Frankly, I am very interested in uniting all Americans. I want them to unite together and reject the hypocritical and blind hatred which I find in the Democratic Party. As soon as everyone unites behind that common purpose, then one of our problems will be solved, and maybe we can consider a few others.

Democrats Routinely Ignore the Lessons of Literature

I've got another beef with Democrats and the left which I wasn't sure where to add, but seems appropriate to place it here. I am very disturbed by their complete lack of sensitivity and understanding of many of the classics of literature. More than that, I am angered by the complete distortion regarding the point of such works as *1984* and *Animal Farm*.

Many literary works which attack totalitarianism so obviously attack leftist varieties that there is no possibility to distort them. I have in mind works like Arthur Koestler's *Darkness at Noon*, Heinlein's *The Moon is a Harsh Mistress*, and Ayn Rand's novels *Anthem*, *Atlas Shrugged*, and *We the Living*. Leftist reaction to these masterpieces of literature is generally to ignore or dismiss them, and to denigrate them when pressed.

Other works are more subtle, or are written in such a way that they can be interpreted ambiguously when read uncritically. For example, the novel *1984*, by George Orwell, is often praised by leftists. It condemns a system of government that takes away freedom. I think that if you ask most leftists, they would say that Republicans were the target of Orwell's condemnation.

But to any serious readers of the work and of Orwell's other masterful novel *Animal Farm*, Orwell was attacking political systems which took away economic freedom, i.e. communism and socialism. Some individual leftists may argue that they are not socialistic, and that their ideas are not socialistic, but the reason we classify them on the left is precisely because they want to restrict freedom in the economic sphere. The oblivious nature of many leftists in this regard really frightens me. How it is possible to miss the fact that these works are criticizing and attacking one's own totalitarian impulses?

Besides this, leftists are the source of almost all forms of political correctness. Political correctness is the tendency to alter language for ideological purposes. This tendency was one of the principal targets of criticism in *1984*! For someone not to realize this takes a massive amount of contorted thought, on a truly extraordinary level.

A college professor I know who self-describes himself as a convert from staunch leftism was incredulous at the thought that these classics of literature actually targeted leftist ideology. He seemed to think that fact would indicate that teachers had indoctrinated him and other students and completely distorted the point of these novels. I tried to tell him that if he was taught and accepted that Orwell was targeting American conservatives, then he had indeed been misled. Sadly, he is far from alone.

Fahrenheit 451, by Ray Bradbury, condemns government censorship. Leftists will pretend that censorship comes solely from the authoritarian right, but librarians know that the impulse for censorship is equally represented on both sides of the political spectrum. Besides, there are more sinister forms of mind control than outright censorship, which we all should fight against.

Various books and movies condemn societies which are modeled on utopian visions of the left. I believe *The Giver*, by Lois Lowry, is one of these, and I think *Brave New World*, by Aldous Huxley, probably qualifies, although I wish now that I had finished reading it in high school.

I also recently had the pleasure of viewing the movie *Equilibrium* in a viewing shown by the Santiago Canyon College Philosophical Society. In a conversation I had with a committed leftist student after the movie, it was clear that he had underestimated, if not overlooked, the fact that his political views were exactly the ones condemned in the movie. I had to point out that the villains in the movie were advocating his values. He meekly admitted that they were, but still tried to argue that only their methods were faulty, and not their values themselves. As is so often the case, I believe he missed the entire point of the movie.

I never expected it when I first saw the movie, on a plane, I think, but the movie *Coach Carter* is a paean for the individual and for individual decision making and responsibility instead of group responsibility, which is pretty close to an oxymoron. I didn't realize it immediately, but the movie pretty directly condemns the same strains of thought in leftist circles which I have been criticizing in this book.

Again, I think all of the works I've mentioned here are fantastic, and young people should be encouraged to read them. I only object to the fact that leftists also praise them, while simultaneously advocating the policies condemned within them! Then they try to twist them and portray them as condemning Republican policies so as to gain political advantage. All while blindly failing to recognize the incongruity.

The Smoking Gun

For anyone to still think that Republicans are negative and pessimistic and Democrats are the opposite takes quite a bit of obstinacy, but I realize that I have presented mostly anecdotal evidence, or at least only partial evidence. I have not conducted a large scientific survey of Americans upon which to base my conclusions. But fortunately, others have.

Imagine that you thought you lived in a country that was neither fair nor decent. I suspect you wouldn't be very happy about it. It would likely fuel all kinds of negative and cynical thoughts and attitudes. The widely respected pollster Scott Rasmussen asked Americans whether they thought America was basically fair and decent. His results were truly remarkable.

Fully 84% of Republicans felt that they were living in a fair and decent country, while only 49% of Democrats felt the same. On the other side, 41% of Democrats held that the country was unfair and discriminatory. I looked at results from January of 2008, but surveys in other months appear to be consistent with this one.[72]

Arthur C. Brooks also looked at the data, and found enough information to fill his book, *Gross National Happiness: Why Happiness Matters for America—and How We Can Get More of It.* He doesn't do his own research, but pulls it from the work of James A. Davis, Tom W. Smith, and Peter V. Marsden. They found that 44% of people who call themselves conservatives reported being happy, as opposed to 25% of those who call themselves liberals.[73] This "happiness gap" has persisted for at least thirty years. Around 40% of self-described conservatives each year report being very happy, whereas on average 30% of self-described liberals describe themselves as very happy.

Brooks also reports on the results of a more recent Gallup survey which actually asks about party affiliation, and not just political ideology. According to the Gallup survey, 58% of Republicans report having excellent mental health, while only 38% of Democrats said the same thing. These results persisted even when factoring out age, gender, church attendance, income, education and other variables.[74] I would think that excellent mental health and happiness are correlated.

One might point out that self-reporting of happiness might not be the most accurate way to judge whether someone is happy. It is possible that someone who is very unhappy might still report themselves as happy, or vice versa. Still, this criticism seems a little picayune. Okay, a lot picayune. Happiness is a subjective state of mind. There will be no objective measure of how happy someone is, so what else will we go by except for what people report, the number of times they smile every day? In the absence of any specific reason for why people would misreport their state of mind, I think it is reasonable to conclude that people have generally been accurate in these studies, and that thus Republicans are far happier than Democrats.

Final Thoughts

I'm not saying that being pessimistic is wrong, or morally problematic. People have habits of thought which may be beyond rational control, and this may be one of them. All I'm saying is that I have an optimistic personality, and that I am turned off by bitterness and negativity. I also think that Democrats are more likely to have a negative view of things, and that the Democratic Party in general encourages this view for political reasons. And because of these reasons, I would have a hard time being a Democrat.

I will offer one other piece of advice. As Blaise Pascal encouraged agnostics to hang around religious people, not because they would rationally convince anyone to believe in God, but because the change of perspective might have an effect on one's habits, which might then affect one's state of mind, I would encourage pessimists to hang around people who are more positive. Happiness is a good thing, I think, and I wouldn't want anyone to go without as much of it as possible, within the bounds of what is morally permissible.

Besides that, happy people are less likely to fall for some messianic figure who will solve all of your problems by making your decisions for you. (Hey, even happy people can be annoyed and cynical once in a while.)

CHAPTER NINE
The Imperial Presidency

Washing one's hands of the conflict between the powerful and the powerless means to side with the powerful, not to be neutral.
—Paolo Friere

I became interested in politics around the time of Bill Clinton's presidency. I suppose I had some feeble inklings before then, but I just considered it more of a nuisance. I wanted to live my life as I saw fit, and I thought government was largely irrelevant to my concerns. I can't say completely what changed my attitude, but I suspect it was mostly having a daughter, whom I hoped would long outlive me. One starts thinking about the future and what it will look like when one loves someone who will inhabit that future.

I always considered myself an independent, although I flirted with communism in high school. I think the Catholics from whom I was learning had been influenced by liberation theology or socialism in some form, but I can't say for sure. I do remember insisting that Bolshevism was too drastic, and that perhaps Menshivism was a more practical and less violent solution. I never had a deep understanding of the issues, and never really took a real position either way. I lost interest after high school.

I began thinking about politics a lot more in college, especially after taking a class on Political Liberalism. It was about the same time that Bill Clinton had been accused of perjury.

I followed the case with piqued interest, and think that I learned quite a bit about politics, both theoretical and practical. Ultimately, what I learned made me disgusted with the Democratic Party.

So much has occurred and so much has been written about the impeachment and the whole period that I could never hope to do justice to the entire situation without years of research, which is not my forte. All I can do, which has been my intention throughout this book, is to offer to my readers my impression about what occurred and how it influenced my views of Democrats in general. As always, my readers are free to disagree, but if one wants to change my viewpoint, one will need to offer me good reasoning, or evidence from a strongly credible source.

So, let me give my reconstruction of what occurred during the later years of Bill Clinton's presidency, and offer the conclusions I draw from those events.

The Election of William Jefferson Clinton

I supported Ross Perot the year that Bill Clinton was elected to President. I liked the idea that Perot was an independent, and he seemed to want to try to end corruption in government. I also liked the idea that he was a bit "off". He said what he wanted to say, and didn't couch every word in political doublespeak. Even after the whole pulling out of the race, getting back in thing, I still voted for him, although I was pretty sure he wouldn't win.

No one can say for sure what would have happened if Perot had not been in the race, but in any case, Bush lost his reelection bid, and Bill Clinton became the President. I was a little disappointed, but I didn't really know much about Bill Clinton, so my disappointment was only that Perot, whom I knew was an outsider and not a "typical" politician, was not elected, and not because I knew much about Mr. Clinton and didn't like him or his policies specifically. I did get the sense that he was a bit phony, but no more so than I thought most politicians were.

One of his first moves as President, I recall, was to institute the "Don't ask, don't tell" policy on homosexuals in the military. I thought it was a lot of show without much substance. Being in the military, I was pretty sure that homosexuals were not routinely rounded up and harassed until they confessed and could be dismissed from service. I don't ever remember being asked whether I was homosexual, other than by other homosexuals who were looking for sex.

Now, any serviceman who let it be known that he was gay would be questioned, their lives investigated, and they would be discharged, but if they kept it to themselves, and either never acted on their sexuality with another person, or were able to keep those interactions private, then they would continue to serve. As I saw it, the new policy did not change things one iota.

I must admit that I didn't work in an area that would investigate such matters, so I could be wrong. There may have been some minor changes and maybe some significant changes in how these matters were pursued, but I still doubt it.

It was at this point that I started thinking that maybe Mr. Clinton was even phonier than most politicians. He portrayed this new policy as revolutionary: an incredible compromise which would give both sides of the issue most of what they wanted. I was a little baffled that the mass media seemed to echo his rhetoric. How could the cynics in the media be so easily fooled?

Of course, military leaders grumbled, but didn't seem overly upset. After all, their policy was basically intact. Homosexual groups seemed much more disappointed, as they should have been. They wanted to be able to serve in the military while being openly gay. The "Don't ask, don't tell" policy did absolutely nothing for them. Sure, it allowed them to stay in the military if they were able to keep their homosexuality a secret, but they were already able to do that.

This episode began to solidify my skepticism toward Bill Clinton. It also made me begin to think about my own political views. I began to think about homosexuality as a social issue. I didn't think that homosexuality was immoral, but I knew that many, probably most, of the people in the military did. That wasn't because the military was unrepresentative of the general population, but rather because it was. Still, I thought it was a person's right to be homosexual and act on it, regardless of the judgments of the majority. That was just a basic political freedom.

The real question, however, was whether homosexual people had a right to serve in the military. If they did, then it seemed to me that they should be able to serve regardless of what people knew about their sexuality. If they did, then Bill Clinton's policies were a violation of their fundamental civil rights.

The thing that really began to bug me was that I was pretty sure that people who supported Bill Clinton did think that homosexual people had a right to serve, which meant that they should think that his policy was fundamentally unjust. And yet, outside of the most strident activists, very few were willing to criticize Mr. Clinton's policy as if it were fundamentally unjust. Many seemed to praise his actions, and his ability to compromise. I take it to be an important principle that one not compromise with justice.

After long consideration, I concluded that homosexuals do not have a right to serve in the military. Before you begin condemning me, let me explain why, in a way with which you might even agree. At least my logic will be impeccable here. I do not believe homosexual people have a right to serve in the military because I don't believe that anyone has a right to serve in the military.

Serving in the military is honorable, and anyone who wants to serve in the military is to be admired, but whether one serves in the military should be purely a matter of efficiency. The military should generally operate in whatever way allows it to accomplish its mission most effectively and efficiently, as long as it doesn't violate basic rights. No one has a right to serve, which means that denying homosexuals the ability to serve does not, I think, violate their rights, at least not directly.

Perhaps one can argue that all people still deserve to be treated fairly, and thus we must treat homosexual people and heterosexual people equally. This argument also seems to get back to an issue of justice, but not as directly. Here's what I would say about this reasoning: it's just wrong.

Fairness does not require equal treatment. It requires equal treatment when two people are equal in every relevant way, and when treating them differently denies one of them something of which they are due. Let me put it this way. I don't think any government official, even military authorities, should be able to make decisions such as these based purely on their emotional prejudices. But they should be given some latitude at making decisions about the relevance of justifications for differential treatment.

If the question is whether we should adopt policies which treat people differently, the answer is that of course we should. But we should only adopt sensible policies. And we should expect authorities to adopt policies which they can explain. The military has adopted a policy which disallows openly homosexual people from serving. Is this a sensible policy, or not?

Military commanders generally say that allowing homosexual people to openly serve will reduce morale and unit cohesion. It seems to me that this is sufficient to justify the ban. You see, I'm really not looking for much in terms of justification. Almost anything would work. Some might object that this is just a rationalization, but I think military commanders are in the best position to judge. Even if I think their judgments are skewed, they still seem to be a lot more reliable than people who are not in the military and who have never served.

One might also argue that troop cohesion will be damaged only because of the prejudices and biases of many of the troops, to which I answer, "so what?". Does it matter why? Even if it were just biases in most military personnel, as long as they exist, I would say they are enough to justify a ban. Perhaps one might be saddened or disappointed at what one looks at as a flaw in these personnel, but that doesn't seem to me to justify changing the policy.

Moreover, it seems to me that the whole attitude driving the argument is one of intolerance. Although I do not find homosexuality to be immoral, I can accept that other people have a morality other than my own. I would never belittle a person's judgment that an action is wrong by labeling it as a prejudice. The fact that most military personnel find an act morally wrong is enough to justify prohibiting people who engage in that activity from serving, at least as long as they make it publicly known that they engage in that behavior, and maybe even if they don't.

If most military personnel thought that gambling was seriously morally wrong, I would think it a prudent policy to keep gamblers out of the military. Would I then question a gambler's right to serve? I don't think so. As I've said, I don't think people have a right to serve in the military.

Before anyone tries to use the silly argument that my policies would have supported keeping black people out of the military, that criticism would only hold if one thought that being black is considered a moral failing. I don't see how even the most strident racist could think that.

More generally, it also seemed to me that there were other practical matters that many leftists wanted to sweep under the rug regarding homosexuals in the military. This led me to be even more skeptical of leftists, and their ability to be consistent and wise.

For example, one reason that we segregate men and women in places like bathrooms is because of privacy. Most women wouldn't want men ogling them in the restroom, as let's face it, men will tend to do. Would men want other homosexual men ogling them in the restroom or showers? Presumably not. When I shower, I don't care about other men in the room, because I generally assume that they are not interested in me sexually. That would completely change if I knew that there were homosexual men in the same room. Leftists seem not to be capable of recognizing this simple fact, much less of taking it seriously.

It would seem to me that allowing homosexual men to serve openly would require us to eliminate common bathing facilities, or at least segregate them over sexual preference. In fact, even that wouldn't work. Heterosexual men could all shower together, but unless we want to encourage sexual activity among troops, homosexual servicemen should each have their own bathing facilities. Barracks might be a bad idea as well.

I know there are competent homosexual men and women who could serve (and have served) admirably and nobly in the military, and that in some ways it is a tragedy if they are not able to do so, but unless the practical problems could be worked out, it seems to me to be a reasonable policy to exclude them from serving. This policy may force many people to make a difficult decision: whether to serve in the military, or to be open about their sexuality. I may be sympathetic toward people forced into this dilemma, but I don't think that sympathy should drive all public policy decisions.

I bring up this incident to show that I had already soured on Bill Clinton early into his presidency. Shortly afterwards, he chose his wife, Hillary Clinton, to head a committee to decide what to do about healthcare in America. The more I heard about it, the more it seemed the solution she offered was a massive takeover of healthcare by the government. The solution was to nationalize healthcare as Democrats had already nationalized retirement (social security) and charity (welfare). I began to realize how far I was in terms of political philosophy from the Clintons, and other leftists.

These episodes, and numerous others, convinced me that the Clintons were duplicitous, power-hungry, hypocritical, double-talking nearly paradigmatic politicians. But Bill Clinton, especially after the healthcare debacle and the disastrous showing of Democrats in his first mid-term elections, governed in a decidedly moderate way. I believe he called it triangulation.

Ultimately, my attitude toward Mr. Clinton leading up to the impeachment was not positive. I know many people were willing to overlook many of Mr. Clinton's flaws because he supported their policies, or at least he did in his rhetoric, but that just made it worse in my eyes. I didn't support his policies, and was grateful that he often governed differently than he spoke. But it certainly didn't make him more honorable to me, though I was able to appreciate his craftiness.

Leading Up to the Impeachment

I feel that I must make it clear that at the time I couldn't care less about Bill Clinton's personal life. I was young, and accepted the general wisdom that such things didn't matter. So, no matter how many affairs he had, I still wouldn't have supported his impeachment. I thought it was a little distasteful to do it just off the oval office, but even that, I thought, could be overlooked in a President who wasn't violating his oath of office in any way.

It was eminently clear to me, however, that Bill Clinton's real crime was far from personal. It was legally a crime. But before we get there, let me relate what I believe got us to impeachment.

Bill Clinton clearly appreciates women. No problem there. But he seems to do it in a less than respectful way. When he was governor of Arkansas, he saw a pretty young thing with whom he wanted to spend some time. Her name was Paula Jones. She was apparently flattered at meeting the governor, and she, being a government employee, was working for him, at least indirectly.

Paula Jones told us that he made a rather crude advance on her. He exposed himself, and asked her to "kiss it". Apparently, smooth he ain't. She was married, a fact Bill Clinton didn't care about, and uninterested, which fortunately he did care about. She got up to leave, and Mr. Clinton stopped her at the door with the pro forma warning not to tell anyone, and something about knowing her supervisor.

Paula Jones was let go from her position soon afterward. My understanding is that she was going to let the whole episode pass, and didn't even go public with her allegations when Mr. Clinton was running for President.

In his first year as President, Mr. Clinton's political opponents were scouring Arkansas for something with which they could slime him. Shortly thereafter, an Arkansas State Trooper told *The American Spectator* that Mr. Clinton *had* met with Paula Jones, implying that he had achieved the purpose of his meeting. At this point, Paula Jones came forward and said that the story was false. She had met with him, and he had propositioned her, but she had turned him down. She also asked for an apology.

I think that if the President had sincerely apologized, the whole impeachment episode could have been avoided. After all, he is a gifted speaker when it comes to making public pronouncements. Even the Republicans wouldn't have had the fortitude to fight for impeachment if he had seemed to be sincerely remorseful early on. Instead, he decided to deny that the incident had ever occurred. James Carville, Mr. Clinton's attack dog defender, even said "Drag a hundred-dollar bill through a trailer park, you never know what you'll find." Apparently, he didn't think too highly of Mrs. Jones. Not finding any contrition in Mr. Clinton, Paula Jones decided to sue.

Her legal claim was that she had been sexually harassed, although Arkansas didn't have a specific law against sexual harassment. I think it was some other civil employee protection statute which the lawsuit cited. I should say right now that I am extremely skeptical of sexual harassment laws. I suppose that conditioning employment on sexual contact should perhaps be considered soliciting prostitution, and that would be a crime. But I'm not sure about civil damages even in clear cases like this.

If Paula Jones told the truth, and I have every reason to believe she did, with little reason to believe she didn't, then Bill Clinton's actions constituted a form of "sexual harassment" that even I would condemn using legal force. For many Americans, those who think that calling a woman a "broad" in the workplace constitutes an actionable offense, Bill Clinton's behavior would be off the chart persecution.

I think it is important to point out that Bill Clinton was the governor at the time, and so it would be appropriate for citizens to place restraints on his employment policies which would not be appropriate for private businesses. That distinction seems to be overlooked all too often. In any case, it is undeniable that Paula Jones was alleging that she had been sexually harassed, and that under laws which are often championed by leftists, she was pressing her case as far as she could.

Democrats and Leftists generally like to think, and generally want the rest of us to think, that they support the little guy over the oppressive power of people in authority. I like to think that I stand up for the little guy as well. Nothing can anger me as much as when a person with little power has their rights violated by a person or people in power.

I think it should already be clear, but let me make it explicitly so. In this story, Paula Jones is the little guy. Yet, it was clear that the Democrats didn't look at it this way. In their eyes, she seemed to be the evil witch tearing down the noble hero. I will return to this topic of standing up for the little guy in the next chapter.

Mr. Clinton did not roll over when the lawsuit was filed. He used every measure he could to avoid having to face the lawsuit. He and his lawyers filed all sorts of frivolous claims of presidential immunity which served to prolong the lawsuit through the next election, which he won. The Supreme Court was unanimous that the President could be sued. It officially declared that the Office of President was not above the law in any way, as his lawyers argued, and as many Democrats seemed to agree.

How could Democrats even pretend to support these kinds of arguments? Weren't they the ones who didn't think the Executive authority should be absolute? At least, that was what I had been taught, and how their rhetoric always portrayed them. Weren't they the ones who righteously pursued Nixon when he tried to shield himself from the legal repercussions of his actions? Could it really be that even then Democrats were only engaging in partisan politics, and that they would do or say whatever they needed to in order to maintain power, regardless of inconsistency? I ultimately concluded that it was true. Many Democrats, particularly the ones with power in the Federal government, had no principles, except the principle to hold on to political power.

I have seen little since then to change my mind.

Fortunately, these sorts of imperial arguments failed, and Paula Jones's lawsuit entered the discovery phase, where her lawyers would attempt to find evidence supporting her case. Think about the kind of evidence they would be able to find. There was no videotape of the incident, at least none of which we know. Bill Clinton wasn't likely to have told anyone about what he did. Paula Jones had told a few people, but their corroboration could only go so far against the perceived credibility of the President of the United States. Again, why were Democrats so indifferent to the relative lack of credibility of the woman who had no power, in opposition to the attitude they claim to have?

It seems that the only other kind of evidence one could find would be other women who claimed that Bill Clinton had made other sorts of crude advances to them, especially women who worked for him. This evidence might not be absolutely definitive, but it would certainly be highly corroborative. It turned out that Bill Clinton had.

Kathleen Willey admitted that Bill Clinton had taken her hand and placed it on his erect penis, although it was over his clothing. It may be legally relevant that at the time she wasn't working for him, but I doubt it. She did her best to avoid admitting it, but Paula Jones's lawyers persisted in questioning her until she did. It would seem that this would be enough for a slam dunk against Mr. Clinton already, but the lawyers for Paula Jones had heard about other women, including Monica Lewinsky.

All they knew at first was that a White House intern was bragging to another employee that she was engaged in a sexual relationship with Bill Clinton. That fact all by itself seems relevant to the question of whether Bill Clinton propositioned Paula Jones, but it would be even more so if the woman admitted that she was propositioned in a crude fashion by Mr. Clinton.

I don't believe either Mr. Clinton or Monica Lewinsky stated that Bill Clinton made such a crude gesture, and that instead Miss Lewinsky admitted to having flashed her thong. We may never know exactly how their relationship began. It seems indisputable, however, that Paula Jones's lawyers were legally entitled to ask questions to find out.

Monica Lewinsky had offered an affidavit declaring legally under penalty of perjury that she had never had a relationship with the President. It was after she did so that Paula Jones's lawyers had their deposition of Mr. Clinton. This point was the moment of truth. A citizen of the United States had pressed her lawsuit in a court of law, relying on legal protections which Bill Clinton himself strongly supported. Bill Clinton had used every power within the law to avoid facing that lawsuit, and he used every legal tactic he could think of to belittle and besmirch her and the other women who would be witnesses in her lawsuit.

He had been forced to face justice by a ruling of the Supreme Court. If he followed the law and told the truth, he faced humiliation, a decision against him in the lawsuit, and possibly worse repercussions. If he gave Paula Jones what she was legally entitled to as a citizen, he would be hurt professionally and personally.

Ultimately, he decided to lie. He denied ever having any kind of a sexual relationship with Monica Lewinsky.

Lessons of Impeachment

A powerful man using the office of President to pervert the justice system for his own personal ends, in the process denying the legitimate rights of a weak, powerless woman. Up until the point where he committed perjury, I'm not sure whether he deserved to be impeached and removed from office. I can't and couldn't at the time condone his caddish behavior, but I could probably, possibly, tolerate a cad as President. What seemed to me indisputable was that we could not allow a President to remain in office if he took his legal oath so trivially.

Presidents have lied before, but never as far as I know under oath. To lie to the American people to protect state secrets or to prevent an attack, or for some other state reason sounds more than permissible, maybe even admirable in some sense, and possibly to be commended. To lie to the American people in order to protect one's personal life even seems to me to be perfectly acceptable. Even Presidents deserve some privacy, and if some nosy reporter asked a personal question that they have no right to know, then I can see how a President might lie, though I would probably prefer him to refuse to answer, much as President Bush did about his cocaine use.

But to lie in a court of law, to ignore one's Oath in a court case, and to do so for purely personal reasons, that seems to me inexcusable, and at the time I didn't see how anyone could disagree. I was confident that Mr. Clinton would be removed from office.

I was wrong. Democrats disagreed. I'm not sure how. I know they think they had good reason. They offered all sorts of reasons, but none of them made any sense to me. They claimed that Bill Clinton hadn't technically lied, that he lied to the American people, but not to the court, so it wasn't perjury; they said that it wasn't perjury because it wasn't relevant. All of these rationalizations were so transparent I couldn't believe anyone would publicly assert them, but they did. They claimed it was personal and so that we had no right to know about it, but that reasoning would seem to allow any CEO to sexually harass any employee and then claim that it was personal, and so no court had any right to investigate it. Or was this "it's personal" defense only supposed to apply to the imperious President?

One of the stupidest things I had heard came from my graduate advisor in philosophy. He said that Clinton shouldn't be impeached because the Republicans were just out to get him. It was just a political witch hunt, and shouldn't be allowed to succeed. I don't think he realized how disappointed I was in his statement. I wish I had had the courage at the time to ask him if I could excuse cheating on an exam because I thought I had a professor who was out to get me.

Where were the feminists all during this time, generally considered to be politically on the left? Were they AWOL? No, of course not. Amazingly, they were busy *protecting* Bill Clinton. Even when Bill Clinton's first response to Monica Lewinsky's coming clean turned out to be to slime her as a crazy stalker, people who called themselves feminists stood by the president. Even though he treats many of the women in his private life as little more than masturbatory tools, they fiercely defended his actions with all sorts of mental gymnastics.

Selling out one's principles for political power leaves a dirty taste in my mouth, but it apparently didn't phase Democrats. Like I said, many of them were more than willing to support Bill Clinton's wife for President, and most of them supported her selection as Secretary of State. I'm not saying that Secretary of State Clinton had anything to do with the President cheating on her, or lying to the court, but she did have something to do with sliming the women who admitted that they had engaged in sexual activity with her husband, and she did everything she could to shield her husband from being punished for committing perjury. I do feel some compassion for her. I'm not sure what a woman who finds out her prominent political husband is cheating on her should do. She probably should stand by him, but not by attacking the women with whom he cheated. And either way, it shouldn't enhance her political prospects.

If it ever happens that a President for whom I voted has suggested to a woman that she needs to have sex with him in order to keep her job, and then he uses all his power to denigrate her and prevent her from achieving justice, let me just say that I will be on her side, regardless of what party the President is a member or how strongly I supported him. If any President commits perjury to avoid embarrassment, in the process denying an ordinary citizen her civil rights, I will call for that President to be removed from office, even if he is my best friend, especially if he is my best friend. I don't play favorites when it comes to justice.

And if any political party sells its soul to protect that President from the only appropriate consequence for his egregious behavior, I will not support that party in any way, much less join it. When it became known that President Nixon was going to be impeached, because Republicans told him that they would not protect him, he decided to spare the country from the divisiveness of a trial and resigned. Bill Clinton decided that his hold on power was more important than the repercussions of a Senate trial considering his removal from office. And he knew it would be close and divisive. Democrats in the Senate made it clear that they would probably not vote to remove him from office fairly early on.

The partisan divide and the animus and vitriol we experience today is in large part a result of Mr. Clinton refusing to follow President Nixon's example, and putting his own legacy ahead of the country. I am ashamed of him, and I am ashamed of the Democratic Party which supported him. Even if I thought the Democratic Party adopted my political philosophy and supported returning to a country where individual differences were respected and not punished, I would have a hard time becoming a member because of this unseemly episode.

As it stands, I can't imagine that this will ever happen, but as always, I'm open to being convinced.

Final Thoughts

I was unfamiliar with the term "imperial presidency" at the time of Clinton's impeachment. It wasn't until President Bush was tarred with the term that I remember hearing it. Apparently, it was the title of a book by Arthur M. Schlesinger, Jr. in 1973. Helen Thomas, the well-known and fiercely partisan former-member of the White House Press Corps, used the term in a 2002 column in reference to George Bush. Since then, many Democrats seemed to hurl it at President Bush every chance they got. As recently as January 13th, 2009, the House Committee on the Judiciary, led by John Conyers, Jr. released a report entitled "Reining in the Imperial Presidency: Lessons and Recommendations Relating to the Presidency of George W. Bush," and planned to hold hearings on the matter.

As I understand it, the concept of an Imperial President is basically a president who operates outside of the restrictions placed on the office by the Constitution. It is a President who doesn't want to rule like a President, but instead like a king.

There are indeed some reasons to argue that Bush is guilty of acting like an imperial president, which I should make clear is a bad thing in my eyes, and as well there are reasons to think he is not, as it is with most complex judgments. The thing I really don't get, however, is that many of those who most vociferously criticize President Bush for being an imperial president often uphold President Clinton as an ideal President. I suppose I do understand it; it is crass inconsistency used to rationalize one's views.

A President who lasciviously and crudely touches women in sexually inappropriate ways is probably not an imperial President (although I suspect many feminists would say he was, at least if he didn't agree with their agenda), though he may be considered immoral, but a President who uses his office to protect himself from the legal ramifications of his actions is another thing altogether. One who uses his power to shield himself from legal consequences by denying a powerless citizen her due rights is certainly an Imperial President.

If anyone is really troubled by an Imperial Presidency, one should have been thoroughly disgusted with President Bill Clinton.

CHAPTER TEN

"We Are Our Brother's Keeper, Unless He's Not Born Yet"

That the poor are invisible is one of the most important things about them. They are not simply neglected and forgotten as in the old rhetoric of reform; what is much worse, they are not seen.
—Michael Harrington
[As are those who are yet to be born]

Injustice anywhere is a threat to justice everywhere.
—Martin Luther King Jr.

Washing one's hands of the conflict between the powerful and the powerless means to side with the powerful, not to be neutral.
—Paolo Friere

Democrats like to say that they are for the little guy. The disenfranchised. The powerless. The weak. The disadvantaged and underprivileged. In some ways, they may be right, although I have come to believe that much of their rhetoric is cynically motivated. Scare the poor, make them think that the rich are out to screw them over, and you end up with a lot more votes.

Still, Democrats do support things like welfare and minimum wage, which are supposed to help the poor. And they fight for minorities and women, and anyone who is oppressed. Or at least, that's what they would have us believe.

I am convinced that many, if not most, of the programs that Democrats support ultimately make the poor worse off, or at least spread around the misery caused by irresponsible behavior to lots of people instead of concentrating it on those who engage in the irresponsible behavior. The others I tend to think are unconstitutional. Yet, I'm not sure I could present an argument which would even have a chance of convincing anyone who is predisposed to believing anything else.

Instead I want to argue about something which falls under the realm of philosophy, for which I can argue well myself. I want to argue that there are a large group of disadvantaged, powerless people in our country who are being oppressed by people who are stronger and more powerful than they are, and about which the Democrats don't care in the slightest. In fact, they fight hard to ensure that the domination continues. The people of whom I speak are the pre-born.

Expanding the Definition of Personhood

Democrats early on were the fiercest opponents to expand the recognition of humanity beyond its archaic beginnings. Going back to feudal times, a Lord could kill a peasant just for getting in his way, and he could do it with impunity. America never accepted this level of legalized inequality, but it did begin its existence with many forms of it.

Long ago, though not that long ago, only white land-owning men were considered complete human beings. They were the only ones allowed to vote and influence their political institutions. If only certain people are considered *demos* (Greek for "people"), then "democracy" only requires political influence from that subset of the society. We recognized early on in our society that white men who didn't own land were still equally people, and deserved the right to vote and influence their government.

Slavery is the clearest example of legalized inequality which our country has had. Even our Constitution recognizes a difference in worth or fundamental value between slaves and non-slaves. Even after slavery was ended, it was a hard won fight to get our legal institutions to finally recognize that black men were metaphysically equal, and should be jurisdictionally equal, to white men. It took tremendous loss of life, and incredible divisiveness, but most of us think it was worth it. Thank God we didn't value peace and harmony over the basic rights of people.

Keep in mind, as I have already related, it was Democrats who fought the progress every step of the way. Perhaps even then they were keen on fighting for "Unity", even at the sake of diversity or justice. Think about it. During the Civil war, those who were for peace, and those who fought for unity, really were just fighting for an unjust status quo. It's easy to argue for unity when I think my values are winning the day. Imagine arguing for unity when your opponent's values are carrying the day. That just amounts to handing over your society to their values.

Based on the undisputed historical record, it is undeniable that Democrats fought hard to ensure that black men would still be seen as sub-human, and not entitled to fundamental political and civil rights. Even when they were given those rights, Democrats fought hard to ensure that political and social institutions continued treating black men and women as sub-human. If Democrats in the early to mid part of the twentieth century felt guilty for their partisan forebears, then they should have, but I think sometimes guilt makes people do horrible things.

Moving forward, even after black men were granted civil and political rights, and were struggling to get individuals to accept their fundamental equality, women were still not allowed to vote. They were never legally barred from working or owning companies, although most men who controlled those institutions prevented them from achieving high positions, but women were prevented by law from voting. I think they had a great case that a legal proscription from voting was the enforcement of an unjust legalized inequality. I'm not informed enough to know who fought against feminine suffrage, but I suspect it was across the ideological, or at least political, spectrum.

Sometime in the early to mid twentieth century, the Democrat party experienced a transformation. Perhaps it was guilt for their previous provincialism, but they decided to stand for the expansion of civil rights, and the demand for further recognition of the equality of mankind. And they threw their hearts into it.

The legal recognition of women and minorities had already been achieved largely over their objections, so they turned instead to society itself. Women and minorities were still rarely seen in positions of great power and authority. The Democrats were going to change that. Because they couldn't do so through persuasion within a decade or two, they turned to legislation. They tried to enforce a legalized equality, not in terms of jurisdiction of law, but in actual circumstance of position. This is where some Republicans started to balk, though still not the majority. It seems like they were skeptical of using law to push values on people who were unwilling to accept them.

For example, if a man owns a restaurant, and he only wants white people to eat there, should we use the force of government to require him to live according to our values. Democrats, at least today, wholeheartedly say "Yes". This impulse is not liberal. It is not democratic. It is not respectful of freedom.

Should we refuse to eat there until he changes his policy? Absolutely. But to not see the difference between these two responses, and to recognize that the latter is to use our own freedom to encourage others to adopt our values, and the former is to use the force of government to punish someone who doesn't share our values, is the cause of tremendous problems. And the ignorant, but rampant, tarring of people who recognize this distinction as "racist" is not only wrong, but shortsighted and illiberal.

There is a faulty understanding of human nature being applied here. Democrats seem to think that if they just alter the law and government to declare these forms of bigotry illegal, then everyone will just accept it as being immoral and they will abandon it. This assumption reveals a tendency I have sometimes seen in Democrats to equate law and morality, possibly due to their relativistic attitude toward morality.

In my experience, the old saw is true: you catch a lot more flies with honey than with vinegar. When people use their freedom in such a way that one suffers because of their values, they are a lot more willing to abandon those values than when one uses the force of government to punish them when they act on their values. Counterintuitively, perhaps, Democrats have actually prolonged the racism in society that they supposedly condemn.

One negative consequence of the Democratic worldview is the fighting over spoils. Is there anything more sickening than seeing minority groups fight over who was more oppressed, and so who deserves to be handed more of the pie? Looking at the entire world in terms of who is oppressing and exploiting whom, is damaging to self as well as to others. It must sometimes be done, but one can't revel in it and hold onto it forever.

The Redirection Effect and the Fetus

One other related negative aspect of a group coming out of oppression is that they sometimes just redirect that oppression onto another group. Sometimes, such groups will fight the hardest to keep out other groups from the ranks of the "human." Fortunately, before Democrats got involved, Black people coming out of slavery experienced little of this. Unfortunately, these tendencies were reignited in the sixties.

Here is my point, if it hasn't been clear where I was headed. Women since the sixties have been encouraged to view the world in terms of how it oppresses them. It's hard to read "the world" in any other way than "men", or perhaps "men in power." This attitude has only been encouraged by the political left and the Democratic Party. Leftists have encouraged women to "liberate" themselves, by coming out from under the oppression from men.

Talk about divisive. Oh, that's right, sometimes it is important to be divisive. A big part of this liberation was supposed to be sexual. Sometimes Democrats call it "reproductive freedom," but what they really seem to mean is "unreproductive freedom." The fact that a woman could not have sex without worrying about getting pregnant was unacceptably oppressive. They should be able to have sex like men, who never seemed to worry about the consequences. Men just used women for sex, and then threw them away, without having to worry about whether she got pregnant or had to drop out of school. At least, that was rhetorically the picture they drew. So, women should be able to have sex equally as cavalierly and carelessly.

One advance, in their eyes, was oral contraceptives, but these had their own problems, and were not completely effective, in any case. Many women would not use them properly, or forget them, or just not use them, and still ended up pregnant. And then evil, oppressive men compelled them to give birth, in the process ruining their lives.

So, in this version of events, from a Marxist perspective, the situation was about men oppressing women and keeping them in their place, not allowing them to experience guiltless, worry-free sex, or more precisely, keeping guiltless, worry-free sex for themselves, and not sharing this golden prize with women. And in this version, there is a simple solution: allow women to terminate their pregnancies.

Then they could engage in sex and not worry about having to raise a child. You might object that they could always give up their child for adoption, but who even wants to go through a pregnancy? No one wants to get fat and throw up, and have a hard time getting up and sleeping for six to nine months, just so that another human being has a chance to live. Even this is too much to give those oppressive men. No. Women must be able to terminate their pregnancies before they even start showing that they are pregnant.

I have a different way to think of things. I don't accept the idea of viewing the world solely in terms of who is oppressing whom, but I will accept that one group of people can oppress another group.

So, some women have sex for their own pleasure, to appease their own sexual gratification. Excluding the issue of rape, no one is forcing women to have sex, they do it of their own free will (unless you think women have no minds of their own and can be easily pressured and manipulated into having sex by wily men). They attempt to prevent pregnancy, but it doesn't work, and they end up pregnant. And instead of giving birth to the child and giving her up for adoption, they ask a doctor to kill the developing human who is growing inside of them.

Talk about oppression. Not since the middle ages has one person held that they had the right to kill another person because their existence was inconvenient. Even slave-holders did not think they could kill any person who was in their way, but only their slaves. The ancient Romans adopted the principle of *paterfamilias*, where a father could kill his own children no matter what age they were, but that philosophy has long been abandoned in the modern world.

But here it was, resurrected by leftist feminists in order to "throw off their chains." And the first casualty of their newfound freedom was a group of the smallest, weakest human beings we can imagine: infants in their mother's wombs.

I know, I know. I can already hear you as I type this. Many of you are saying that fetuses are not people, as was declared by the Supreme Court in Roe v. Wade. But guess what. The Supreme Court had ruled that black people were not complete people, too. It doesn't have the best record on figuring out who counts as a person. And throughout history, all sorts of groups have gone through rationalistic contortions in order to deny the basic humanity of all sorts of other human beings.

I believe that every fetus is indeed a person, and has full moral rights, and I think that claim is really indisputable. I think most people who reject this claim do so only because they think this fact has consequences which they really don't like: namely, that women can't engage in sexual activity with the wild abandon that some disgusting men think they can. Rejecting the truth of a claim because it has unwanted consequences is a poor method of reasoning.

I don't know if I can convince anyone who already has their mind made up, because, well, closed minds sometimes can't be pierced, but those who are open to cogent reasoning should be able to follow it. One way to get at my argument is to consider what science says about the issue.

What Does Science Say?

I have heard students say that science proves that the fetus is not a person. I have no idea where they could be getting this information, because first, science can't prove anything of the sort. The question of the conditions for humanity is a philosophical question. Second, if science does anything, it would only confirm that a fetus is a person.

Consider the history of scientific consensus on procreation. Ancient people knew that there was a connection between sex and childbirth, even if they weren't sure what it was. The entire process was a complete mystery.

At some point, someone conjectured that semen contained a "homonculous", or a miniature human being in microscopic form. This homonculous could only grow inside a female uterus. This theory relegated women to the status of an incubator, with no contribution to the child. It sounds awfully, naively hyper-masculine.

Still, between the act of impregnation and quickening, no one knew what the heck was going on. This lack of knowledge led many to conclude that it was not until quickening, the point where the mother could feel the fetus kick, that a person was present. The womb may have been getting ready, but there was no human fetus present until quickening.

A more likely story was that the animal nature of the fetus was present since impregnation, but that the human soul was not imparted to the fetus until the point of quickening. I think this pre-scientific view influenced many early laws concerning abortion (to which, by the way, the Supreme Court appealed in its decision in Roe v. Wade).

Of course, now we have a much better understanding of the process. The male gamete, hundreds of millions of which are found in every ejaculate, contains half of the genetic material which can constitute a human being. The female gamete, the egg, also contains half of the material which can constitute a human being. Human sperm cells and egg cells are human cells, but neither of them can be called a human being, and neither one can be considered an organism.

So, when does a human being become a human being. If we look at it in a purely scientific fashion, there is one point, and only one point, which it is even possible to seriously consider. It is the point at which a new organism enters the world. That point is conception.

At the point when a sperm cell merges with an egg cell, a new and unique human DNA sequence is instantiated in the world. This DNA sequence has never been seen before in the world and will never be seen again. The new cell that is created no longer takes orders from the biology of the mother, but takes on its own biological imperative.

I don't believe in any religious or metaphysical concept of a soul, or ensoulment, which arguably indirectly influenced the Supreme Court's decision in Roe v. Wade, and instead accept that DNA is it. We are our DNA, and the body instantiated through that DNA. Our genes tell us who we are, although it only influences our psychological and philosophical natures in conjunction with our environment. But it dictates the scope over which even our philosophy can expand.

One's physical nature is not necessarily unique. There are biological twins. But each of those twins is a separate instantiation of the same DNA sequence.

If it is not conception, then when is a new human organism created? Birth is so far from a possible answer, it can only be supported by someone who has not considered or doesn't know what an organism is.

One can say that the fetus is a parasitic organism, but even a parasite is still considered an organism.

One prominent supporter of abortion rights argued that a fetus is not a person, just as an acorn is not an oak tree. Many readers of her works think this is a very important and strong analogy. But it misses the point entirely. A child is not an adult either, but that doesn't mean that we can deny children every right belonging to adults, such as the right to life.

The real question, and a more appropriate analogy is this: would any society that found oak trees to be sacred dismiss acorns as trivial and unimportant. I dare say that they would not. If an oak tree is sacred, then the acorn that develops into the oak tree is sacred as well. If an oak tree deserves respect and a right to life, then the living organism which turns into that oak tree deserves a right to life as well. Anyone who thinks that butterflies are sacred and should be respected, but thinks that caterpillars are trivial and don't deserve any respect, is not a very thoughtful person.

The fetus is indisputably a human organism from a biological perspective. Perhaps, however, one can argue that the fetus is not a person in a moral sense, in the sense in which we use human rights. I take it to be accepted by every one that "human" rights would be given to a creature who was not human, but was capable of a high level of communication and emotion. We do not deserve our "human rights" merely because of our biological natures, but because of our psychological natures. I think it is important to understand, though, that our psychological natures are only possible because of our biological natures.

I believe that it is at least a defensible position to say that the fetus is biologically human, but might not be human in the more fundamental moral sense. I disagree with it, but at least one can make some kind of case in its favor. Science, however, can tell us nothing about this sense of humanity. So, as far as science is concerned, which can only address the biological, the fetus is a human organism, case closed.

Why do I still think the fetus is a human in the more important moral sense? There are a variety of overlapping, related reasons. It is the only theory which matches many of my other moral intuitions. I believe that any other theory would exclude certain groups of human beings which should not be excluded. I don't know of any other consistent theoretical framework which allows us to exclude fetuses, and only fetuses.

For example, the issue of viability, which can be used to exclude fetuses from the ranks of humanity, seems to me to exclude many disabled people, as well as bed-ridden people. I recently became aware of a man who was so obese that he could not get out of bed himself. It seems to me that he is just as dependent on other human beings as is a fetus, but that fact does not reduce his personhood in the slightest. So, the fact that a fetus cannot exist independently of another human being should not reduce the fetus's personhood, either. Perhaps one can argue that a fetus is dependent on a specific human being, whereas the bed-ridden man is dependent on any human being, but I don't see how this is a relevant distinction.

One might say that fetuses, at least in their early stages, don't look like human beings, and so that excludes them from being human. I think this distinction eliminates anyone with any kind of deformity. Perhaps we can say that fetuses don't have functioning lungs, but then anyone on a heart/lung machine is no longer a person, and can be summarily destroyed.

Perhaps one can say that fetuses are not self-conscious, or that they don't have the capability of reasoning, or that they lack some other function of being a human being. It seems to me that this line of reasoning might have some epistemological value, but I don't see that it carries any real strength. Let me explain. If I came across an object which I had never seen before, and someone asked me whether that object was a person in the moral sense, I would not be in a position to know.

Epistemologically, or in terms of my ability to know, I would be very limited. The thing might be a person or not, and I would have to compare that thing to other things in my background which might be persons. If it were completely unlike any person I had ever seen before, it would be reasonable for me to conclude that it is not a person. But again, that is a question of my belief and the best grounding of my belief, and not a question of what is real, or metaphysically true.

Ultimately, if that thing started to communicate with me, I would have to alter my conclusion. But it seems to me that an entity can be a human being in the moral sense even if it is currently incapable of communicating with me.

The Butterfly Analogy

In comparison, imagine I come across a caterpillar, and it is just like any caterpillar. It is eating my plants, so I put poison on the plant, and it kills the caterpillar. I would have to conclude that I did nothing wrong (barring any concern one might have for organic farming or the rights of caterpillars). After all, in my experience, no caterpillar has ever spoken, or communicated, or reasoned, or felt anything in a self-conscious way. So, it would be reasonable for me to conclude that caterpillars are not persons in a moral sense.

I go away for a month, and when I get back, I find that there are several chrysalises on my bushes, and I go out to get something to get rid of them. When I get back, one of the chrysalises has opened, revealing a butterfly. Amazingly, the butterfly begins asking me questions! Who am I? What am I? What is he? I may have a difficult time answering the butterfly's questions, but at this stage, I think I would have to conclude that butterflies are persons in a moral sense.

Now, what would you think if I took my shovel, and immediately began to smash the remaining chrysalises? Would you think I was just being practical, or would you think me a horrible monster? Would you defend my right to protect my bushes? Would you say it's none of your business, or would you try to stop me?

Imagine that all the butterflies emerged from their chrysalises and flew away, and a week later I saw a group of caterpillars munching on the leaves of my bush. Would you object if I sprinkled poison over the top of them? Let's say you do object to what I am doing, and I responded by saying that even though butterflies might count as moral persons, caterpillars are not butterflies. Thus, anyone can destroy caterpillars for whatever reason they desire. How fortunate for me that I can kill them off before they emerge as butterflies. If I wait until then, they would have rights and I would have to allow them to live. Can anyone honestly admit that they would stand by and defend my freedom of choice in this case?

I can see someone argue that there is an important disanalogy between my situation and a pregnancy. Caterpillars don't grow inside human women. That's true, but it only brings out an important point in my favor. If we recognize caterpillars as moral persons because they are the same organism which emerges as a butterfly, the same should apply to a fetus. We would not be able to deny the personhood of the fetus merely because of its location. One cannot define away personhood (at least not justifiably so) by focusing on dependence or location, although we might be able to discuss a conflict of rights in this situation.

If the fetus is a person, and the mother is a person, then how do we settle any dispute between the two of them? Whatever way we do it, you can bet that the government is going to be involved, and that it should be. Whenever one person or group of persons claims a right to destroy another person or group, then it is the role of the government to step in and arbitrate.

This reasoning alone doesn't mean that abortion will always be illegal. It just means that the default position would be for the life of the fetus. If a woman can demonstrate that without separating herself from her fetus she would be at serious risk to her life or health, then even a fetus's guardian *ad litem* would respect her right to do so. But it would mean an end to elective abortion for trivial reasons. It would end abortion as simply a last ditch effort at avoiding pregnancy when contraception failed, or when no contraception was used. And it would probably end abortions which seek to kill the fetus, and not merely to separate the fetus from his mother.

Who Has the Power?

I don't intend to completely settle this issue here, but mostly just to point out another blatant hypocrisy of Democrats and leftists in general. Fetuses are the least powerful members of society, and in the relationship between a woman and her fetus, she has all the power. Whereas leftists completely deplore this type of situation in general, and demand that the government step in and equalize such power relations, in the case of a woman and her fetus, they vigorously defend a completely unequal power distribution. Many of them would even argue that a woman has the right to kill her fetus, and for any reason she decides.

The blatantly confused reasoning on the left can be illustrated most clearly by reflecting on the fact that many leftists strongly support animal rights. They vehemently condemn anyone who kills an animal in a cruel, sadistic way. Think about Michael Vick. Many of them object to factory farming, where animals are stunned using electricity, and then killed by slashing their throats. Some animal rights groups even compare chicken ranching to the holocaust.

Yet, I have never heard of any leftist group condemning the way abortions are performed. In fact, most of them even defend the procedure called partial birth abortion, where a living fetus which is as capable of pain as most animals are, has its head punctured by a pair of surgical shears. Many abortions involve cutting up a fetus so it can be removed through the vagina more easily. Some also include injecting a strong saline solution which can burn the skin of the fetus and other tissues, so that the fetus is spontaneously aborted.

Consider that, and consider that fetuses are never stunned by an electric pulse or given any kind of analgesic so that they can't feel the pain they must experience, at least neurophysiologically, as do animals, if not self-consciously. Why do leftists care so much about the pain of animals, but not one iota about the pain of a fetus?

I don't think that neurophysiological pain matters, but I still think that the fetus is a person in a moral sense, and deserves to be treated as one. This means that every fetus has a right to life, and thus, the wishes of the mother can't be the only thing we consider.

Do I want to force my moral view on others? You're damn straight I do. When that morality is that one person does not have the right to destroy another human being without some compelling, overriding reason, such as self-defense, then of course I want to see government enforce that morality. Would any of you say that you wouldn't?

As I'll explain more in the next chapter, liberalism doesn't say that all government is illegitimate. It only says that government should step in to make sure that those who are physically strong don't violate the rights of those who are weaker than they are. It seems to me that abortion falls precisely under this definition.

Maybe you can convince me otherwise.

Final Thoughts

Democrats, and their supporters in the mainstream media, portray themselves as defenders of the disenfranchised, but the group of people with the fewest rights in our entire society is the group of those who are not yet born. Why is it that Democrats want to grant citizenship and recognition to every other group in society except this one? Why is this the one group that they vociferously refuse to accept as persons? Why do they fight so hard to exclude them from the ranks of humanity?

I don't suppose that I have all the answers, but I suspect that no one does. I suspect that most Democrats don't know themselves. They have committed to the idea of being "pro-choice" (those that fall under that appellation, that is), and they won't let anything stand in the way, especially not some weak, powerless non-person who is just an inconvenience to a woman wanting to live her life the way she pleases.

I have heard it said that if I were a woman, I would be more sympathetic to women who desire to kill the fetus growing inside of them (dang, there goes my sympathy again). To that I say that I only have so much sympathy to give, and currently it is all being used up in sympathy for the fetuses who are callously being destroyed and discarded. (Obviously, I'm a little emotional about this issue).

Given current political realities, I don't think the legal status of abortion will change much in the short-term. With that in mind, as a pragmatist, I could join a political party which wasn't organized around trying to end the practice of elective abortions, but I would find it difficult to join one which unabashedly supports and defends the supposed right of every woman to kill the fetus growing inside her for any trivial reason which she can use to rationalize her actions.

Perhaps I have not convinced anyone that the fetus is a person and indeed deserves the rights of personhood, but I hope that it is clear to every reader that those who want to allow women to choose to get abortions are equally imposing a moral viewpoint on those who disagree with them. And I hope it is clear why I don't see myself joining the Democratic Party anytime soon.

CHAPTER ELEVEN

Democrats Are Not Liberals!

The sole end for which mankind are warranted, individually or collectively, in interfering with the liberty of action of any of their number, is self-protection. That the only purpose for which power can be rightfully exercised over any member of a civilised community, against his will, is to prevent harm to others. His own good, either physical or moral, is not sufficient warrant. He cannot rightfully be compelled to do or forbear because it will be better for him to do so, because it will make him happier, because, in the opinion of others, to do so would be wise, or even right.

—John Stuart Mill

The urge to save humanity is almost always a false front for the urge to rule it.

—H. L. Mencken

I consider myself a liberal, and that is why I cannot stand the Democratic Party. For those readers who are astute, you will have noticed that I have assiduously avoided using the term liberal, at least in reference to the leftist political philosophy of the Democratic Party. There is a reason for this omission. I do not believe the Democratic Party is anywhere near being liberal.

I know this goes against most of the rhetoric one hears in American media these days, but once one understands why liberalism was invented, it is undeniable that what is generally referred to as "liberal" these days is hardly anything like liberalism was when it was invented. Nor does it reflect the usage of the term throughout the world even today. Liberalism was supposed to capture the political philosophy which gave people a maximal amount of freedom, without the interference of governmental busy-bodies. Today, at least as the term is used in political discourse in America, the word "liberalism" seems to have the exact opposite connotation. It strikes me that some kind of incredible manipulation must have occurred to accomplish this Copernican revolution. I am convinced that this manipulation continues to cause a great deal of confusion and misunderstanding today. Perhaps one day I will write a more complete history and analysis in a book dedicated to the purpose, but here I will summarize my main points.

The History of Liberalism

Throughout the history of the world, governmental authority, wherever it was found, was considered absolute. Citizens falling under such governments had freedom only inasmuch as the rulers didn't regulate every aspect of their lives. No ruler dictated to every citizen every act the citizen would have to perform, yet every government claimed the authority to do so. There was no sphere of action which was in principle off limits from governmental jurisdiction. The government may not have wanted to dictate behavior in a certain area, either because it didn't see any reason to do so, or because it thought it best for individual citizens to make up their minds, but every government claimed that no area was out of bounds in principle.

Even vaunted, democratic Athens accepted this model of governmental authority. The only difference in governments was who, and how many people, controlled governmental decision-making. But, no matter who grabbed the reins of power, they always ruled with this model in mind.

Kings throughout time have believed that they had the right to kill their subjects for any perceived violation of the good or the right, including disobedience. The king's word was law. Even Democratic governments claimed that if they made a law, it was the obligation of every citizen to follow it, and they did not place limits on the kinds of laws they could make, unless one includes the displeasure of the gods as a limit.

As "small-d" democrats realized, when a large group of people is making a decision, it is less likely to pass a law which makes the majority of them unhappy, as can sometimes occur with a single monarch. Unfortunately, that's not necessarily a good thing. If the majority of the people are happy violating the rights of the minority, then a democracy can be worse than a monarchy, for the minority, that is.

What helped propagate and sustain this view of governmental authority was that governments had so often been so strong, at least in comparison to any of the subjects falling under them. During the later middle ages, governmental authority began to be fractured in Europe, partly because secular authority had been placed under religious authority, and people began to question religious authority. Individuals gathered armies to themselves, and then demanded that the authority over them was limited. One clear example of this phenomenon was the Magna Carta.

As a result, governing authorities began to lose the absolute strength which they had been so used to wielding, at least over their own subjects. Thomas Hobbes[75] observed this lack of strength and was troubled by it. He thought that there should be one central authority which had absolute reign over every aspect of life for every subject of that authority. Of course, that central authority could allow as much free activity as it judged was prudent, but ultimately it had the authority to command anything, and no one had the right to question it.

Hobbes was a rational man, though, and he thought he needed to provide some kind of rational justification for this authority, which paradoxically provided the intellectual resource to throw off absolute sovereignty. For Hobbes, it made sense for every individual in society to turn over every right he had, in order for the sovereign power to make things better for everyone. Hobbes thought that in a "state of nature", everyone had the right to do whatever he thought best for himself, but that this freedom would necessarily lead to a "war of all against all", where life would be "nasty, brutish, and short." In Hobbes' view, it would be infinitely beneficial to turn over all of one's rights and powers to the sovereign, who could ensure that life is at least longer than in a state of nature (if one were obedient to that sovereign, that is).

If the sovereign, however, only ruled by the consent of those who are governed, and that rule was legitimate only if there is a rational basis for the governed to allow it to rule, then it would seem that one's individual rationality is the highest source of authority. In a sense, Hobbes's fundamental premise undermined his ultimate conclusion.

As John Locke[76], following in Hobbes's wake, put it, the government has only that authority which the people give it, and the people would only give it a limited authority. They only transfer that authority by which the government can achieve its purpose, which is the settling of disputes in a fair manner, and the guarantee that's one's rights will not be violated by someone who is stronger, and that one has control over his own property. John Locke is widely recognized as one of the first liberal political philosophers. There is academic dispute about whether anyone before him was a liberal, such as Baruch Spinoza, but no one questions Locke's liberal credentials.

Locke did not call his philosophy "liberalism", but it eventually came to be known by that term, and it's easy to see why. The term "liberalism" derives from the same root as "liberty". Locke's theory allowed for a realm of activity which belonged to an individual by right, such that the government could not interfere with that person's activities without violating the rights of the individual. This was a true sphere of Freedom, not just the pitiable leftovers from an absolute government which just hadn't gotten around to regulating some behavior, as it was for Hobbes. Notice that if one of the fundamental purposes of government is to protect one's rights, and the government itself is violating those rights, then it is vitiating the very reason for its existence, and as Locke realized, deserves to be annihilated. Liberalism was truly a revolutionary doctrine.

Adam Smith put another face on liberalism. He was an economic philosopher who provided a rational basis for a liberal government, instead of one based on justice, as Locke's was. He argued that no governmental authority could understand the economy well enough to control it. The best it can do is to muck it up, while allowing certain interests liked by those in authority to profit immensely. So, it would be better, from a rational point of view, to allow the free market to work on its own. It was a mistake to try to require citizens to act from moral motives, because we would all benefit by relying on each person's self-interest. As Smith puts it "By pursuing his own interest [the individual] frequently promotes that of the society more effectually than when he really intends to promote it. I have never known much good done by those who affected to trade for the public good." [77] He adds that "It is not from the benevolence of the butcher, the brewer, or the baker, that we expect our dinner, but from their regard to their own interest. We address ourselves, not to their humanity but to their self-love, and never talk to them of our own necessities but of their advantages."[78]

Smith is generally considered a liberal, at least as the term was originally used. Whereas Locke argued for liberalism on the grounds of justice, however, Smith argued for it from a more pragmatic standpoint. I side more with Locke in thinking that the government simply does not have the right to regulate citizen's lives, except within a very limited sphere, but for those who would balk at accepting liberalism because it depends on a deep sense of justice, Smith provides a reason to adopt it anyway.

There were of course many other liberal philosophers, but I want to focus on only one other. John Stuart Mill[79] lived at the end of the nineteenth century, and he noticed a trend in liberalism which he found objectionable. I believe that his diagnosis was brilliant, as was his solution, although ironically, I think some of his other writings led to perhaps worse problems, but I will leave that for another time.

Originally, Mill pointed out, liberalism stood for limiting the authority of governments, and for placing restraints on what is a legitimate exercise of the power of government, along the lines that I have already pointed out. When a king is exercising power for his own good, it's easy to see how the interest of the king might not correspond to the interests of the people. So, liberals saw that the best hope for liberalism was to place limits on the king's authority, but they also dreamt of the possibility of a popular form of government, democracy.

They considered democracy the best way to ensure that the governing power ruled in accordance with the interests of the liberal ideal.

Once the second of these dreams was achieved, some people who also might have fought to limit governmental power began to see things differently, but I would argue only by ignoring what made liberalism what it was. People took the words of Jean Jacques Rousseau seriously, perhaps more seriously than he did. In The Social Contract, he wrote:

> So long as several men assembled together consider themselves a single body, they have only one will, which is directed towards their common preservation and general well-being. Then all the animating forces of the state are vigorous and simple; its principles are clear and luminous; it has no incompatible or conflicting interests; the common good makes itself so manifestly evident that only common sense is needed to discern it.[80]

People who thought that the general will was evident to common sense began to think that limits on governmental authority were no longer required. After all, when the interests of the ruling class were opposed to those of the people, it makes sense for the people to want to limit the power of the rulers. But, when the people were themselves the rulers, it didn't make sense to limit their own power, or at least so they thought. Why would the people, who were now the ruling power, want to limit themselves? Their interests were exactly the ones they were worried about, and why would they accept limitations on the power to act upon those interests?

Mill argued that we still needed to defend the idea of limited governmental authority. He thought that there was still a great possibility for the majority, who rules in a democracy, to tyrannize over individuals, which led him to warn against the "Tyranny of the Majority". As he pointed out, there is an ambiguity in the concept of "self-government." This new philosophy that government need not be limited, which was really a throwback to the viewpoint prior to liberalism, held that a society was free when the people generally could rule over society, without any limits. This viewpoint could be seen as self-government, at least in contrast to monarchies or oligarchies.

But there is a much more important sense of self-government: the ability for individuals to make up their own minds and live their lives as they see fit without being harassed by others. Mill insisted on viewing people as individuals, each with their own mind. The throwback philosophy viewed society as a single whole, and made that whole metaphysically prior to the individual. This view is similar to Organicism, but with the added insistence that the decisions made for society must be made in a democratic fashion. To continue the analogy, it would be as if we got rid of the brain, and let the body be controlled by the decision of the majority of the body's organs.

Mill insisted, as every liberal should, that the individual was of paramount importance. Each person is a whole, and should be treated as one. Of course, individuals can come and join together to create higher wholes, but this cannot obviate the fact that each individual ultimately should have control over his own life, inasmuch as he allows others to control their lives.

In order to more clearly distinguish liberalism from this throwback philosophy, which is basically a form of populism, Mill proposed his "Harm Principle."[81] Society has the right to place limits on a person's behavior only when that behavior harms another person, but never in any other case. The principle is the most sublime expression of liberalism ever made.

It captures the idea that society has no right to impose its morality on individuals, other than the basic proscription against harming others. The fact that certain people, whether the majority, or the influential people, or the ruling party, find certain behavior contemptuous, or distasteful, or horrible, does not mean that they can use the force of government to dissuade people from engaging in that behavior, as long as that behavior doesn't infringe on someone else's rights. No one should be fined, imprisoned, or harassed, simply because they engage in behavior which other people find immoral.

This philosophy is the one properly identified as Liberal. It is the view which was originally identified as liberal even in the United States, up until some point in the twentieth century. Even today, it is the philosophy that the rest of the world, besides the United States, recognizes as liberal. And it is *not* the philosophy of the Democratic Party.

As I have demonstrated throughout this book, the Democratic Party consistently adopts positions which go against the Harm Principle. Minimum wage laws. Most forms of sexual harassment laws. Seatbelt laws. Welfare laws. Paying taxes for the pet projects of legislators. All sorts of regulations on businesses. Hate Crime laws, arguably. The Separation of Church and State, understood by the left as barring all mention of God in the public sphere. Many more, as I've already covered.

Democrats are constantly supporting laws which infringe on the freedoms we all cherish. Yet, somehow, they are never called to task on it. Yes, they may take away freedom for the sake of the poor, or helping out people who are having trouble, but that doesn't mean they are not taking away freedom, and it doesn't mean they are not imposing their own view about how people should live on others with whom they disagree.

Democrats say they stand for choice, but when we really examine their stands on policies, the only choices they fight for are the choice to kill the living, growing, developing human being inside their wombs, and the choice to have sex with almost anyone at any time. Do they support choice when it comes to Social Security? No. Do they support choice when it comes to schools, as in vouchers? No. Do they think I have the right to choose to pay an employee any amount of money they will accept? No. Do they support the choice to own weapons and carry them freely? No. Do they support the choice to make decisions as to how charity should be given? No, they tax us all and spend money on government supported welfare, which is charity by another name. Do they support choice when it comes to healthcare? No. They generally want a single-payer system. Do they support choice when it comes to whom a business owner can hire or fire? No. Or what customers they can serve, or to whom they can rent out their rooms? Sure, but only if you follow the guidelines that they set out.

They do also seem to support the choice of citizens from other countries to immigrate to the United States without any documentation. I forgot that one.

Honestly, can anyone really say that the Democratic Party is the party of choice? Even the choices they fight to allow I find problematic. I personally wish the courts would appoint a guardian *ad litem* for every fetus so that the fetus's choice would be considered.

As I see it, Democrats are not liberals, at least not in the sense of the term which gave liberalism its very name. They rarely adhere to the principle established as the hallmark of liberalism. Call them pseudo-liberals, or anti-liberals, or crypto-socialists, if you want. If they insist on calling themselves progressives, as many are wont to do now, they should be asked whether they are progressive communists, or progressive socialists. My impression of the Progressivism of the early to mid-twentienth century is that it was instituted because early American communists knew they couldn't get a majority of Americans to adopt communism immediately, and so opted to push for a slower, more step-by-step "progression" to a communist country.

In any case, please stop calling Democrats liberals, and stop calling the political ideology associated with them liberalism. To do so is to allow the cross manipulation of language for political gain to have some measure of success.

The Most Misunderstood Saying Ever

Many people have heard the quote attributed to Winston Churchill along the lines of "If a person is not a liberal in his twenties, then he has no heart, but if he is not a conservative by his forties, then he has no brain." Practically everyone in America today completely misunderstands the brilliance of this saying because the definitions have been reversed. I understand that many scholars dispute whether Winston Churchill ever spoke those words, but regardless of who came up with them, most Americans do not fully understand what they mean, and generally understand incorrectly.

I must admit that when I first heard them, and for long afterward, I understood them in the same twisted way. I applied the meanings of the terms liberal and conservative as I had heard them defined in America. It seemed to me that the first part of the saying indicated that liberalism was a caring doctrine, which wanted to help the poor. It pointed to the fact that a person who didn't care about others was lacking an important emotional empathy, which we would expect to be present in young people. An idealism and hopeful attitude is proper for a young person, or so the saying seemed to indicate.

The second part of the saying was more cynical, and indicated that a person who didn't think about what they were doing could bring about horrendous consequences. We should of course have learned that lesson by the time we are forty. The saying thus seems to indicate that having a heart is a good, necessary thing, but must be tempered by pragmatic concerns.

This understanding leads us to think that a young person should be a Democrat, who possibly even recklessly supports welfare payments and social security and any other government program which anyone can possibly argue does anything nice for people, no matter how trivially, nor how destructive it is in the long run. Later, when the person is older, they will of course shift to becoming a little more conservative, realizing that such policies may put us into a never-ending cycle of spiraling debt, or have some other negative consequences.

This understanding pushes us to think of "conservative" in a fiscally conservative light, simply as a contrast to the profligate spending inherent in this understanding of the first phrase. In this light the phrase seems to hold Bill Clinton, in his lurch to the middle after the 1994 Republican landslide win, as the highest ideal. After all, he started his Presidency firmly left of center (although according to the saying, he should have been old enough to know better), but after the mid-term elections of 1994, he slid right so far that he enacted a Republican-sponsored welfare reform program.

Now that I understand how the terms "liberal" and "conservative" have had their meanings twisted in America for political reasons, I am in a position to completely rethink the aforementioned saying. If we use the original meanings, the meanings Winston Churchill, or anyone outside of America, would have intended them to be meant, we have a very different picture of what the saying means.

A "liberal", in this sense, is someone who thinks that the government has no right to tell anyone what to do or how to live outside of basic laws against killing and the like. In this interpretation, the word "heart" simply cannot mean compassion for one's fellow man. It must mean something more like "spirit" or "fire". The kind of fire that stands up to authority and tells it to go away. The spirit that insists that it can keep its own money and would ignore income tax laws because it holds that they are unjust.

This interpretation is almost diametrical to the understanding garnered using the twisted definition of "liberal". In this sense, a person with "heart" might encourage a person who was suffering and possibly even offer money to help out someone in need, but if I told this person that I was going to take some of his money and hand it out to someone in need, he would punch me in the face. In this sense, a person with "heart", a "liberal", refuses the guidance of authority and instead sets his own course, almost the opposite of a person who wants government to take care of every individual in society who can't care for himself.

Given this understanding, I don't think we can interpret "conservative" in the second part of the saying as simply meaning "fiscally conservative". In this sense, a conservative holds that young people need guidance, and that the moral authority of society ought to be respected. In the current American parlance, this appeal was for "social conservatism" to some degree. It was for a respect for authority, grounded in the intellect, which tames not one's impulse to be compassionate toward others, but extinguishes one's desire to lash out at any kind of control exercised by people in authority.

If the saying is correct, that would be the natural progression people make when they age. Perhaps the saying doesn't apply to middle-aged and older professors enclosed within the ivory tower, but it does seem to capture some deep truth about most people. I'm not sure what to make of the saying now, and I may at heart reject the claim, if it means that we should allow government to control our lives more rather than less using coercive measures. I do believe, though, that in America, the saying has been entirely twisted so that it is a shadow of its real self, and its meaning has been completely distorted.

I don't blame this solely on Democrats, but I do think that if the saying were understood properly, it would cause a shift in the conversation. It would cause people to more fully confront our understanding of liberalism and conservatism and where each party ultimately stands in relation to them. In my view, such an honest accounting would be very harmful to the Democratic Party.

Let me summarize my views here. I am not a Democrat because I am a liberal, in the original sense of the word, and most Democrats are not. If my readers are unaware of it, I have been trying to make this case throughout the book, though without using the term. As I see it, Democrats are generally racist, and condemn others for being racist. They are divisive, and condemn others for being divisive. They want to use the government to force their own morality on society, while pointing the finger at Conservatives for doing the same thing. They support policies which only make sense from an organic perspective, dehumanizing the individual. They blindly impose a form of Christian benevolence on everyone in society, while attacking others for minor impositions like having "In God We Trust" on our money. They worship the idol of equality over liberty. They are intolerant and hateful of others who disagree with them. They are shortsighted, cynical, negative, and generally pessimistic. They adopt a Marxist perspective on history and society, thinking the truth doesn't matter and only power does. They often use rhetoric which is relativistic, but only when it suits their purposes. Democrats do not support the concept of self-reliability, and self-responsibility. They support policies which punish those who are responsible and reward those who are irresponsible. On top of all this, they took the wrong side of the issue on the impeachment of Bill Clinton for callous, partisan political reasons.

It is manifestly clear to me that Democrats in general are not liberals, at least not in any way which is consistent with the way the word is used throughout the world. They support liberty only for things which they consider to be morally permissible. And most of all they are hypocritical in a multitude of ways.

For all of the reasons, I am not a Democrat.

Why I Am Not a Republican

Now that you know why I am not a Democrat, perhaps I should briefly explain why I am not a Republican, either. Ever since I can remember, I have not been a "joiner". I've always been more of a lone wolf. Joining a group entails obligations and expectations, and I always preferred keeping my options open and my freedom intact. That way I didn't owe any group allegiance, and could pursue my own interests without having to worry about the group's interests.

I always thought that people putting their college's mascot or logo on their cars was utterly ridiculous. I would have thought that by the time they were in college, people would have gotten beyond the primitive tribalism which I found so prevalent in high school and other areas.

Because of all this, I suppose I have always been predisposed to be a political independent. It made it even easier when people around me criticized politicians constantly, and I could see most of them as incompetent, corrupt imbeciles. Why would I want to get involved in any of that?

I've grown quite a bit, and I no longer see politicians with such a condescending view. I recognize that they are flawed human beings who usually try their best to do what they think is right. Most of them are honest, to the same extent as other human beings, and most of them are in politics for noble reasons, and won't sell out their principles for money (although they aren't always consistent, as I have been arguing throughout most of this book).

Now that I'm older, though, I find my independent streak is fading. I wouldn't mind joining a political group, if I could find one that shares my political values. I'm looking for a group that believes strongly in the individual, that each individual owns himself and what we legally owe each other is the freedom to live our lives as we see fit, and no more. A group which believes that each person should decide moral matters for himself or herself, and that the majority's moral views should only matter in cases where one person is infringing on another person's right to live his life as he sees fit. A group which believes that the government's role is to protect me from infringements from other individuals and groups, and not to impose a way of life on me which I don't want, even one which I do want. A group which expects the government to live within the boundaries of the Constitution, and not put in place judges who will interpret the clear words of the Constitution in whatever way they want in order to impose their moral views on everyone else in the country.

It is eminently clear to me that the Democratic Party is not that group. Neither the people in power in the Democratic Party, nor its general members, believe in the principles I have outlined here. They sometimes say that they do, but a careful examination of their policies reveals the exact opposite. But what about the Republican Party?

Does the Republican Party advocate policies which respect individual autonomy? Although I can't claim to have given it as comprehensive consideration, I must say that I think it does a much better job than the Democratic Party. It is not perfect in this regard, but it seems to me that its policies are generally much more in line with the political principles which I accept. So, why don't I join the Republican Party?

I think there are basically two general reasons. First, the Republican Party fails to live up to these principles in some pretty obvious ways. For six years of George Bush's tenure the Republicans had full control of the federal government, and they could have drastically cut wasteful and inefficient programs, which they failed to do. My understanding is that the government grew under President Bush even faster than under President Clinton. I had believed that they might go so far as cutting clearly inefficient programs which were not Constitutionally mandated, but they seemed to go in the exact opposite direction.

Second, it would be difficult for me to join a Party which was so politically incompetent. How on Earth have Republicans allowed themselves to become the Party of rich, elite snobs who don't care one whit about the poor? I know that this is completely wrong, but it is the impression which many Americans have. Especially Americans in my neck of the woods.

Republicans have allowed leftists to take over the schools, and indoctrinate millions of children. How could I join a Party which would allow itself to be maligned so easily? The only response Republicans in power have offered is a Bushistic "compassionate conservatism", where Republicans offer handouts to the poor in violation of their political principles to curry favor with such groups. Where is the rhetoric that although we would love to use the force of government to rip money and time away from the well-off, we just don't believe the government should be used to impose our moral perspectives. I sometimes hear this kind of rhetoric from regular Republican Party members, but rarely from those with power, or in official positions.

How could I join a Party which has allowed itself to have such a horrible reputation? Their reputation is so bad among young people that I would lose a great deal of respect from at least half of my students the second they found out I was a member. Why would I want to spend any amount of time defending my association with a group that only haphazardly and half-heartedly stands for the same principles as me?

Honestly. How could Republicans allow themselves, against so much evidence, to become seen as the party of racism, of uncaring aristocrats without souls? How could they allow the entire school systems in at least several states to be run like leftist indoctrination centers? How could they allow the mainstream media to range from extreme leftist to moderate leftist?

And how could I join a party that is so incompetent and ineffectual? If you want to know why I'm not a Republican, it's because Republicans don't know what they are doing. They retreat at every opportunity. They run government like Democrats when they have power. They seem consistently unable to articulate the reasoning behind their views and policies, and of limited government in general. I am not a Republican because even though they sometimes seem to talk like they support my values, their extraordinary ineptitude only serves to undermine those values.

Final Thoughts

I am a Liberal. I believe that government does not own its citizens, and that morality is a difficult, but essential idea. I believe that it is proper to impose some kind of morality on everyone in society, but that it should be limited to banning direct harm to another human being's person or rights. I believe that the individual is paramount, and that each person's autonomous actions should be respected. I am sickened by the idea that one man must go to another man or group of men to ask permission to live the way he wants to live his life. I believe in negative rights, and I believe that a positive construal of rights makes the rest of us slaves. I believe in personal responsibility, and that the government should not take from responsible people only to give to those who are irresponsible, punishing some for helping to build society, and rewarding those who do not, even sometimes protecting those who help tear it down. One man's irresponsibility should affect him, and everyone who voluntarily chooses to associate with him, and to some extent his children, but it should not be allowed to affect everyone else in society.

I believe that the Democratic Party disagrees with me on all of these issues. Not all the time, and not every Democrat, but definitely in a general sense. When they do support my values, they do so inconsistently, and condemn others who try to apply these values consistently.

Now you know my views. At least my views as I currently understand them. As a philosopher, I have learned not to become too attached to every single one of my views. But I am committed to many of the central positions I have presented throughout the book.

At this point, perhaps you have found nothing convincing in anything I have said. You can go on with your life and forget about me and my views. But I'd urge you to think carefully about how closed-minded you are.

If you have been convinced by some of my arguments, and you are a Democrat, and a liberal in the historical and etymological sense of the word, you should think carefully about how strong my arguments are, and whether they demand that you sever your ties with the Democratic Party, or whether you can work within the system to fundamentally alter those areas where the Democratic Party is anti-liberal.

If you are a Republican, then you need to think carefully about why your leaders are so incompetent and ineffective. Why do they govern so much like Democrats when they get the chance? You need to think about going into education or the media, to help ensure that those institutions move toward something approaching fairness and balance. And you need to think about trying to push Republicans to live up to their ideals of limited government.

Lastly, if you are neither Democrat nor Republican, you can still consider which, if any, of my arguments have convinced you. Hopefully, we can work together on those areas, and push both major parties in the right direction. Whether you have joined a third political party, or refuse to join any of them, like me, you can still voice your opinions and try to persuade others to adopt them as well.

My aim is not to destroy the Democratic Party; whether it continues or not is not my business. But as long as it continues to adopt the leftist, collectivist, anti-liberal policies which it currently does, I do hope to diminish its power as much as I can. Pointing out the inconsistencies in leftist ideology will hopefully succeed, either in reducing that power, or in convincing Democrats and leftists to move toward a more consistent liberalism. I firmly believe that those who do not support Liberty do not deserve the Blessings which flow from that Liberty. Hopefully, together we can make it so that every American deserves those blessings which are only attainable through Liberty.

Notes

Chapter One

[1] Murphy, Dean E., "In Upstate Victory Tour, Mrs. Clinton Says Electoral College Should Go", November 11, 2000, New York Times http://query.nytimes.com/gst/fullpage.html?res=9507E2D81538F932A25752C1A96 69C8B63&sec=&spon= , accessed February 25, 2008.

[2] Guinier, Lani, "Making Every Vote Count", December 4, 2000, *The Nation*, http://www.thenation.com/doc/20001204/guinier, accessed February 25, 2008.

[3] A better way to elect a president :[Chicago Final Edition]. (2004, November 7). Chicago Tribune,p. 2.8. Retrieved February 25, 2008, from Chicago Tribune database. (Document ID: 731241091).

[4] Matthew Yi (2006, July 24). SACRAMENTO / Stanford professor stumps for electoral alternative :[FINAL Edition]. San Francisco Chronicle,p. A.1. Retrieved February 25, 2008, from ProQuest Newsstand database. (Document ID: 1081996301).

[5] A vote for democracy :[HOME EDITION]. (2006, June 5). Los Angeles Times,p. B.10. Retrieved February 25, 2008, from Los Angeles Times database. (Document ID: 1048411531).

[6] Koza, John R. et al., *Every Vote Equal: A State-Based Plan for Electing the President by the National Popular Vote*, National Popular Vote Press, California, 2006. All following quotes appear in the Forwards or section 1.2, between pages 8 and 19.

[7] Ibid., page 8.

[8] Ibid.

[9] Ibid., p. 12.

[10] CNN Election Center 2008, accessed February 5, 2008, http://www.cnn.com/ELECTION/2008/primaries/results/scorecard/#val=D.

[11] CNN Election Center 2008, accessed February 5, 2008, http://www.cnn.com/ELECTION/2008/primaries/results/scorecard/#R. Republicans have 463 unpledged delegates, but 320 of them are apparently elected.

[12] Larry Elder, "Low Black Voter Turnout -- Who's to Blame?," 11/6/1007, accessed 2/29/2008 at Real Clear Politics,

http://www.realclearpolitics.com/articles/2006/11/low_black_voter_turnout_whos_t. html.

[13] Bill Rankin "11TH CIRCUIT COURT: Atlanta justices uphold overseas ballots arriving after Election Day ELECTION 2000 :[Home Edition]." The Atlanta Constitution, December 12, 2000,   http://voyager2.lbcc.edu:2058/ (accessed March 3, 2008).

[14] "Nader sues Democrats, citing his failed White House bid :[FINAL Edition]." Orlando Sentinel, October 31, 2007, http://voyager2.lbcc.edu:2058/ (accessed March 4, 2008).

[15] Transcript of interview between Amy Goodman and Carl Mayer, on DemocracyNow!, October 31, 2007, "Ralph Nader Files Lawsuit Accusing Democratic Party of Conspiring to Block Presidential Run", accessed March 4, 2008. As of March 5, 2008, a copy of the lawsuit can be found online at http://www.newjerseyuntouchables.blogspot.com/.

[16] Katharine Q. Seelye, New York Times, "Democrats' Legal Challenges Impede Nader Campaign", August 19, 2004, accessed March 5, 2005 at http://query.nytimes.com/gst/fullpage.html?res=9A03E7DB1E3FF93AA2575BC0A 9629C8B63.

[17] Dennis B. Roddy and Tracie Mauriello, Pittsburgh Post-Gazette, "E-mails show how Dems tied staffers' bonuses to campaign work", December 16, 2007, accessed on March 4, 2008 at http://www.post-gazette.com/pg/07350/842079-85.stm.

[18] H. Quach & D. Bunis, *All Bow to Redistrict Architect*, Orange County Register, Aug. 26, 2001 , at A1.

[19] I should disclose that I attempted to get on the ballot to run against Rep. Sanchez as an independent, but was unable to gather the required signatures.

[20] Mark Murray, for MSNBC, accessed February 5, 2008, http://firstread.msnbc.msn.com/archive/2008/01/17/585015.aspx.

Chapter Two

[21] See *The American Heritage History of the Congress of the United States*, Alvin M. Josephy, Jr., American Heritage Publishing Company, 1975, pp. 230-238.

[22] Mitgang, Herbert, Ed., *Washington D.C. in Lincoln's Time: A Memoir of the Civil War Era by the Newspaperman Who Knew Lincoln Best: Noah Brooks*, pg. 188, as quoted in the website of the Lincoln Institute: www.mrlincolnandfreedom.org/inside.asp?ID=59&subjectID=3, on July 30,2007. Number of members of Congress taken from website of the Office of the Clerk of the House of Representatives: http://clerk.house.gov/art_history/house_history/index.html, on July 30, 2007.

[23] Linden, Glenn M., "A Note on Negro Suffrage and Republican Politics", in The Journal of Southern History, Vol. 36, No. 3, Aug. 1970, pp. 411-415, ultimately from *Cong. Globe,* 40th Cong., 3rd Sess. 745, 1428, and 1563-64, which can be accessed on the Library of Congress website at http://memory.loc.gov/ammem/amlaw/lwcg.html.

[24] *These United States: Our nation's geography, history and people,* The Reader's Digest Family Reference Series, The Reader's Digest Association, Pleasantville, New York, 1968, pp. 95-96. I also relied upon this source for many other historical details.

[25] The Dirksen Congressional Center website accessed August 1, 2007: http://www.congresslink.org/print_basics_histmats_civilrights64text.htm.

[26] One example of many can be found on page 37 of the 2004 Democratic National Platform found at http://www.democrats.org/pdfs/2004platform.pdf.

[27] http://transcripts.cnn.com/TRANSCRIPTS/0804/30/lkl.01.html

[28] from March 5, 2001. Accessed on http://findarticles.com/p/articles/mi_m1355/is_12_99/ai_71704802.

[29] Greg Gilderman, "King of East New York", New York Press, http://www.nypress.com/17/3/news&columns/feature.cfm, accessed August 8, 2007

[30] For example, see Michael Meyers, who is executive director of the New York Civil Rights Coalition, "Blacks must reject Barron's race-baiting", New York Daily News, at http://www.nydailynews.com/opinions/2007/08/01/2007-08-01_blacks_must_reject_barrons_racebaiting.html, accessed August 8, 2007. Meyers catalogs other racist remarks of Barron.

[31] See, for instance Media Matters article on the Coulter misquoting Donna Brazile: http://mediamatters.org/items/200412020004, or the one on Larry Elder misquoting Donna Brazile: http://mediamatters.org/items/200503020008.

[32] http://www.washingtonpost.com/wp-srv/politics/special/clinton/frenzy/jackson.htm

[33] Jet, June 26, 1995, accessed from http://findarticles.com/p/articles/mi_m1355/is_n7_v88/ai_17108826, on August 8, 2007.

[34] Salon.com, "Is Willie Brown Playing the race card?", at http://archive.salon.com/politics/red/2001/04/05/blue/index.html, accessed August 8, 2007.

[35] Roll Call reported on Representative Bonilla's demand for her to resign. Bonilla is a Republican. http://www.rollcall.com/issues/1_1/breakingnews/4513-1.html.

[36] Larry Elder, *The Ten Things You Can't Say in America*, St. Martin's Press, New York, 2000, p. 20.

[37] See the CNN website, http://www.cnn.com/2005/POLITICS/09/30/bennett.comments/, accessed August 9, 2007.

[38] CNN, http://archives.cnn.com/2002/ALLPOLITICS/12/09/lott.comment/, accessed August 9, 2007.

[39] See the platform at The American Presidency Project, http://www.presidency.ucsb.edu/showplatforms.php?platindex=SR1948, accessed, August 9, 2007.

[40] From the New York Times archives, http://query.nytimes.com/gst/fullpage.html?res=9F0CEFDF123BF935A25757C0A9629C8B63, accessed August 8, 2007.

[41] CNN archives, http://archives.cnn.com/2001/ALLPOLITICS/03/04/byrd.slur/, accessed August 8, 2007.

[42] The New York Times, "Ferraro's Obama Remarks Become Talk of Campaign", March 12, 2008, http://www.nytimes.com/2008/03/12/us/politics/12campaign.html, accessed May 3, 2008.

[43] Interview with Amazon.com, http://www.nytimes.com/2008/03/12/us/politics/12campaign.html, accessed May 3, 2008.

[44] The Boston Globe, "Another year of hate speech from the left, December 31, 1996, http://www.boston.com/news/globe/editorial_opinion/oped/articles/1996/12/31/another_year_of_hate_speech_from_the_left/, accessed August 8, 2007.

[45] Larry Elder, *The Ten Things You Can't Say in America*, p. 17.
[46] Amy Ridenour blog on the National Center for Public Policy Research website, http://www.nationalcenter.org/2005/11/michael-steele-oreo-incident.html, accessed August 8, 2007.

[47] Derald Wing Sue, *Overcoming Our Racism: The Journey to Liberation*, Jossey-Bass, 2003, pp. 30-31.

[48] Marion Barry was the Mayor of Washington, D.C. who was caught on video taking cocaine. He was later reelected as mayor.

[49] Iyengar, Shanto and Richard Morin, "Natural Disasters in Black and White: How Racial Cues Influenced Public Response to Hurricane Katrina", June 8, 2006, WashingtonPost.com, http://www.washingtonpost.com/wp-dyn/content/article/2006/06/07/AR2006060701177_pf.html, accessed May 3, 2008. Shanto Iyengar later coauthored a paper with Kyu S. Hahn at U.C.L.A., with the

same title, which is available on Stanford's Political Communications Lab website: http://pcl.stanford.edu/common/docs/research/iyengar/2007/katrina-cues.pdf, as of May 3, 2008.

[50] Morin, Richard, "John Stewart, Enemy of Democracy?" under subheading "Miserly Republicans, Unprincipled Democrats", June 23, 2006, WashingtonPost.com, http://www.washingtonpost.com/wp-dyn/content/article/2006/06/22/AR200602201474_pf.html, accessed May 3, 2008.

Chapter Three

[51] John Stuart Mill, *On Liberty*, edited by David Spitz, W. W. Norton & Company, 1975, pp. 10-11.

Chapter Four

[52] Lawrence Summers, "Remarks at NBER Conference on Diversifying the Science & Engineering Workforce", January 14, 2005, accessed at http://www.president.harvard.edu/speeches/2005/nber.html, on May 12,2008.

[53] Michael Molloy, *Experiencing the World's Religions*, McGraw-Hill, , p.230.

[54] John L. Esposito, et. al., *World Religions Today*, Oxford University Press, 2006, p. 436.

[55] Thomas Hobbes, *Leviathan*, edited by Edwin Curley, Hackett Publishing Inc, 1994, pg. 3.

[56] *Social and Political Philosophy*, ed. John Somerville and Ronald E. Santoni, Anchor Books, 1963, pp. 425-6.

[57] Ibid., p. 455.

[58] David G. Hale, "Analogy of the Body Politic", in the *Dictionary of the History of Ideas*, edited by Philip P. Wiener, Charles Scribner's Sons, New York, 1973-74, as found online maintained by The Electronic Text Center at the University of Virginia, http://etext.virginia.edu/cgi-local/DHI/dhi.cgi?id=dv1-11, accessed 9/9/2007.

[59] From U.S. National Archives and Records Administration website, clinton4.nara.gov/textonly/WH/New/html/19990120-4091.html, accessed 9/17/2007.

[60] PR Newswire website: prnewswire.com, division of United Business Media, "Nicholson to Clinton: 'It Is Too Our Money!'", accessed 9/18/2007.

[61] Thomas Hobbes, *Leviathan*, edited by Edwin Curley, Hackett Publishing Inc, 1994, pg. 76, chapter 13, paragraph 9.

[62] John Locke presented his views in his Second Treatise of Government, published in 1690. I will present a more complete historical overview and analysis in Chapter 11.

Chapter Five

[63] Cybercast News Service, CNSNews.com, Susan Jones, "House Speaker Invokes God and Bible in Earth Day Declaration", April 22, 2008, accessed July 1, 2008, http://www.cnsnews.com/ViewCulture.asp?Page=/Culture/archive/200804/CUL200 80422c.html.

[64] As an example of the controversy, see the Catholic News Agency, "Nancy Pelosi criticized for using false 'environmentalist' Bible quotation", April 24, 2008, accessed July 1, 2008. http://www.catholicnewsagency.com/new.php?n=12458.

[65] Taken from Barack Obama's campaign website, delivered March 18, 2008, http://my.barackobama.com/page/content/hisownwords, accessed July 1, 2008.

[66] Ariel Sabar, "Barack Obama: Putting faith out front", The Christian Science Monitor, July 16, 2007, accessed online July 1, 2008 at http://www.csmonitor.com/2007/0716/p01s01-uspo.htm.

Chapter Six

[67] Thomas Sowell, *Applied Economics: Thinking Beyond Stage One*, Basic Books, second edition, 2008, p. vii.

[68] San Francisco Chronicle editorial, "A New Low Point", October 22, 2007, B6, accessed July 9, 2008 at SFGate, http://www.sfgate.com/cgi-bin/article.cgi?f=/c/a/2007/10/22/EDGNST4V7.DTL&hw=pete+stark+editorial&sn=001&sc=1000.

[69] You can read the extensive study at http://www.ksg.harvard.edu/presspol/miscellaneous/invisible_primary.pdf.

Chapter Eight

[70] Transcribed from video clip accessed at http://www.thedailyshow.com/watch/mon-march-3-2008/sen--hillary-clinton-pt--1, accessed July 10, 2008.

[71] CNN archives, accessed 10/ 29/2010, http://archives.cnn.com/TRANSCRIPTS/0805/20/se.06.html.

[72] Rasmussen Reports, "62% Think American Society is Fair and Decent", January 12, 2008, http://www.rasmussenreports.com/public_content/politics/mood_of_america/bench marks/62_think_american_society_is_fair_and_decent, accessed November 2, 2008.

[73] As reported in Arthur C. Brooks, *Gross National Happiness; Why Happiness Matters for America—and How We Can Get More of It*, Basic Books, 2008, p. 27, originally from James A. Davis, Tom W. Smith, and Peter V. Marsden, principal investigators, *General Social Surveys, 1972-2004* (Chicago: National Opinion Research Center; Storrs, Conn,: The Roper Center for Public Research, University of Connecticut, 2004).

[74] Gallup, "Republicans Report Much Better Mental Health Than Others," November 30, 2007, http://www.gallup.com/poll/102943/Republicans-Report-Much-Better-Mental-Health-Than-Others.aspx.

Chapter Eleven

[75] The version of Hobbes classic *Leviathan* with which I am familiar is: Thomas Hobbes, *Leviathan*, edited by Edwin Curley, Hackett Publishing Inc, 1994. For Hobbes's view on the state of nature, see Chapter XIII. For his view on the formation of civil society, see Chapter XVII, especially 12-13. For his view of liberty see Chapter XXI. *Leviathan* was originally published in 1668.

[76] The version of Locke's Second Treatise with which I am familiar is: John Locke, Two Treatises of Government, edited by Peter Laslett, Cambridge University Press, 1988. For Locke's view on the state of nature, see the Second Treatise, Chapter II, especially §§4-8. For Locke's view on the formation of political societies and the requisite consent of the governed, see Chapter VIII, §§95-99. For Locke's view on the purpose of government, which in turn specifies the limits or the extent of governmental authority, see Chapters IX and XI. Locke's Two Treatises of Government was first published in 1690.

[77] Adam Smith, *An Enquiry into the Nature and Causes of the Wealth of Nations*, first published in 1776, Book IV, chapter II.

[78] Ibid. Book I, chapter II.

[79] The version of Mill's *On Liberty* with which I am familiar is: John Stuart Mill, *On Liberty*, edited by David Spitz, W. W. Norton & Company, 1975. See especially Chapter I, pp. 3-11.

[80] Jean-Jacques Rousseau, *The Social Contract*, originally published in 1762, Book IV, Chapter One, ¶ 1.

[81] See Mill, p. 10.